Shaping of America, 1783–1815

Biographies

Shaping of America, 1783–1815

Biographies

Volume 2: L–Z

**Richard C. Hanes,
Kelly Rudd, and
Sharon M. Hanes**

Lawrence W. Baker,
Project Editor

U·X·L

*An imprint of Thomson Gale,
a part of The Thomson Corporation*

Detroit • New York • San Francisco • San Diego • New Haven, Conn. • Waterville, Maine • London • Munich

Shaping of America, 1783–1815: Biographies

Richard C. Hanes, Kelly Rudd, and Sharon M. Hanes

Project Editor
Lawrence W. Baker

Editorial
Jennifer York Stock

Rights Acquisition and Management
Emma Hull, Jackie Jones, Lisa Kincade

Imaging and Multimedia
Randy Bassett, Dean Dauphinais, Lezlie Light, Mike Logusz, Dan Newell, Christine O'Bryan

Product Design
Pamela A. E. Galbreath, Kate Scheible

Composition and Electronic Prepress
Evi Seoud

Manufacturing
Rita Wimberley

For permission to use material from this product, submit your request via Web at http://www.gale-edit.com/permissions, or you may download our Permissions Request form and submit your request by fax or mail to:

Rights Acquisition and Management Department
Thomson Gale
27500 Drake Rd.
Farmington Hills, MI 48331-3535
Permissions Hotline:
248-699-8006 or 800-877-4253, ext. 8006
Fax: 248-699-8074 or 800-762-4058

Cover images (clockwise from top right): Absalom Jones (Fisk University Library); Aaron Burr (Library of Congress); Betsy Ross (Corbis Corporation).

While every effort has been made to ensure the reliability of the information presented in this publication, Thomson Gale does not guarantee the accuracy of data contained herein. Thomson Gale accepts no payment for listing; and inclusion in the publication of any organization, agency, institution, publication, service, or individual does not imply endorsement by the editors or publisher. Errors brought to the attention of the publisher and verified to the satisfaction of the publisher will be corrected in future editions.

LIBRARY OF CONGRESS CATALOGING-IN-PUBLICATION DATA

Hanes, Richard Clay, 1946–
   Shaping of America, 1783–1815, Reference Library.
     v. cm.
   Includes bibliographical references and index.
   Contents: [1] Almanac / Richard C. Hanes and Sharon M. Hanes ; Lawrence W. Baker, editor — [2] Biographies / Richard C. Hanes, Kelly Rudd, and Sharon M. Hanes ; Lawrence W. Baker, editor (2 v.) — [3] Primary sources / Sharon M. Hanes and Richard C. Hanes ; Lawrence W. Baker, editor — [4] Reference library cumulative index / Lawrence W. Baker, index coordinator.
   ISBN 1-4144-0181-7 (set) — ISBN 1-4144-0182-5 (Almanac : hardcover : alk. paper) — ISBN 1-4144-0183-3 (Biographies : set : hardcover : alk. paper) — ISBN 1-4144-0184-1 (Biographies : v. 1 : hardcover : alk. paper) — ISBN 1-4144-0185-X (Biographies : v. 2 : hardcover : alk. paper) — ISBN 1-4144-0186-8 (Primary sources : hardcover : alk. paper) — ISBN 1-4144-0187-6 (Cumulative index)
   1. United States—History—1783–1815—Juvenile literature. I. Hanes, Sharon M. II. Rudd, Kelly, 1954– III. Baker, Lawrence W. IV. Title.

E301.H29 2005
973.4—dc22   2005019664

This title is also available as an e-book.
ISBN 1-4144-0471-9
Contact your Thomson Gale sales representative for ordering information.

Printed in United States of America
10 9 8 7 6 5 4 3 2 1

Contents

Volume 2

Introduction

I n 1783, the United States, having just won independence from Britain in the American Revolution, was the only republican form of government known in the world, a nation run by the people for the people. Britain assumed the new nation would not last long and eventually return to the British Empire. Americans had long relied on Britain for manufactured goods and profitable trade with other British colonies, such as the West Indies. Britain was not eager to set up a trade relationship with the new nation after the war, believing that the United States, left on its own, would soon economically collapse. Britain even kept troops at outposts in the western territories granted to the United States in the Treaty of Paris, knowing that the United States was too weak to enforce the treaty's terms.

Through the 1780s, it looked like Britain might be right. After freeing themselves from the heavy hand of British rule, Americans were fearful of giving away the freedoms they spilled blood for to another strong government, albeit one of their own creation. Therefore, the newly adopted Articles of Confederation established a very weak central government with no single executive position and no taxing power. Even the ability to raise an army for national defense was dependent on the individual states agreeing to supply the soldiers. As the 1780s progressed, the states bickered more and more with each other, to a large extent over trade competition. Each state had its own currency, making interstate commerce almost impossible.

On the frontier, rapid population growth was leading to settlements spilling over the Appalachian Mountains into the fertile Ohio and Mississippi river valleys. However, many Native American groups still controlled the region, joined by remnants of Native American groups displaced from the Atlantic Coast. The Cherokee and Creek controlled much of the land south of the Ohio River, and a number of tribes controlled lands between the Ohio and Mississippi Rivers northward to the Great Lakes. Hostility was high among the Native American population and violent attacks were frequent on U.S. settlements often followed by brutal retaliations. In addition, Spain, like Britain, did not respect the new U.S. boundaries and kept Spanish forces on U.S. soil. Both countries encouraged Native Americans to combat the spread of U.S. settlement. In addition, Spain controlled use of the Mississippi River and refused to sign a commercial treaty. The river was vital for western frontier farmers in getting their produce to East Coast markets since roads were few and primitive, especially through the Appalachians. Frontiersmen were resentful that the new national government could not protect them and exert control over the region.

Indeed, the national government offered little help to its citizens. Though the nation's economy remained fairly healthy, the national government, unable to tax that wealth, was broke and could not pay the debts it accumulated through the war, or even pay the interest on those debts. The nation's leaders were becoming gravely concerned that the new nation was nearing collapse. Those fears increased further in late 1786 when farmers in western Massachusetts rebelled against state taxing practices. Threatening to capture a U.S. ammunition supply depot in January 1787, the national government was helpless to defend its armory or protect U.S. citizens. The day was saved when the state quelled the uprising with its own militia. Lawlessness and lack of civil order seemed to be brewing. It was time for action.

From May to September 1787, fifty-five delegates from twelve states met with the intent of fixing the Articles of Confederation. However, immediately upon starting the convention, they determined that a whole new government was needed. Under a veil of secrecy, they began drafting a new Constitution. This time, the national government would have two strong legislative houses, a chief executive, and a federal court system. Power would be shared among the three branches of government and with the states. The new government had the power to tax, raise an army, and regulate commerce between states. These were bold new directions that attracted considerable debate and controversy at the state ratification conventions and among the public in general. Nonetheless, by June 1788, enough states had ratified the Constitution to make it effective. The contentious debate led to the creation of the Bill of Rights, the first ten amendments to the Constitution that guaranteed certain basic rights held by citizens of the country and protections from government actions. Now the task was to prove the new government could work across the expansive area that this republican form of government would be stretched.

The new U.S. Congress met on April 6, 1789, with the first order of business to count the electoral ballots for president. War hero General George Washington was the unanimous choice for the nation's first chief executive. Americans believed he would preserve the freedoms gained from the fight for independence. In fact, if it were not for Washington's participation at the Constitutional Convention two years earlier, a single executive position may not have been created. Perhaps there would have been a committee to run the country. President Washington's task was enormous. He had to fill hundreds of government positions and put the new government into operation. At the top positions, he appointed Thomas Jefferson as secretary of state, Alexander Hamilton as secretary of the treasury, Edmund Randolph as attorney general, and Henry Knox as secretary of war. These were President Washington's most trusted advisors—the Cabinet.

The first U.S. census was taken in 1790, a necessary step to determine how many seats each state would be assigned in the U.S. House of Representatives. The census was revealing about the makeup of the new nation. The United States had a population of almost four million people, including seven hundred thousand slaves and sixty thousand free blacks. Black Africans and their descendants composed some 16 percent of the population. In the South, that percentage was higher. In South Carolina, they amounted to over 40 percent of the population. Most of the white population was from England, Scotland, and Ireland, with a large number from Germany as well. Landowner-ship, a hallmark of the new society, was also reflected in the census, as 97 percent of the population lived in rural areas.

One of the most important first tasks of the new govern-ment was to make the nation economically independent just as it was now politically independent. Congress gave Hamilton a direct charge: develop a plan for economic growth. The resulting complex plan, which Congress mostly enacted, charted a course for the nation that proved successful. The economy began to grow. By 1790, only three banks existed with little capital for business investment. Creation of a national bank provided a major source of loans to new busi-nesses and the new U.S. mint developed a national currency system to improve internal trade. Hamilton's plan raised expectations of economic improvement in the business com-munity, spurring their support for the new government, just as Hamilton had anticipated.

However, Hamilton's success did not bring political unity in the nation. Just the opposite occurred. Hamilton was so committed to a strong national government, that others such as Jefferson and James Madison, principal author of the Con-stitution, became increasingly alarmed. They believed Hamil-ton was recreating the British political and social systems in the United States. Earlier political division over ratification of the new Constitution was now renewed in a new form. Supporters of a strong central government and industrial growth became known as Hamiltonians, or Federalists. Those who believed most governing power should reside with state governments and the continuation of agriculture as the primary economic driving force became known as Jeffersonians, or Republicans. A two party system of politics was beginning to take shape.

Foreign affairs issues drove the political wedge deeper. When the new republic of France declared war on Britain in 1793, the Federalists supported continued relations with Britain, a vital market for U.S. goods and produce. The Repub-licans favored close relations with France, America's ally during the American Revolution. Some, including President Washington, were dismayed over the rise of political parties as the Republicans evolved into the Democratic-Republican organization. They feared the parties would only represent their own interests, not necessarily the national interests. Nonetheless, the war between France and Britain was an economic boon to the United States as new foreign markets opened up. There were large profits but great danger on the hostile seas.

While deep schisms were forming in the East during the 1790s, the western frontier was experiencing the increasing hostility of the Native Americans. A developing Native American alliance defeated U.S. military forces sent to pacify the situation in 1790 and 1791. Not until 1794 was the United States able to mount a sufficiently large enough force to subdue the strengthening Native American alliance.

John Adams, President Washington's vice president for two terms, followed Washington into the presidency. However, the Federalist hold on power in the nation was fading as public differences over the French and British war escalated. The Federalist-controlled Congress passed the Alien and Sedition Acts in 1798 in an attempt to suppress opposition to the administration's policies. This legislative action backfired, causing greater distrust of the Federalist leaders by the public. As a result, in 1801, the Democratic-Republican Jefferson became the nation's third president. This also marked the first peaceful transition of government control from one political party to another, a historic event of major proportions. Jefferson would be followed by two fellow Virginia Democratic-Republicans in the presidency, James Madison and James Monroe.

After a brief lull, the war between France and Britain was renewed in 1803. America was caught again in the middle as both European nations disrupted U.S. trade. The prosperity that had been building in the nation began to quickly sink by 1808. Everything Americans had fought for since 1775 was jeopardized by new economic policies from President Jefferson and the headlong rush into war once again with Britain. Believing the United States carried more economic clout than it really did, Jefferson cut off all trade with foreign countries through the Embargo Act of 1807. He believed Britain and France would back off their policies of seizing U.S. merchant ships and seamen. However, the Embargo Act proved far more harmful to U.S. businesses than it did to foreign countries and Congress soon passed less rigid economic measures. Even though the nation's economy had been greatly damaged, public opinion led some young firebrand congressmen from the West and South known as War Hawks to push the nation's fourth president, James Madison, toward war with Britain. Finally, in June 1812, Madison relented and asked Congress to declare war. The War of 1812 was in a sense the second revolutionary war.

The United States was woefully unprepared. It had almost no navy and a very small army. Many of its military leaders were aging Revolutionary War veterans. In addition, the nation was severely split over the war. New England merchants and financiers were strongly opposed. They relied on trade with Britain for their livelihood and they were already angry over the economic policies Jefferson had established. Worst of all, the nation's government had no money.

The war results were predictable. Relying on state militia, highly reluctant in some cases, and navy privateers, the U.S. military suffered one humiliation after another. It ineptly prosecuted a war strategy of avoiding direct battles with Britain, both on land and the high seas, and invading Canada instead. The capture of Canada from Britain was a leading goal of the war for land hungry Americans. Thanks to critical naval victories on Lake Erie and Lake Champlain, the United States was able to outlast the British who were war weary after decades of war with France. A great moment of indignity for the United States came in August 1814 when British troops marched largely unopposed into Washington, D.C. They proceeded to burn most of the young capitol's public buildings, including the President's House and the Capitol building. The biggest military victory for the United States in the war came in January 1815 in the Battle of New Orleans, ironically two weeks after a peace treaty was signed in Europe. With communications slow, word had not reached the United States yet of the treaty, signed on Christmas Eve 1814. The belated military victory catapulted General Andrew Jackson to national fame and ultimately the White House.

Word of peace with Britain and the major victory over seasoned British forces at New Orleans sent the nation into a major period of optimism and growth. Though the war was largely a draw settling little, the United States had now survived two wars with Britain, a world power. Self-confidence was at a new high and foreign nations showed new respect. The United States was a young nation as well. The population had grown dramatically—from less than 4 million in 1790 to 5.3 million in 1800 and 7.2 million in 1810—largely due to the very high birthrate. Immigration during the period was primarily slaves shipped from Africa.

The economic blockades and War of 1812 had invigorated America's infant industries to produce goods no longer available through international markets. New factories mass-produced goods by employing semiskilled wage laborers who had replaced the traditional craftsmen working in their home shops. The Era of Good Feelings was dawning and the growing pains of a new nation felt between 1783 and 1815 had come to an end. People now thought of themselves as Americans foremost, rather than as Virginians, New Yorkers, or some other state affiliation.

Independence had affected almost all aspects of life in America since 1783. Even religion saw a major change away from the older traditional denominations led by figures of authority to more democratic denominations such as Methodists and Baptists, in which individuals openly expressed their own religious conversions.

Sadly, by 1815, equality of rights had still not reached everyone. White males enjoyed the most rights, more so than they enjoyed before independence. However, women and free blacks had far fewer rights than white men. Slaves and Native Americans had none. Women could not vote and married women could not own property or file lawsuits. Aside from keeping their households and spinning thread and weaving cloth, their primary role was to raise sons who would contribute to the new nation's development. When educational opportunities did begin to surface through the early period, such as the opening of private female academies, it was primarily to better equip women in raising their sons.

One other major issue left unresolved by the Founders was slavery. The Founders had hoped slavery would die out on its own. However, the invention of an improved cotton gin by Eli Whitney in 1793 led to a rapid increase in slavery as the South's economy boomed. That issue would not be resolved for several more decades when America faced another major crisis, the Civil War.

Reader's Guide

Shaping of America, 1783–1815: Biographies presents in two volumes the life stories of fifty-one men and women who played key roles from 1783 to 1815 when the United States was forged into a politically and economically independent nation. Individuals from all walks of life are included. They all took an active role in the creation and early development of the United States whether they were aware of it at the time or not. Some were Founding Fathers who signed the 1776 Declaration of Independence and drafted the U.S. Constitution at the 1787 Constitutional Convention. Many held prominent national positions in government, religious organizations, educational institutions, businesses, and the military. Some were victims of the swift national growth. Native Americans lost extensive life and their lands to the onslaught of frontier expansion. African slaves were vital to the economic growth of the South at the expense of all personal freedoms. They all guided America through its first years as a nation in some way.

Coverage and features

In *Biographies*, part of the amazing legacy of the period are the sons of Virginia—George Washington, Thomas Jefferson,

John Marshall, James Madison, and James Monroe—all born within 150 miles of each other to wealthy and influential families. In addition to Washington, Jefferson, and Madison, two other presidents of the era are featured— John Adams and James Monroe—as well as a future president, Andrew Jackson. Other biographees are first ladies Martha Washington, Abigail Adams, and Dolley Madison; treasury secretaries Alexander Hamilton and Albert Gallatin; diplomat Benjamin Franklin; Supreme Court chief justice John Jay; Secretary of War Henry Knox; Attorney General Edmund Randolph; authors Hugh Henry Brackenridge and Mercy Otis Warren; black social activists Benjamin Banneker, Elizabeth Freeman, and Prince Hall; religious leaders Richard Allen, Francis Asbury, John Carroll, Absalom Jones, and John Witherspoon; educators Elizabeth Ann Seton and Sarah Pierce; inventor and engineer Eli Whitney; midwife and health care giver Martha Ballard; Native American leaders Little Turtle, Alexander McGillivray, and Tecumseh; explorers Meriwether Lewis and William Clark; and many more.

Shaping of America, 1783–1815: Biographies also features sidebars containing interesting facts about people and events related to early America. Within each full-length biography, boldfaced cross-references direct readers to other individuals profiled in the two-volume set. Finally, each volume includes approximately 125 black-and-white illustrations; a timeline of important events of the era; a Words to Know section that introduces students to difficult or unfamiliar terms (terms are also defined within the text); a general bibliography; and a cumulative subject index.

Shaping of America, 1783–1815 Reference Library

Shaping of America, 1783–1815: Biographies is only one component of the three-part U•X•L Shaping of America, 1783–1815 Reference Library. The other two titles in this set are:

Shaping of America, 1783–1815: Almanac (one volume) presents a comprehensive overview of the early history of the United States. The *Almanac* is divided into fifteen chapters. The first ten chapters chronologically address different timeframes during this early age in U.S. history. Featured subjects include the signing of the Declaration of Independence, the Articles of Confederation, and the U.S. Constitution; the early battles between those who favored a strong central government and those who favored strong state governments; foreign relations with Britain and France; the presidential administrations of George Washington, John Adams, Thomas Jefferson, and James Madison; the War of 1812; and the dramatic Louisiana Purchase, which instantly more than doubled the United States. The final five chapters describe topics that are of importance throughout the period—farming, religion, women's roles in everyday life, black slaves and Native Americans, and the westward expansion of the United States.

Shaping of America, 1783–1815: Primary Sources (one volume) tells the story of early America in the words of the people who lived and shaped it. Eighteen excerpted documents provide a wide range of perspectives on this period of history. Included are excerpts from presidential addresses; treaties with other nations and Native American tribes; national and state legislation; speeches by prominent early Americans; an everyday diary; and letters by individuals who lived through the eventful period.

A cumulative index of all three titles in the U•X•L Shaping of America, 1783–1815 Reference Library is also available.

Dedication
These volumes are dedicated to Hazel Hanes, who has a love of history.

Special thanks
Gratitude to Sue Van Leuven for assistance on literature research. Much appreciation also goes to copyeditor Jane Woychick, proofreader Amy Marcaccio Keyzer, indexer Theresa Murray, and typesetter Integra Software Services.

Comments and suggestions
We welcome your comments on *Shaping of America, 1783–1815: Biographies* and suggestions for other topics to consider. Please write: Editors, *Shaping of America, 1783–1815: Biographies,* U•X•L, 27500 Drake Rd., Farmington Hills, Michigan 48331-3535; call toll free: 1-800-877-4253; fax to (248) 699-8097; or send e-mail via http://www.gale.com.

Timeline of Events

February 10, 1763 Britain and France sign a treaty ending the French and Indian War and securing British control over Canada and all French territory east of the Mississippi River south of Canada.

1763–67 British Parliament passes a series of taxes to pay for the defense of the colonies and asserts greater control over colonial governments. Among the new taxes is the Stamp Act of 1765, which requires colonists to purchase seals to be attached on a wide range of documents.

May 29, 1765 Patrick Henry introduces the Virginia Resolutions, which contest Parliament's right to tax the colonies.

1765–66 Several colonial legislatures pass "non-importation agreements," restricting the importing of British goods into America.

October 1, 1768 Britain sends troops to Boston to enforce import taxes and keep watch on Boston's "radicals."

March 5, 1770 In an event that becomes known as the Boston Massacre, British troops fire on an angry mob of Boston citizens, leading to the injury or death of eleven colonists.

December 16, 1773 Bostonians board British trade ships and dump 342 chests containing 90,000 pounds of tea into Boston Harbor in protest of the tea tax and other trade policies.

March–June 1774 British Parliament passes the Coercive Acts, which punish the colonists for rebellious behavior but lead to greater colonial resolve for independence from British rule.

September 5, 1774 The First Continental Congress meets in Philadelphia and sends a list of grievances to Britain.

April 19, 1775 Massachusetts militiamen and British troops fire shots at each other at Lexington and Concord; this marks the beginning of the American Revolution.

May 10, 1775 The Second Continental Congress convenes in Philadelphia and creates the Continental Army with **George Washington** as its commander.

March 31, 1776 Future first lady **Abigail Adams** writes a letter to husband **John Adams** (the future second president), asking him to "remember the ladies and be more generous and favorable to them than [were] your ancestors."

July 2, 1776 Congress adopts a resolution that makes the colonies free and independent states; the thirteen new states develop state constitutions through the following year.

July 4, 1776 Congress adopts the Declaration of Independence.

October 7, 1777 The United States' victory over the British army at Saratoga, New York, convinces France to ally with the Americans in the war.

November 15, 1777 The Second Continental Congress, meeting in York, Pennsylvania, adopts the Articles of Confederation; this creates a national government with little authority, including no taxing powers.

February 6, 1778 The United States signs an alliance treaty with France for defense and trade.

March 1780 Pennsylvania becomes the first state to ban slavery.

March 2, 1780 Massachusetts adopts a new state constitution that maintains the Congregational Church as the official state church.

March 1, 1781 The Articles of Confederation go into effect as the nation's first constitution after Maryland becomes the thirteenth state to ratify them.

August 21, 1781 Lawyers on behalf of **Elizabeth Freeman** and another slave argue before the Bershire County Court of Common Pleas that slavery is not lawful and they were free people; the court rules in Freeman's favor.

October 19, 1781 British General Charles Cornwallis surrenders his force of seven thousand soldiers to General George Washington at Yorktown, Virginia, bringing victory in the war for independence within reach, though the war drags on for another two years.

1783 In a case involving slave Quock Walker, the Massachusetts Supreme Court rules that slavery is inconsistent with the state constitution's Declaration of Human Rights; as a result, slavery would no longer be supported by the state courts.

May 1783 The Society of the Cincinnati, originated by General **Henry Knox** for the purpose of providing fellowship and assistance to those who served as officers in the American Revolution, has its first meeting in Fishkill, New York.

September 3, 1783 The United States and Britain sign the Treaty of Paris, ending the Revolutionary War; the treaty recognizes America's independence and grants the United States control of lands extending westward to the Mississippi River.

December 20, 1783 Virginia legislature adopts a plan for ceding its western land claims to the United States.

1784 **Francis Asbury** and Thomas Coke organize the Methodist Episcopal Church, a new denomination in the United States.

1784 Betsy Ross, famed flag maker of the "Stars and Stripes" in the Revolutionary War, joins the Free Quakers, who believe in military action for defense; she continues a successful upholstery and flag-making business in Philadelphia, Pennsylvania, a unique businesswoman of the early Republic.

March 1784 John Sevier is elected governor of the newly independent state of Franklin, which is composed of North Carolina land claims west of the Allegheny Mountains; he serves in that post until his arrest for treason in 1788 by North Carolina.

December 1784 Soon after the end of the Revolutionary War, Francis Asbury becomes North America's first Methodist bishop as the American and English Methodist organizations formally split.

1785 William White is elected president of the first General Convention of the Protestant Episcopal Church meeting in Philadelphia, Pennsylvania; he is consecrated bishop in February 1787.

January 1, 1785 Massachusetts midwife **Martha Ballard** begins a diary she will faithfully keep until her death in 1812, providing many details of daily life in New England.

March 1785 Representatives of Virginia and Maryland, meeting at Mount Vernon to resolve issues over navigation of the Potomac River, call for a more general meeting of states the following year at Annapolis to discuss growing national problems.

May 20, 1785 The Continental Congress passes the Land Ordinance of 1785, which establishes a process for surveying and selling western public lands.

January 10, 1786 The United States signs the Treaty of Hopewell with the Chickasaw tribe of Native Americans, one in a series of treaties with Southeastern tribes that establishes a boundary between Native American and U.S. settlements.

January 16, 1786 The Virginia legislature adopts the "Virginia Statute of Religious Freedom," written by **Thomas Jefferson**, establishing a model for the protection of religious beliefs in America.

February 1786 Former slave **Richard Allen** permanently settles in Philadelphia, Pennsylvania, where he is invited by St. George's Methodist Church to preach to its black congregants.

September 14, 1786 Representatives from only five states attend a meeting in Annapolis, Maryland, to address growing national concerns; they send a request to the Continental Congress to call for a national convention of all states the following year in Philadelphia to fix the shortcomings of the Articles of Confederation.

1787 **Prince Hall** becomes first Grand Master of black Masons after the African Grand Lodge receives a charter from England for full recognition as a regular Masonic lodge; Hall could now issue charters to African Masonic lodges elsewhere in the new republic.

January 25, 1787 At the peak of Shays's Rebellion, a revolt begun in August 1786 among western Massachusetts farmers against state taxing policies, some two thousand rebels are dispersed by the state militia while trying to capture a U.S. military arsenal in Springfield.

February 21, 1787 The Continental Congress passes a resolution calling for a meeting of all states in May to amend the Articles of Confederation.

April 12, 1787 A group of black Methodists meet in a Philadelphia, Pennsylvania, home and form the Free African Society (FAS), the first organization among free blacks in the young nation; the group elects **Absalom Jones** its leader.

May 25, 1787 A convention of state delegates convenes to correct shortcomings of the national government and by September 17 adopts a new U.S. Constitution.

May 29, 1787 Virginia delegate **Edmund Randolph** presents **James Madison**'s "Virginia Plan" to the Constitutional Convention in Philadelphia; the proposal calls for a powerful two-house legislature, a president, and a national court system.

July 13, 1787 The Continental Congress passes the Northwest Ordinance, which establishes the Northwest Territory from lands obtained from Britain in the 1783 Treaty of Paris and provides a three-step plan on how U.S. territories can gain statehood; the region includes the future states of Ohio, Indiana, Illinois, Michigan, and Wisconsin, as well as parts of Minnesota.

September 17, 1787 Pennsylvania delegate **Benjamin Franklin** explains to fellow delegates at the Constitutional Convention why they should sign the Constitution.

October 1787 Alexander Hamilton, James Madison, and **John Jay** begin publishing a series of eighty-five anonymously written essays in New York newspapers through May 1788, later called the *Federalist Papers,* carefully explaining why the Constitution should be ratified.

June 21, 1788 New Hampshire becomes the ninth state to vote in favor of ratification, the minimum needed to make the Constitution the law of the land.

September 1788 Pierre-Charles L'Enfant's plans are approved for converting New York's City Hall into Federal Hall, the new home for the U.S. Congress.

1789 Newly appointed treasury secretary Alexander Hamilton encourages editor John Fenno to regularly publish pro-Federalist articles in the *Gazette of the United States,* thereby promoting Hamilton's vision of what the U.S. government should be.

April 6, 1789 The first U.S. Congress convenes in New York City under the new U.S. Constitution.

April 30, 1789 In the nation's capital of New York City, George Washington is inaugurated as the country's first president and John Adams the first vice president.

May 16, 1789 At ten years of age, **Nelly Custis Lewis,** brother George "Wash" Custis, and grandmother **Martha Washington** depart for New York City to join newly inaugurated President George Washington at the President's House; Nelly becomes one of the first children to grow up while residing in a U.S. presidential mansion.

July 14, 1789 French crowds storm the Bastille, a Paris prison, releasing prisoners and capturing stored arms and munitions; this marks the start of the French Revolution.

September 1789 Edmund Randolph is appointed by newly inaugurated President George Washington to serve as the nation's first attorney general; he later replaces Thomas Jefferson as secretary of state in December 1793.

September 12, 1789 President George Washington appoints Henry Knox secretary of war in the newly established federal government, making Knox the only high-ranking official who remains in the same position he held in the previous confederation government.

September 24, 1789 President George Washington appoints foreign secretary John Jay as the first chief justice of the newly formed U.S. Supreme Court; he proceeds to establish many rules and procedures for the new Court.

September 24, 1789 Congress passes the Judiciary Act, organizing the Supreme Court and creating district and appellate levels of federal courts.

1790 The national government moves from New York City to Philadelphia.

1790 The first national census shows that 97 percent of the population of four million people live in rural areas and fewer than sixty thousand are free blacks.

January 1790 Treasury secretary Alexander Hamilton delivers the first of several proposals to Congress that map out a complex and controversial program for economic recovery of the nation.

February 2, 1790 The U.S. Supreme Court meets for the first time, with one chief justice and five associate justices; the Court hears its first case two years later.

May 1790 President George Washington appoints William Blount governor of the new Southwest Territory and superintendent of Indian affairs in the region.

July 22, 1790 Congress passes the Indian Trade and Intercourse Act, establishing a foundation for future U.S.–Native American relations; the act expands the national government's role in Native American affairs by controlling all interaction with Native Americans, including regulation of all trade between U.S. citizens and Native Americans.

August 14, 1790 Secretary of War Henry Knox, eager to bring peace to the South's frontier, personally signs the Treaty of New York with **Alexander McGillivray**, leader of a Creek confederacy, recognizing the Creek tribe as an independent nation and establishing a border between Creek and Georgia settlements.

August 15, 1790 Father **John Carroll** is ordained bishop of the new diocese of Baltimore by Pope Pius VI in Dorset, England, as Church ties with England end; Carroll would become Archbishop of Baltimore on April 8, 1808.

October 20, 1790 Over 180 Americans die after a combined force of Miamis, Shawnees, and Delawares in northern Ohio, led by Miami member **Little Turtle**, defeat an American force led by General Josiah Harmar.

November 1, 1790 The Brown Fellowship Society is founded in Charleston, South Carolina, one of several organizations established in the country to provide support to the local black American and African slave population.

December 20, 1790 America's first factory, Slater Mill, located in Pawtucket, Rhode Island, begins producing cotton yarn.

January 1791 Pierre-Charles L'Enfant is selected to design the Capitol and all other public buildings for the new nation's capitol in Washington, D.C.; he soon sketches out a plan for the city.

February 25, 1791 President George Washington signs legislation to establish the First National Bank of the United States after hearing arguments from James Madison and Alexander Hamilton concerning Congress's power to create a bank; the legislation expires in 1811.

March 3, 1791 Congress approves a site selected by President George Washington on the Potomac River between Maryland and Virginia to become the permanent capital of the nation.

March 4, 1791 Vermont is admitted as the fourteenth state of the Union, the first addition to the original thirteen states.

May 1791 President George Washington stops at the home of agriculturalist **Eliza Lucas Pinckney**, mother of prominent early American statesmen Charles Cotesworth Pinckney and Thomas Pinckney, during his Southern tour to rally support for the new national government; Washington would soon serve as pallbearer at her funeral.

July 2, 1791 U.S. territorial governor William Blount signs a treaty with the Cherokee tribe of Native Americans that guarantees the Native Americans land in Georgia and North Carolina and establishes a boundary between U.S. and Native American settlements.

July 4, 1791 The First National Bank of the United States opens in Philadelphia with branches in Boston, New York, Baltimore, and Charleston.

August 19, 1791 Free black **Benjamin Banneker** writes a letter to Secretary of State Thomas Jefferson asking for the freedom of slaves in America; Jefferson responds in an August 30 letter.

October 31, 1791 Poet and editor **Philip Freneau** publishes the first edition of the *National Gazette* that attacks the domestic and foreign policies of Alexander Hamilton and defends those of Thomas Jefferson.

November 4, 1791 A growing Native American confederacy in the Ohio region defeats an American military force led by General Arthur St. Clair; 647 soldiers are killed, making it the worst defeat of the U.S. military by Native American forces in U.S. history.

December 1791 Benjamin Banneker publishes his first almanac, which will continue to be annually published until 1797.

December 15, 1791 States ratify the first ten amendments to the Constitution, originally drafted by James Madison and known as the Bill of Rights, that identify certain basic rights held by citizens of the country. The Bill of Rights covers such freedoms as speech, press, and religion, and certain protections from government actions such as unreasonable search and seizure.

1792 Author **Hugh Henry Brackenridge** publishes his novel titled *Modern Chivalry;* because of its popularity, it would see a series of additions and revisions until its final publication in 1815.

1792 Sarah Pierce obtains local government approval in Litchfield, Connecticut, to open the Litchfield Female Academy, the first school in the United States dedicated to the higher education of women.

February 1792 Author **Judith Sargent Murray** begins publishing a monthly series of essays titled "The Gleaner" in the *Massachusetts Magazine;* written from the point of view of an imaginary man to promote education and economic self-sufficiency for women, the series continues until August 1794.

April 2, 1792 Congress passes the Coinage Act, establishing the U.S. mint in Philadelphia to coin money and create the nation's first monetary system; this national system replaces the previous individual state monetary systems.

June 1, 1792 Kentucky, previously the western portion of the original Virginia colony, is admitted as the fifteenth state of the Union.

September 21, 1792 France is proclaimed a republic as the French monarchy is overthrown; soon, war on Britain is declared by the new government and the Reign of Terror, a period of excessive bloodshed within France, follows from June 1793 to July 1794.

1793 Some thirty-five organizations in support of France, calling themselves Democratic-Republican societies, voice opposition to the policies of the George Washington administration.

1793 Judith Sargent Murray becomes head of the Universalist Society of Boston that later would become the Universalist Church of America and eventually the Unitarian Universalist Association.

February 12, 1793 President George Washington signs into law the Fugitive Slave Law, making it a crime for persons to harbor runaway slaves or interfere with their apprehension. The law asserts that escaped slaves and those accused of being escaped slaves hold no rights to a jury trial or any other formal opportunity to prove they are free blacks.

March 4, 1793 George Washington is inaugurated for a second term as president after being a unanimous selection of the electors, also for the second time.

April 1793 **Eli Whitney** invents an improved version of the cotton gin on the Georgia plantation of **Catharine Littlefield Greene** that more readily removes seeds from the green seed cotton; the machine substantially affects the economy of the South and makes slavery an expanded institution.

April 22, 1793 President George Washington issues the Neutrality Proclamation in an effort to keep the nation out of the war between Britain and France while continuing to trade internationally with all nations as long as war materials are not involved.

August 1793 An angry President George Washington asks the new French republic to recall Edmond Charles Genet as the first foreign minister to the United States after he violates international procedures in seeking support of U.S. citizens for France's war with Britain.

December 1793 Thomas Jefferson resigns as secretary of state; attorney general Edmund Randolph replaces him.

July 17, 1794 The Free African Society (FAS) dedicates the African Church in Philadelphia, which is associated with the Episcopal Diocese of Pennsylvania.

July 29, 1794 The Bethel African Methodist Episcopal Church, led by former slave Richard Allen, is dedicated.

August 7, 1794 President George Washington issues a proclamation to organize thirteen thousand militiamen from several states that he personally leads to western Pennsylvania to subdue farmers rebelling against a 1791 federal tax on whiskey producers, known as the Whiskey Rebellion.

August 20, 1794 General **Anthony Wayne** leads U.S. troops in a crushing defeat of the Native American confederacy of the Ohio River valley at the Battle of Fallen Timbers.

November 15, 1794 **John Witherspoon** dies after serving twenty-eight years as president of Princeton

University; he taught and greatly influenced many of the future leaders in early American public life.

November 19, 1794 U.S. diplomat and Supreme Court chief justice John Jay signs a treaty with Britain, known as the Jay Treaty, maintaining peace between the two nations and opening up markets for U.S. trade; after much controversy, the U.S. Senate ratifies the treaty on August 14, 1795.

December 28, 1794 Henry Knox resigns as secretary of war, the position he had held since March 1785 in both the confederation and federal governments.

January 1795 Treasury secretary Alexander Hamilton retires from public service but remains the recognized political leader of the Federalist Party.

February 7, 1795 The Eleventh Amendment to the U.S. Constitution is ratified, limiting the federal courts' authority over disputes between citizens of one state filing suit against another state.

August 3, 1795 General Anthony Wayne signs the Treaty of Greenville with the Miami Confederacy of the Ohio River valley led by Little Turtle, establishing peaceful relations for further U.S. settlement.

October 27, 1795 U.S. diplomat Charles Cotesworth Pinckney signs the Treaty of San Lorenzo with Spain, guaranteeing navigation rights for U.S. citizens to the Mississippi River and the port of New Orleans and resolving a disputed Florida boundary; the U.S. Senate ratifies the treaty on March 7, 1796.

December 1795 Young **Andrew Jackson** is elected delegate to the state convention to draft a Tennessee constitution and becomes Tennessee's first member of the U.S. House of Representative.

March 30, 1796 John Sevier is inaugurated as Tennessee's first governor and serves for twelve years; he completes the organization of the state and confronts problems of establishing a government on the frontier.

June 1, 1796 Tennessee, previously the western portion of North Carolina colony, becomes the sixteenth state to join the Union.

September 19, 1796 Having decided to retire from public service and not run for a third term as president, George Washington publishes his farewell address in the Philadelphia newspaper *American Daily Advertiser.*

March 4, 1797 After narrowly defeating Thomas Jefferson in the presidential election the previous fall, John Adams is inaugurated in Philadelphia as the nation's second president.

1798 Benjamin Franklin Bache, grandson of Philadelphia's first citizen, Benjamin Franklin, is arrested for publishing articles in his newspaper *Aurora* that are critical of President John Adams's administration, but dies from yellow fever before going to trial.

1798 Black activist Prince Hall organizes the African Masonic Lodge in Philadelphia, Pennsylvania, with Absalom Jones as its worshipful master and Richard Allen its treasurer.

January 14, 1798 Inventor and engineer Eli Whitney receives a federal government contract to manufacture muskets; he becomes the first manufacturer in America to make a product with interchangeable parts.

June–July 1798 Congress passes the Alien and Sedition Acts, making it more difficult for emigrants, or "aliens," to become citizens and establishing that writing, publishing, or speaking critically of the government is a federal crime punishable by fines and imprisonment.

1799 James McGready holds a summer camp revival meeting in rural Kentucky that draws hundreds of peoples for several days; it becomes the pattern for all religious camp meetings in America for the next few years, a staple of the frontier culture that ignites the "Second Great Awakening" that not only meant spiritual renewal for the churches, but also significant increases to their membership.

1799 U.S. bishop Francis Asbury ordains Richard Allen as deacon of the African Methodist Episcopal Church, making him one of the first black Americans to receive formal ordination in any denomination in America.

1800 Author Hugh Henry Brackenridge establishes the *Tree of Liberty,* a Pennsylvania newspaper to voice Jeffersonian political perspectives among the frontiersmen in opposition to *The Pittsburgh Gazette,* a Federalist-associated newspaper.

1800 The Northwest Territory is first split into the Ohio Territory and the Indiana Territory, with two more territories carved out a few years later, the Michigan Territory in 1805 and Illinois Territory in 1809.

February 22, 1800 At the invitation of Congress, Bishop John Carroll presents the eulogy at President George Washington's funeral in Baltimore's St. Peter's Church.

May 10, 1800 To spur settlement of the Northwest Territory, Congress passes the Land Act. It maintains a low price per acre, reduces the minimum number of acres per purchase, and allows a buyer to pay back the loan over several years.

September 30, 1800 To repair relations, the United States and France agree to a treaty known as the 1800 Convention, renewing trade between the two nations.

October 7, 1800 A young slave, Gabriel Prosser, and thirty-four other slaves are hanged for plotting a slave revolt in Virginia.

January 20, 1801 President John Adams appoints his secretary of state **John Marshall** to be chief justice of the U.S. Supreme Court, a position he will hold for the next thirty-four years.

February 17, 1801 On the thirty-sixth ballot, the U.S. House of Representatives select Thomas Jefferson as the third president of the United States after tying in electoral votes with fellow Democratic-Republican **Aaron Burr** in the previous fall election.

March 4, 1801 President Thomas Jefferson presents his First Inaugural Address in Washington, D.C., marking the first change in governmental rule from one political party to another.

March 4, 1801 Foreign-born **Albert Gallatin** becomes the fourth U.S. secretary of the treasury and remains in that post until 1814, longer than any other person in U.S. history.

August 1801 Thousands claim religious conversion as twenty thousand people attend a revival meeting held at Cane Ridge, Kentucky; attendance at revival camps peaks across the nation during what becomes known as the Second Awakening.

January 7, 1802 Congress establishes a permanent committee called Ways and Means that oversees both government taxing and spending policies.

April 18, 1802 President Thomas Jefferson writes a letter to U.S. diplomat Robert R. Livingston in France providing instructions on acquiring western lands from France.

February 19, 1803 Ohio becomes the seventeenth state in the Union.

February 24, 1803 In *Marbury v. Madison,* U.S. Supreme Court chief justice John Marshall establishes broad powers of the Court through judicial review; the Court can rule whether laws are constitutional—if the law agrees with the intent of the Constitution.

April 30, 1803 U.S. diplomats **James Monroe** and Robert R. Livingston sign a treaty with France for the purchase of the expansive Louisiana territory for $15 million, doubling the size of the United States.

June 20, 1803 President Thomas Jefferson issues instructions to Captain Meriwether Lewis, establishing the many goals of the Lewis and Clark Expedition.

May 14, 1804 Army officers **Meriwether Lewis** and **William Clark** set out from St. Louis, Missouri, with thirty-one men known as the Corps of Discovery, on an exploratory expedition of the West to the Pacific Ocean; they return to St. Louis on September 23, 1806, with extensive records of their experience.

June 15, 1804 States ratify the Twelfth Amendment to the U.S. Constitution, changing how electors vote for president and vice president by now having separate ballots for each position.

July 11, 1804 Aaron Burr mortally wounds Founding Father Alexander Hamilton with a single shot in a duel at

Weehawken, New Jersey, that resulted from personal comments Hamilton had made about Burr's character.

September 1804 Episcopal bishop William White ordains the fifty-eight-year-old Absalom Jones to the priesthood, the first black American ordained by a major religious denomination.

November 1804 Riding a wave of economic prosperity and international peace, President Thomas Jefferson easily defeats Federalist Charles Cotesworth Pinckney for a second term as president.

1805 Author **Mercy Otis Warren** publishes *History of the Rise, Progress and Termination of the American Revolution,* a three-volume set that provides an insider's view of the Revolutionary War and the founding of the nation.

February 1805 A young Native American woman from the Shoshone tribe named **Sacagawea** and her husband, Toussaint Charbonneau, join the Lewis and Clark Expedition at a Hidatsa and Mandan village in North Dakota as interpreters for the journey west to the Pacific Ocean.

May 1806 With French leader Napoléon Bonaparte gaining control of much of Europe, Britain imposes a naval blockade of northern European ports that shuts off trade routes to U.S. merchants; Napoléon retaliates by banning foreign trade with Britain.

March 2, 1807 U.S. Congress passes an act prohibiting the importation of slaves in the United States, effective on January 1, 1808.

June 22, 1807 The British warship *Leopard* opens fire on the American frigate *Chesapeake,* killing three American sailors and wounding eighteen after the *Chesapeake* resists British demands to search for recent British deserters; public demands for war with Britain escalate.

August 17, 1807 Inventor Robert Fulton, in partnership with U.S. diplomat Robert R. Livingston, demonstrates the capabilities of a steamboat by carrying passengers up the Hudson River from New York City to Albany in the record time of thirty hours on the *Clermont.*

September 1, 1807 Aaron Burr is found not guilty of treason before Chief Justice John Marshall in U.S. Circuit Court in Richmond, Virginia; Burr was accused of a conspiracy in the western states against the U.S. government.

December 22, 1807 Congress passes the Embargo Act, banning all U.S. merchant ships from sailing to foreign ports and prohibiting foreign ships from carrying American goods away from U.S. ports.

March 1, 1809 With the Embargo Act proving a disaster to the U.S. economy, Congress passes the Non-Intercourse Act, which lifts the trade ban on all nations but Britain and France.

March 4, 1809 Outgoing secretary of state James Madison is inaugurated as the fourth president of the United States.

June 1, 1809 Elizabeth Ann Seton establishes the Sisters of Charity of Saint Joseph's, the first religious order of women in the United States; she is elected Mother Superior, or head, of the Sisters of Charity in 1813.

September 30, 1809 Indiana territorial governor William Henry Harrison and Native American leader Little Turtle sign the Treaty of Fort Wayne, the last of a series of treaties paving the way for further settlement in the Northwest Territory but also increasing hostility of other Native American leaders toward U.S. expansion.

November 1810 President James Madison announces that trade with France will resume while restrictions on British trade will continue; this drives the United States and Britain further apart.

1811 Shawnee leader **Tecumseh** and his brother Elskwatawa, known as "The Prophet," begin organizing an alliance of Native Americans from Ohio to the Gulf Coast to resist the further spread of American settlement onto Native American lands.

February 30, 1811 Vice President **George Clinton**, known as the Father of New York for his many years as the state's first governor, casts the tie-breaking vote as president of the U.S. Senate to deny rechartering the First Bank of the United States; the country would economically suffer from the decision through the War of 1812 and it would be chartered again in 1816.

November 1811 Elected by a wide margin, Kentuckian **Henry Clay** begins service in the U.S. House of Representatives, joining a group of newly elected Republican representatives from the West and South known as War Hawks, who pushed the nation toward war against Britain.

November 8, 1811 While Native American leader Tecumseh was away in the South recruiting for his alliance, Indiana territorial governor William Henry Harrison leads a force against Tecumseh's village of Prophetstown on the Tippecanoe River, burning it to the ground.

April 30, 1812 Louisiana, formerly called the Territory of Orleans, enters the Union as the eighteenth state.

June 1812 Suffering from poor economic conditions and social turmoil, the British government removes its longstanding trade restrictions with the United States.

June 18, 1812 Unaware of British actions in repealing trade restrictions, U.S. Congress declares war on Britain; this marks the start of the War of 1812.

August 2, 1812 The *U.S.S. Constitution,* also known as "Old Ironsides," under the command of Isaac Hull, captures the British ship *Guerrière* several hundred miles off the coast of Newfoundland.

February 1813 Britain establishes a naval blockade of American ports from New York in the North to Georgia in the South and including the mouth of the Mississippi River at New Orleans.

August 30, 1813 A warring group of Creeks called Red Sticks attacks Fort Mims, an American post near Mobile, Alabama, killing some 250 whites and Native American allies.

September 10, 1813 U.S. naval commander Oliver Hazard Perry uses a fleet of nine wooden ships constructed on the banks of Lake Erie to defeat a British fleet of six ships, breaking a key British supply route and forcing British land forces to withdraw from Detroit and surrounding areas.

October 5, 1813 U.S. ground forces led by General William Henry Harrison overtake the retreating British and defeat them at the Battle of the Thames; Shawnee leader Tecumseh is killed in the battle, essentially ending Native American resistance to American settlement in the Ohio and Mississippi river valleys.

March 14, 1814 General Andrew Jackson leads a large militia force and crushes the Creek Red Sticks in the Battle of Horseshoe Bend in Alabama; the U.S. victory leads to the Treaty of Fort Jackson in August, in which fourteen million acres of Native American lands are ceded to the United States.

April 1814 The British navy extends its blockade of American ports along the entire East Coast, shutting down all U.S. trade and further crippling the U.S. economy.

August 24, 1814 Launching an attack on the Mid-Atlantic coast, British forces enter Washington, D.C., and burn many public buildings, including the Treasury, the War Department, the Capitol, and the President's House. First Lady **Dolley Madison** waits until the last minute to evacuate and courageously removes out of the city vital government papers and some of the young nation's few treasures including a full length portrait of George Washington painted by Gilbert Stuart.

September 11, 1814 A small American fleet of four ships commanded by U.S. commodore Thomas Macdonough intercepts and defeats a British supply fleet on Lake Champlain near Plattsburg, New York; with its supply line broken, an invading British land army quickly retreats to Montreal.

September 13, 1814 British ships begin bombarding Fort McHenry, a military installation protecting the entrance to Baltimore's harbor; the following morning, the fort remains in U.S. control, inspiring American lawyer **Francis Scott Key** from nearby Georgetown to write "The Star-Spangled Banner," America's future national anthem.

December 24, 1814 The United States and Britain sign the Treaty of Ghent, ending the War of 1812; the treaty restores British-American relations and reopens trade but resolves few other issues that led to the war.

January 5, 1815 Unaware of the recently signed peace treaty, representatives from several New England states, secretly meeting since December 15 in Hartford, Connecticut, send off three representatives to Washington, D.C., to express their grievances toward and make demands to the U.S. government; public exposure of the meeting leads to the final demise of the Federalist Party.

January 8, 1815 Unaware of the peace treaty, General Andrew Jackson commands a U.S. force of seven thousand soldiers and others that crushes a massive assault by eight thousand British troops in the Battle of New Orleans.

December 1815 Free black captain Paul Cuffee sets sail for Sierra Leone in West Africa with thirty-eight free black emigrants and a cargo of goods that pioneers could use to begin a colony of free blacks away from the United States.

March 14, 1816 U.S. Congress revives the national bank system with the Second National Bank of the United States, located in Philadelphia.

November 1816 Following in the steps of earlier Virginian presidents George Washington, Thomas Jefferson, and James Madison, outgoing secretary of state James Monroe is elected the fifth U.S. president; the nation is at peace, feeling strong and confident, and ready to move forward.

Words to Know

A

abolition: The prohibition of slavery.

academy: A high school or college where special subjects are taught.

agrarianism: A belief that farming is the most respectable way of life and should remain the most important sector of the nation's economy.

alien: A person who holds citizenship in one country but resides in a different country.

alliance: An agreement of mutual aid between groups or nations.

amendment: A formal change to a legal document, such as the U.S. Constitution.

American Revolution: The American colonies' battle to achieve independence from Great Britain that took place from 1775 to 1783.

Anti-Federalists: Those who opposed the U.S. Constitution during its ratification process in 1787 and 1788 because they preferred to have a weak central government with most governing powers held by the states.

appellate: Courts that do not hear original cases, but review lower trial court decisions to determine if proper legal procedures were followed.

aristocracy: A government or ruling class made up of royalty and wealthy individuals.

articles: Sections of a formal document.

B

bankruptcy: A financial condition in which a party is unable to satisfy claims against it, such as paying back loans or making payments on something purchased.

Bill of Rights: The first ten amendments to the U.S. Constitution, identifying certain basic rights that the government cannot take away from U.S. citizens.

blockade: Barriers positioned at a seaport entrance to prevent ships from entering or leaving.

bond: A paper certificate the government sells to raise money; the government buys back the certificate (repays the money) at a later date.

C

Cabinet: A group of people, including heads of major governmental departments, who advise the U.S. president.

capital: Money invested in a business and used to operate that business.

capital offense: A crime that involves the death penalty.

catechism: The teaching of religious principles.

cede: To give land away by treaty.

chain: A measuring device used by surveyors; a chain had one hundred links of equal length.

charter: A formal document issued by a government that defined rights and privileges of an organization, such as the area to be settled by a land company or rights of a corporation.

checks and balances: The specific powers in one branch of government that allow it to limit the powers of the other branches.

colony: Settlements in a new land still governed by the nation from which they came.

commerce: The buying, selling, or exchange of goods transported between states or foreign countries, conducted on a large scale.

common law: A legal system in use for several centuries in England that provides a set of judicial rules commonly applied to resolve similar disputes; it is built on a history of judge's decisions rather than relying on legislative-passed codes, or laws.

compromise: The settlement of a dispute between two sides that is achieved by each side giving up something in order to gain a desired end.

confederation: A loose alliance of governments that share a common purpose.

consecrate: To provide permanent religious authority to a person.

Constitution: The legal document establishing the main principles and structure of the U.S. government.

cotton gin: A machine that separates seeds from cotton fibers.

craftsmen: Highly skilled persons who make certain hand-crafted items from wood, leather, or metals such as furniture, saddles, and cooking utensils.

credit: The reputation—good or bad—that a person, company, or country has for paying bills or debts on time.

creditor: A person, bank, or nation to whom money is owed.

currency: Coins and paper bills that serve as money.

D

debt: Money or something of value owed to another.

defendant: A person against whom a legal action is brought.

deist: A person who believed that the universe was created by a rational and reasoned supreme being, but questioned traditional religious organizations such as official state churches in early America that regulated how people lived and worshiped.

delegate: A person chosen or elected to represent others at a meeting such as a political convention or a legislature.

democracy: A government whose laws and functions are determined by the will of the majority.

Democratic-Republican Party: A political party that formed around 1793 from a loose organization of people calling themselves Republicans; they were largely rural farmers who maintained sympathies with France, America's ally during the American Revolutionary War, and distrusted a strong national government.

dissenter: One who rejects the doctrines of an established church.

duty: A tax on goods traded into a country.

E

electors: A certain number of persons in each state who are elected by the general public or legislature to cast votes for the president and vice president.

emancipation: Freedom from slavery.

embargo: A government order prohibiting merchant ships from leaving ports with goods.

emigrants: Those who leave their country of residence to live elsewhere.

Enlightenment: Also called the Age of Reason, a period that began in Europe in the 1600s and lasted through the 1700s; a philosophy emphasizing human ability to apply reason over ignorance and religious superstition.

established church: The official church of a colony, state, or country; the established church commonly received a portion of taxes collected from all the people.

evangelist: A spirited traveling preacher who preaches a personal relationship with God that is based on faith in the scriptures of the Bible.

excise tax: A payment of a percentage of the price of a product manufactured or sold within a nation.

executive: A head of government who enforces the laws, such as a state governor or nation's president.

executive branch: The branch of the federal government that enforces the nation's laws.

export: Goods shipped out of a country to another country.

export duties: Fees paid on goods shipped out of a state or country to another state or country.

F

Federalist Party: A political party whose members largely included wealthy and well-educated merchants, manufacturers, and shippers who believed in a powerful central government and distrusted democratic processes.

Federalists: Those who supported a strong central government for the United States and promoted adoption of the U.S. Constitution during its ratification process.

flax: A plant whose silky stem fibers are used to weave linen cloth.

foreclosure: The removal of property from an individual or company to sell and pay off loans on that property.

Founding Fathers: Prominent citizens who took an active role in the creation and early development of the United States, including the signing of the 1776 Declaration of Independence and drafting of the U.S. Constitution at the 1787 Constitutional Convention.

fraternal organization: A group of men who associate with each other for a common purpose, often sharing a common background, such as the same profession.

free black: A person of African birth or ancestry who was not the property of a slave owner.

French and Indian War: A series of military battles between Great Britain and France (and France's Native American allies) that took place on the American frontier and in Canada between 1754 and 1763.

frigate: A sailing warship with tall masts and numerous large guns, sometimes positioned on two levels of decks.

frontier: The furthest point of settlement in early America.

G

grievance: A complaint over what is considered an unjust act by another person or a government.

gristmill: A mill for grinding corn and wheat into flour, often located near most communities in early America.

H

habeas corpus: The right of a person to be brought before a judge to determine if he or she can be legally detained.

heir: A person inheriting property or a title of a position.

house raising: An event in which frontier neighbors came together to help construct a cabin or barn, frequently leading to social gatherings.

I

immigrant: A person who comes into one country from another to establish a permanent residence.

impeach: To bring formal charges of misconduct against a public official.

import: To bring goods into the country from another country.

import duties: Fees or taxes paid on goods brought into the colonies or states from another country.

impressment: A long-standing British practice of seizing sailors from foreign ships and forcing them into military service on British warships.

inaugurate: To install into public office with a formal ceremony.

indigo: A plant that produces a deep purple dye.

industrial revolution: A major change in the economy, caused by the introduction of power-driven machines and factories that produce goods in large quantities.

inflation: Rapidly increasing prices of goods and property.

interchangeable parts: Identical parts made by machine tools that may be quickly assembled into identical products and can easily replace broken parts on existing products, such as muskets in early America.

intolerance: Unwillingness to accept the beliefs of another person.

investor: A person who puts money into something that is likely to make a profit.

J

judicial: Resolving legal disputes in a court of law.

judicial branch: The branch of the federal government that resolves legal disputes in a court of law.

judicial review: The process by which federal courts review laws to determine whether they violate the U.S. Constitution.

jurisdiction: The geographic area and type of law a court has legal authority to hear.

L

land title: Official government document showing property ownership.

legislate: To make laws.

legislative branch: The branch of the federal government made up of an elected body of representatives responsible for making laws.

legislature: An elected body of representatives responsible for making laws.

Loyalists: Colonists who supported the king of Britain during America's fight for independence.

M

magistrate: A person appointed to hear minor disputes and legal cases.

manumission: The process of freeing a person from slavery.

market: A place to sell goods.

merchant: A person who earns a living by buying and selling goods for profit.

midnight judges: Federal judges appointed by President John Adams in the last days of his presidency in an effort to maintain a Federalist Party influence in the national government, which was soon to be led by Democratic-Republican president Thomas Jefferson.

midwife: A woman experienced in helping the birthing process of other women.

militia: An organized military force, made up of citizens, that serves in times of emergency.

monarchy: A government in which a person who inherits the leadership position, such as a king or queen, holds absolute power.

mulatto: Early American term for a person with a black parent and a white parent.

N

nationalism: Loyalty to a nation and devotion to its interests (over the interests of individual states or regions within the nation).

naturalization: The process by which immigrants become citizens of the country in which they reside.

necessaries: An early American term for outhouses.

neutrality: A political policy of not publicly favoring any one warring nation over the other and not taking part in the conflict.

O

ordination: A ceremony for giving priestly authority.

original jurisdiction: A court's authority to rule on a legal dispute first.

P

pamphlet: A short essay of several pages; a common means in early America for distributing viewpoints on controversial topics.

Patriots: American colonists who supported the rebel cause to gain independence from British rule.

pickled: Vegetables and fruits from spring, summer, and fall harvests sun-dried and soaked in sugar and vinegar for long-term preservation.

plantation: A farm worked by one hundred or more slaves.

planter: A large landowner living in a large house, or mansion, and often owning many slaves.

plat: A formal map of surveyed land.

plowshare: The blade on a plow that makes furrows in the ground.

pluralism: Many people of diverse ethnic, religious, and social backgrounds coexisting peacefully while sharing common cultural experiences.

political factions: Groups of people who hold viewpoints on political matters different from other groups.

preamble: The introductory part of a law or legal document summarizing the reason for the document and what it contains.

precedent: A previously established practice to be followed in the future.

privateers: Privately owned small ships recruited to fight or harass the enemy.

protective tariff: A high tax on imported goods to protect domestic producers against foreign competition.

Protestant: A Christian religious denomination that separated from the Roman Catholic church in the 1500s.

Protestant Reformation: An effort in Western Europe beginning in the sixteenth century to reform the Catholic Church, resulting in new denominations, such as the Lutheran Church.

public works: Roads, ports, or other facilities made for public use, often with government funds.

R

ratification: Approval that makes something officially valid or sanctioned.

rebellion: Resistance by an individual or group to the political control of an authority or government.

reexport: To import certain items (such as coffee, sugar, pepper, and cocoa) from one country and then export them to other markets.

religious freedom: In colonial days, the ability to establish specific religious principles in a colony; not the freedom of individuals to worship in the church of their choice.

republic: A country governed by the consent of the people and for the benefit of the people through elected representatives.

Republicans: Those who favored a weak central government and strong state governments; became the Democratic-Republicans.

revenue: The total income a government collects from taxes and other sources.

revival: Renewing interest in religion often in highly emotional meetings.

revolutionary: Supportive of a fundamental change in political organization.

root cellar: An underground structure that remains cool throughout the year, providing conditions for good preservation of fruits and vegetables.

S

salt-curing: A process by which meat is soaked in salty water and hung to dry for long-term preservation.

secession: The formal withdrawal of a state from the union.

sect: A religious body that has separated from a larger religious group.

section: A square piece of land measuring 1 mile on each side and containing 640 acres.

sectionalism: Inflated devotion to the interests of a particular section of the country, at the expense of other regions.

sedition: Behavior or language intended to incite rebellion against an authority or the government.

sovereignty: A government largely free from outside political control.

speculators: People who take financial risks by buying something at a low price with the hope that its value will rise and a profit can be made by reselling.

squatters: Pioneers who settled on unoccupied land without paying the owner.

staples: The chief crops of an area that provide economic stability.

survey: A detailed inspection of a piece of land.

surveyor: A person who precisely measures and marks the location of a piece of property.

T

tariff: A tax on imported goods (goods from another country).

tavern: A central meeting place that included rooms in which to eat, drink, and spend the night.

toleration: A government policy of allowing various forms of religious belief not officially established.

township: A large square piece of land measuring 6 miles on each side and precisely divided into 36 sections of land.

tyranny: The state of possessing absolute rule and making decisions for the benefit of the rulers rather than for the good of the people.

U

unalienable rights: Individual rights that cannot be rightfully taken away.

unanimous: In complete agreement.

unicameral: A one-house or one-assembly legislature.

W

writ of *habeas corpus:* The right of a person to be brought before a judge to determine if he or she can be legally detained.

writ of *mandamus:* A court order directing a government official to perform a specific administrative act.

Shaping of America, 1783–1815

Biographies

Pierre-Charles L'Enfant

Born August 2, 1754 (Paris, France)
Died June 14, 1825 (Prince Georges County, Maryland)

Engineer, architect

Pierre-Charles L'Enfant was a French artist who excelled in architecture and engineering. He is best remembered as the city planner who designed Washington, D.C., under the direction of President **George Washington** (1732–1799; served 1789–97; see entry in volume 2). L'Enfant was also responsible for remodeling Federal Hall in New York City, where Washington took the oath of office as the first president of the United States.

L'Enfant was a soldier in the American Revolution (1775–83) and a charter member of the Society of the Cincinnati, an organization created to help maintain ties among veterans of the American Revolution. He designed the society's certificate and its insignia. L'Enfant's use of symbolism and his practical use of topography (natural features of the ground surface) made him an influential urban planner into the twentieth century. Elements of L'Enfant's plan for Washington, D.C., were adopted in numerous cities nationally and internationally.

"The plan should be drawn on such a scale as to leave room for that . . . embellishment which the increase of the wealth of the nation will permit it to pursue at any period however remote. . . ."

A revolutionary man

Pierre-Charles L'Enfant was born in Paris on August 2, 1754. His mother was Marie Charlotte Lullier, the daughter of an official of the French Court. His father was Pierre L'Enfant

Pierre-Charles L'Enfant. *(National Archives and Records Administration.)*

(Lenfant), a painter for the French Crown whose specialty was landscapes and battle scenes. Pierre-Charles was baptized August 3, 1754, in the Church Royale of the Parish of Saint Hippolytus, one of the oldest Catholic churches in Paris. He had a sister and a brother, but his brother, Pierre Joseph, died in 1758 at the age of six. Pierre-Charles grew up in a privileged home and spent time in the courts of Louis XV (1710–1774; reigned 1715–74) and Louis XVI (1754–1793; reigned 1774–92). In 1771, he became a student at the Royal Academy of Painting and Sculpture, where his father was an instructor. Pierre-Charles studied fine art and learned to draw battle scenes, which involved sessions on how to draw fortifications. Included in his studies at the academy were detailed instructions in the art of landscape architecture.

At the age of twenty-two, L'Enfant accepted a lieutenancy in the Continental Army to help America in its fight for independence from Britain. France threw its support behind the American colonies in 1777 when it became evident that the Americans had a real chance of defeating Britain. The French were longtime enemies of Britain and had lost land to the British in North America during the French and Indian War (1754–63). L'Enfant was among the first to enlist, although he had no military training or experience as an army engineer (who built bridges, roads, and earthworks for troop defense). He joined with other commissioned and noncommissioned officers, including engineers, artillerymen, miners, and trained laborers. L'Enfant set out aboard the *Amphitrite* and arrived in Portsmouth, New Hampshire, in April 1777. Almost immediately he changed his first name to Peter Charles, the English version of his original name, and committed his talents to supporting the American cause.

L'Enfant was sent to Boston, Massachusetts, in December 1777. He joined the staff of Friedrich Wilhelm von Steuben (1730–1794), newly appointed inspector general of the army. Steuben was training General George Washington's raw recruits and preparing the official military manual of the U.S. Army. L'Enfant drew eight illustrations for Steuben's *Regulations for the Order and Discipline of the Troops of the United States* while stationed at Valley Forge, Pennsylvania, in 1778. He also drew a number of landscapes while he was there, including a panoramic view of West Point. It was at Valley Forge that L'Enfant was first introduced to George Washington. Washington requested a pencil portrait of himself after seeing L'Enfant sketch similar pictures for his fellow officers during the long, dreary days at Valley Forge. A talented artist, L'Enfant was able to catch a clear likeness of his subject in his drawings. His service in Pennsylvania earned L'Enfant an appointment as captain in the Army Corps of Engineers on April 3, 1779. With the promotion, L'Enfant was sent south to his next assignment.

In October 1779, L'Enfant was present at the Battle of Savannah, Georgia. He received a serious leg wound while attempting to set fire to the British-built defenses. Thereafter, he relied on a cane to walk. L'Enfant participated in the defense of Charleston, South Carolina, in May 1780, and was captured by the British. He was released in a prisoner exchange in January 1782 and allowed to return to active military duty with the engineers. L'Enfant immediately asked General Washington for a promotion to the rank of major. The commander in chief sent his personal praise, but Congress did not immediately grant a rank increase. L'Enfant's request for a promotion was granted on May 2, 1783. He was commissioned brevet major in the Army Corps of Engineers.

Design work

In 1783, L'Enfant helped found the Society of the Cincinnati. The organization was created to help maintain the bonds of friendship among military officers who had served during the American Revolution. It also worked to promote their interests with the government and aid the widows and orphans of deceased officers. The Society of the Cincinnati was named after the famous Roman general Lucius Quinctius Cincinnatus (born c. 519 BCE). A branch of the organization was formed in each of the original thirteen states as well as France. Just over two thousand of the nearly six thousand officers eligible to join the society in 1783 applied for membership.

L'Enfant was selected to design the society's membership diploma, badge, and medal. He chose a bald eagle with the society's emblem on its breast because the bird's range was limited to the North American continent. The design was presented to George Washington, who had been elected president of the organization. L'Enfant was sent to France in December 1783 to help organize the French branch of the Society of the Cincinnati. He was commissioned to have the society's diploma engraved and the eagle insignia made by a good jeweler in Paris. L'Enfant used the time in France for personal business as well, visiting his aging father and family members, whom he had not seen in seven years.

L'Enfant was back in America by April 1784. Like most soldiers of the Continental Army, he received his official discharge papers in January of that year. In December, L'Enfant sent Congress a proposal for the creation of a department of engineers that he would command. He proposed that this new federal corps would be responsible for the fortification of the nation's harbors, for defense purposes as well as for the protection of trade. The department would also erect frontier posts for the supervision of Native American trade and the protection of Americans immigrating to the West. L'Enfant documented the need for city planning, road and bridge construction, and sanitation controls. His plan for the country's general growth and defense included the idea that the federal government create a separate territory held by the states for their common use. L'Enfant's suggestions for expanding federal control came at a time when Congress, operating under the Articles of Confederation, believed the government should exercise only minimal responsibilities. Congress gave L'Enfant's proposal the dignity due a war hero by submitting it to a committee. The committee studied the documents, and unconvinced, they reported back to Congress that the United States did not need a department of engineers.

The move to New York

In 1785, Congress chose New York City as the seat of the federal government. L'Enfant decided to move to the new capital as well. He settled in New York and supported himself as an artist and architect, designing ceremonial and monument pieces for private and governmental projects alike. He quickly established a reputation as an outstanding designer and engineer. In 1787, L'Enfant supervised the erection of a monument to General Richard Montgomery (1736–1775) at St. Paul's Church in the city. The following year, L'Enfant designed the facility used for New York's ratification convention, where delegates from the state considered whether to approve the new U.S. Constitution. The pavilion was built to seat six thousand people for a grand banquet that took place on July 23, 1788. Three days later, the New York convention ratified the Constitution, and New York became the eleventh state in the union. New York City busily made plans to grow and build in hopes of becoming the permanent residence of the federal government.

L'Enfant enjoyed a pleasant and prosperous decade in New York City. He built numerous mansions and monuments. In September 1788, his plans for converting New York's City Hall into Federal Hall were approved. The restored building faced Broad Street where it intersected with Wall Street. It was to be the new home for the U.S. Congress. On April 30, 1789, George Washington took the oath of the presidency on the second-story balcony of the newly completed Federal Hall.

A capital affair

In 1790, the U.S. House of Representatives approved the creation of a national capital city in the new District of Columbia. Washington had personally chosen the location, which included land in both Maryland and Virginia. President Washington turned to L'Enfant to plan the capital. L'Enfant's grand vision for the city greatly excited Washington. In January 1791, the eager architect was selected to design not only the city's layout but all of the public buildings as well. L'Enfant immediately set about surveying the terrain of the district, which at the time was a wilderness of swamp and forest. He sketched out a plan for the city and outlined a program for its prompt development.

L'Enfant completed his preliminary plan by July 1791. His plan made excellent use of the area's natural features; the proposed city fit the topography of the site perfectly. L'Enfant's "Congress House," which was later renamed the Capitol, was situated on a hill with a large park extending westward to the Potomac River. L'Enfant used long avenues that joined at key points marked by important buildings or monuments. The greatness of the plan was evident in its simplicity and symbolism, with the avenues of power radiating from a central source. By August 1791, L'Enfant submitted a report to President Washington that included a more complete map and numerous plans for proposed buildings. The president brought L'Enfant's work before Congress that December. The cornerstone of the President's House was laid in 1792.

From the beginning, L'Enfant demanded complete control over the entire project. He was unwilling to submit himself to the authority of the federal overseers assigned to work with him. President Washington was finally forced to dismiss L'Enfant in February 1792, after just one year of intense planning activity. The first engraved map of the city of Washington was published that March. It credited the plan to Andrew Ellicott (1754–1820), the surveyor who had worked with L'Enfant. This plan for the district, known as the "Ellicott Map," was a version of the L'Enfant plan.

Post-Washington years

After his dismissal, L'Enfant left Washington, D.C., and moved to Philadelphia, Pennsylvania. **Alexander Hamilton** (1755–1804; see entry in volume 1) hired him to plan a town and an aqueduct (structure that conveys flowing water) for the Society for Establishing Useful Manufacturers in Paterson, New Jersey. Others were later hired to carry out a simplified version of L'Enfant's extravagant design; this was the case with most of his projects over the years. Between 1793 and 1795, L'Enfant designed and partially constructed a famous house for financier Robert Morris (1734–1806). Unfortunately, financial problems forced Morris to declare bankruptcy, and L'Enfant stopped work on the mansion. It became known as "Morris's Folly" and was demolished in 1801.

In 1810, L'Enfant accepted a settlement of several thousand dollars from the U.S. government for his work on the federal city plan. It was far short of the nearly $100,000 he had originally demanded in 1800. L'Enfant was offered a professorship at West Point in the summer of 1812, but he declined to accept. His last public employment was a commission to reconstruct Fort Washington after it failed to protect the city of Washington from invasion by British troops in the War of 1812 (1812–15).

L'Enfant remained in his adopted country until his death in 1825 at the age of seventy. He spent his final years in poverty, depending on the charity of friends in Maryland. His body was buried in an unmarked grave at "Green Hill," a Digges family estate in Prince Georges County, Maryland. Early in the twentieth century, L'Enfant's plan for the city of Washington was readopted, and his contribution to the unique capital city brought him official recognition. In 1909, L'Enfant's body was exhumed and then, after lying in state in the Capitol Rotunda, was buried in Arlington National Cemetery. His tomb overlooks the city he planned. A monument marking L'Enfant's grave includes his map of Washington.

For More Information

Books

Bowling, Kenneth R. *Peter Charles L'Enfant: Vision, Honor, and Male Friendship in the Early American Republic.* Washington, DC: George Washington University, 2002.

Bryan, Wilhelmus Bogart. *A History of the National Capital.* New York: Macmillan, 1914–16.

Caemmerer, H. Paul. *The Life of Pierre Charles L'Enfant: Planner of the City Beautiful—The City of Washington.* Washington, DC: National Republic Publishing, 1950. Reprint, New York: Da Capo Press, 1970.

DeConde, Alexander. *Entangling Alliance: Politics & Diplomacy under George Washington.* Durham, NC: Duke University Press, 1958. Reprint, Westport, CT: Greenwood Press, 1974.

Kite, Elizabeth S. *L'Enfant and Washington, 1791–1792.* Baltimore, MD: Johns Hopkins Press, 1929. Reprint, New York: Arno Press, 1970.

Web Sites

"Explore DC: Pierre L'Enfant." *WETA: The Public Broadcasting Station in the Nation's Capital.* http://www.exploredc.org/index.php?id=181 (accessed on August 14, 2005).

"Pierre Charles L'Enfant." *Arlington National Cemetery.* http://www.arlingtoncemetery.net/l-enfant.htm (accessed on August 14, 2005).

Lewis and Clark

Meriwether Lewis
Born August 18, 1774 (Albemarle County, Virginia)
Died October 11, 1809 (Nashville, Tennessee)

William Clark
Born August 1, 1770 (Caroline County, Virginia)
Died September 1, 1838 (St. Louis, Missouri)

Explorers, governors

M eriwether Lewis and William Clark are two of the most celebrated heroes in American history for leading an extraordinary expedition. With some forty crew members, known as the Corps of Discovery, they journeyed by boat, canoe, horseback, and foot for three years in uncharted territory from St. Louis, Missouri, to the Pacific Northwest coast and back. President **Thomas Jefferson** (1743–1826; served 1801–9; see entry in volume 1) sent them to explore and map the new American lands, find a route to the Pacific Ocean, establish an American presence in the Pacific Northwest, make friends with Native Americans, and see to what extent European influence already existed, if any.

Lewis and Clark shared leadership responsibilities on the expedition and worked so close in harmony that history almost considers them one. They combined their skills, frontier experience, and resourcefulness to accomplish their large and dangerous task. Lewis was the more intellectual man, while Clark possessed greater wilderness and leadership skills. They encountered some thirty Native American tribes, many of

"[At] a village of 7 houses . . . we found the Chief we had Seen at the long narrows . . . we entered his lodge and he gave us to eate Pounded fish, bread made of roots, Filbert nuts, & the berries . . . we gave to each woman of the lodge a brace of Ribon of which they were much pleased."

From William Clark's journal

Meriwether Lewis and William Clark, with Sacagawea. *(© Corbis.)*

whom had never seen a white person. They produced a journal of historic importance that recorded natural and cultural conditions in the West at the beginning of the nineteenth century. Their trek represented the beginning of the great westward expansion of the United States that peaked in the mid-nineteenth century.

Lewis and his love of the wilderness

Meriwether Lewis was born in rural Albemarle County, Virginia, in August 1774, on the eve of the American Revolution

(1775–83). Lewis was the oldest child of William Lewis and Lucy Meriwether, both from influential families of wealth. His great-grandfather arrived in Virginia in 1638 with a large land grant—over 33,000 acres—from the king of England. Lewis's father, William, later inherited almost 2,000 acres with slaves and a house. William served as an officer in the Continental Army during the war and died in 1779 when Lewis was just five years old.

Lewis's mother remarried John Marks, and when Lewis was ten years old, the family moved with other relatives to rural northern Georgia. There they lived on several plantations on the Broad River in Oglethorpe County. Lewis grew up exploring the woods around the plantation and becoming an expert hunter. He learned wilderness skills while living in an upper-class plantation society. Lewis developed a scientific interest in the plants and animals of the area. His mother became an expert in herbal medicines, and others from around the region frequently sought her advice. Lewis learned much about native plants from her.

Meriwether Lewis. (© Bettmann/Corbis.)

Educational opportunities were few in rural Georgia, so at age thirteen Lewis returned to Virginia to be privately tutored for the next five years. He studied various subjects including mathematics, science, and Latin. He also enjoyed reading the journals of British explorer Captain James Cook (1728–1779), who sailed to exotic places in the Pacific Ocean and encountered natives across the region. At age eighteen, Lewis was ready to enter the College of William and Mary in Virginia. However, his stepfather died, and his mother returned from Georgia to live on the "Locust Hill" plantation near Charlottesville, Virginia. Being the oldest son of the family, Lewis felt obligated to forgo his plans for college and help manage the plantation. The home of Thomas Jefferson, future president of the United States, was nearby. They became good friends as well as neighbors.

Lewis as soldier and presidential confidante

In 1794, Lewis joined the Virginia militia as a private and was among the troops sent to western Pennsylvania to quell the Whiskey Rebellion, a revolt by farmers in protest of high taxes on the whiskey they produced from their corn crops. Lewis quickly found a soldier's life to his liking, and he joined the U.S. Army in May 1795. Lewis was sent to the Ohio River valley as part of the force commanded by General **Anthony Wayne** (1745–1796; see entry in volume 2) to end Native American resistance to expanding white settlement. He served under William Clark in a special company of sharpshooters. By 1799, Lewis rose in rank to lieutenant and then became a captain in 1800. While stationed at various posts west of the Appalachian Mountains, Lewis learned about Native American culture.

In 1800, shortly after Lewis was transferred to the post at Detroit under the command of General James Wilkinson (1757–1825), Thomas Jefferson was elected president. Jefferson was a widower, and his daughters, who were married, would be at the president's mansion only on limited occasions. So immediately after his election, Jefferson wrote to Lewis, offering him a position as his private secretary. Jefferson was not only familiar with Lewis's intellectual abilities, but his wilderness skills and familiarity with Native Americans as well. They also had shared through the years an interest in western exploration. Jefferson was eager to have Lewis's knowledge of the West and the military close at hand. Lewis immediately accepted the position and went to live in the President's House. He was in charge of the operation of the mansion and the eleven slaves brought by Jefferson from his Monticello plantation. Jefferson entertained endlessly, and Lewis overheard discussions on all matters by the world's leaders.

The topic of westward exploration had long been of keen interest to Jefferson, and on occasion it surfaced in his discussions with Lewis. Lewis had for years expressed interest in participating in such an adventure. As early as 1792, Lewis had asked Jefferson, who was secretary of state at the time, about the prospects of conducting an exploration of the Far West.

In early 1803, President Jefferson finally decided it was time. On January 18, he sent a secret note to Congress, requesting funds to pursue exploration of the West. Secrecy was necessary at the time because the land to be explored was not part of the United States but Jefferson was interested in possible future expansion and acquisition of the territory. Congress responded with $2,500. Of course, Jefferson asked Lewis to lead the expedition. Lewis already had many of the skills he would need for the journey. Jefferson sent him to the American Philosophical Society in Philadelphia to gain other skills that would be necessary. There, Lewis learned about biology (the study of living organisms), botany (the study of plants), and paleontology (the study of fossils) from the nation's leading scientists. He learned how to make scientific observations and use astronomical instruments to plot locations and directions. He then traveled to Lancaster, Pennsylvania, where surveyor Andrew Ellicott (1754–1820) taught him mapmaking.

On June 30, Jefferson sent Lewis detailed instructions for the expedition along with passports to travel through French-controlled territory west of the Mississippi River. Lewis's tasks were many: to determine if a large river existed that could provide a means for commerce to the Pacific Coast from the interior; to make contacts and friends with Native American tribes; to collect samples and make scientific observations of wildlife, plants, and geography; and to determine what Spanish presence might be in the region. Jefferson asked Lewis to select a companion officer. Lewis's choice was William Clark, his former commander in the U.S. Army.

About the time the expedition was to begin, stunning news arrived from Europe. U.S. diplomat **James Monroe** (1758–1831; see entry in volume 2) and others had negotiated the $15 million purchase of a vast area east of the Mississippi River—800,000 square miles stretching from the mouth of the Mississippi at New Orleans all the way to Canada and west to the Rocky Mountains. Now much of the territory that Lewis would explore was part of the United States.

The Clark family in the military

William Clark was born in August 1770 in rural Virginia, the ninth child of John and Ann Rogers Clark. The Clarks were planters and slave owners, farming many acres. Clark enjoyed

Explorer William Clark. *(© Bettmann/Corbis.)*

exploring the wilderness around his home and received little formal education. He learned the basic skills of the frontier, including horseback riding, hunting, and land surveying.

During the American Revolution, William's older brother, George Rogers Clark (1752–1818), became a national hero. He had much military success in the West, protecting settlements from attacks by Native Americans who had allied with the British against the United States. He rose in rank to general. After the war, in the autumn of 1784, the Clark family moved to Kentucky to join George, who remained stationed there. They built a new home called Mulberry Hill.

In 1785, Congress commissioned George to negotiate treaties with the Native Americans of the Ohio River valley to open up the new Northwest Territory to American settlement. However, hostilities mounted as tribes continued to resist the spread of settlements into their traditional territories, and George ended up leading an expedition against Native American forces on the Wabash River in Indiana in 1786. Hostilities continued to grow. William joined the militia three years later in 1789 when they went back to the White River area near the Wabash. Through the winter months of 1789–90, William helped defend the Kentucky settlements from occasional Native American assaults and joined another militia expedition in the early summer of 1791.

Following the disastrous defeat of General Arthur St. Clair's (1735–1818) force by the Native American alliance later in 1791, Clark joined the regular army. He received a commission of lieutenant on March 7, 1792, and served for the next four years under General Anthony Wayne. He became commander of a sharpshooting rifle corps in September 1793. In August 1794, Clark's rifle corps took part in the Battle of

Fallen Timbers, where the Native American alliance suffered a crushing defeat. Meriwether Lewis had joined Clark's company by that time. During this four-year period of Clark's military career, Clark was also sent on assignments to meet with Spanish officials on the lower Mississippi River to resolve territorial disputes.

By the summer of 1796, Clark was ready to return home to help with the plantation at Mulberry Hill. He resigned his commission in July. Clark worked the plantation and traveled around the country over the next several years, often related to settling his brother's war debts that the government refused to pay. It was not uncommon for Revolutionary War leaders to finance their own expenses in military campaigns and hope for repayment following the war. However, Clark was unsuccessful in getting full repayment from both the state of Virginia and U.S. Congress for his brother's debts. When both of his parents died in 1799, Clark inherited the family home. He fought hard to save their property from creditors.

In 1803, Clark received Lewis's invitation to help command an expedition to the West. Clark eagerly accepted. Though the army failed to raise Clark's rank to captain, Lewis, who had that rank, would always treat Clark as an equal and call him captain.

Corps of Discovery

Later in 1803, Lewis and Clark journeyed west toward the Mississippi River. Along the way, they recruited their crew. They established camp on the Mississippi not far from the mouth of the Missouri River. Much of the crew was recruited from southwestern Illinois, near St. Louis. Throughout the winter of 1803–4, Lewis and Clark drilled the expedition recruits in military fashion and gathered supplies and equipment in preparation for their launch the following spring. For food, they carried pork, flour, salt, and biscuits. They would add wild game and fish as they traveled.

In the spring of 1804, Lewis was taking part in official ceremonies transferring the Louisiana Purchase to U.S. ownership; this was part of his job as Jefferson's private

Lewis and Clark's Slave, York

Until the late twentieth century, few people were aware that the Lewis and Clark expedition included a black slave. Rarely mentioned in the journals kept on the journey, York was a slave brought along by William Clark. York was about the same age as Clark and grew up with him in the woods of Kentucky on the Clark farm. What is remarkable is that York shared much the same privileges on the expedition as the other members, even voting on different issues as they arose. While on the journey York shared in everyday duties and even risked his life in attempting to rescue Clark when he was caught in a flash flood in Montana.

The Native Americans along the route had never seen a black man. They were in great awe of York, who was large, very muscular, and athletic. Full of curiosity, some Native Americans even tried rubbing York's black skin with sand or dirt to remove the color. Native American children regularly followed York, fascinated by his appearance. As a participant in the expedition, York was the first black American to cross the North American continent.

Yet after living for three years as a free man on the expedition, York was forced to return to a life of slavery upon the crew's return to St. Louis in September 1806. He begged Clark for his freedom, but Clark refused. York also wanted to be closer to his wife, who worked near Louisville, Kentucky; Clark refused that, too. Finally, Clark relented and sent York to Kentucky and later gave him his freedom. It is reported that York later worked hauling freight in Kentucky and Tennessee and died sometime before 1832.

secretary. Clark and the Corps of Discovery departed on May 14, traveling in three boats up the Missouri River. Lewis caught up at St. Charles, Missouri. They spent the summer working their way up the Missouri River before selecting their wintering spot on the upper Missouri. They built Fort Mandan near present-day Bismarck, North Dakota, among the Mandan Sioux tribe. There, they recruited the young Native American woman **Sacagawea** (c.1786–1812; see entry in volume 2) and her husband, French Canadian trapper Toussaint Charbonneau (1758–1843). Sacagawea and Charbonneau would serve as guides and interpreters for the journey over the mountains. Their infant son, whom Lewis helped deliver in February, would accompany the expedition.

In 1805, the expedition journeyed up the Missouri River to its source and then across the Rocky Mountains and down the Snake and Columbia Rivers to the coast, where they arrived on November 8, 1805. They established Fort Clatsop near Astoria, Oregon, for the winter of 1805–6. After experiencing a rainy winter, they returned on roughly the same course, arriving in St. Louis on September 23, 1806. By then, Jefferson and the public had thought the expedition was lost and not returning.

The expedition was successful in achieving the goals set out by President Jefferson. Simply surviving the journey was a success in itself. It took great daring and skill to complete the trip, and crew members often had to improvise, whether dealing with Native American encounters or building canoes for the trip on the west side of the Rocky Mountains. The expedition lost only one crew member, who died of appendicitis at the beginning of the journey, and had only one violent skirmish with a Native American group, which occurred on the way back; in the skirmish, two members of the Blackfoot tribe were killed, and Lewis had a near miss with a musket ball. Not long after this incident, Lewis was mistaken for a deer by one of the crew members and wounded. Though his condition was poor, he made a quick recovery on the remainder of the journey.

Lewis and Clark kept detailed journals and maps, recording various observations and locations on a daily basis. Clark was the primary mapmaker and sketch artist, drawing in detail many of the new kinds of animals they observed. Other crew members also kept diaries. Lewis showed greater interest in his scientific observations and human encounters. Upon their return, Lewis and Clark immediately began working on their journals and materials, with plans of publishing an account of their adventures very soon.

Lewis and Clark journeyed to Washington, D.C., in November 1806 and received a hero's welcome. They each received 1,600 acres of public land and double their salary for the time they were gone. The other crew members received 320 acres and double pay.

New government assignments

On February 28, 1807, Lewis resigned his army commission to accept Jefferson's appointment as governor of Louisiana Territory, later to become the Missouri Territory.

The territory included all land in the Louisiana Purchase deal north of the present-day state of Louisiana. Clark had resigned the previous day, February 27, to accept an appointment as superintendent of Indian affairs and brigadier general of the Louisiana Territory militia. Lewis and Clark would both be stationed in St. Louis.

In the summer of 1807, Lewis unsuccessfully tried to finish editing his journals before returning to his new post in St. Louis. He found great turmoil in the wild frontier town of St. Louis: American settlers were moving in, strong competition raged between British and American fur trappers, and Native Americans in the region were resisting the Americans' forced entrance onto their homelands. Lewis did well as he organized a militia, adopted new territorial laws, and assisted Clark in resolving Native American issues in the territory. In January 1808, Clark married Julia Hancock of Virginia; they would have four children, including a son they would name Meriwether Lewis Clark.

In the summer of 1809, Lewis became greatly frustrated with Congress for its failure to provide funds to cover his expenses. In September, Lewis decided to go to Washington, D.C., to resolve the administrative problems. He was to travel with two servants down the Mississippi River to New Orleans and then board a ship to Washington, D.C. However, Lewis became ill with fever along the way, and in the present-day Memphis area he changed his plans. He decided to follow the Natchez Trace (a trail extending from Natchez, Mississippi, to Nashville, Tennessee), across the Appalachians, and into the east. On the night of October 11, he stopped at a rural inn near Nashville. That night, Lewis died of two gunshots. Some think Lewis committed suicide (with the first shot missing its mark). Others believe he was murdered. At the time, the route saw much crime, including robberies and murders. No money was found on Lewis, and his watch was later discovered in New Orleans. He was buried at the location without a gravestone. In 1848, the state of Tennessee erected a monument on the grave. Later, Congress designated the gravesite a national monument.

Clark becomes governor

Jefferson appointed Clark to take Lewis's place as governor of the Louisiana Territory, but Clark at first declined in honor of his friend. In 1813, Clark was appointed as the territorial governor (by that time, the area was known as the Missouri Territory) and served in that position until 1821. With the start of the War of 1812 (1812–15), Clark became busy protecting settlements in the Missouri Territory from attacks by Native Americans who received support from the British. This included leading an expedition of two hundred up the Mississippi River. They established a log fort known as Fort Shelby at the mouth of the Wisconsin River. It was the first American settlement in the future state of Wisconsin.

After the war ended, Clark was responsible for establishing treaties with the Native Americans in the regions that had warred against the United States. Native American relations occupied much of his time for the next several years, both through treaty negotiations and skirmishes.

Clark's later life

Clark's wife, Julia, died in 1820; the following year, he married her cousin, Harriet Kennerly, who was a widow. They had a son named Jefferson Clark. Clark remained in the post of Indian superintendent for the rest of his life. He was considered for governor of the new state of Missouri in 1821 but was not elected. He then served as surveyor general for Illinois, Missouri, and Arkansas in 1824 and 1825. In 1828, he laid out the town of Paducah, Kentucky. Clark died in September 1838.

Lewis and Clark's journal of the expedition, edited by Nicholas Biddle (1786–1844), was first published in 1814, with subsequent editions appearing over the next two centuries. In the twenty-first century, Lewis and Clark still inspire considerable public attention through film documentaries, books, and tourism. Many Americans look to relive the experience of the Corps of Discovery by reading their journals and retracing their route.

For More Information

Books

Ambrose, Stephen E. *Undaunted Courage: Meriwether Lewis, Thomas Jefferson, and the Opening of the American West.* New York: Simon & Schuster, 1996.

Bakeless, John. *Lewis and Clark: Partners in Discovery.* Mineola, NY: Dover Publications, 1996.

DeVoto, Bernard, ed. *The Journals of Lewis and Clark.* Boston: Houghton Mifflin, 1953. Reprint, 1997.

Dillon, Richard. *Meriwether Lewis: A Biography.* New York: Coward-McCann, 1965. Reprint, Santa Cruz, CA: Western Tanager Press, 1988.

Slaughter, Thomas P. *Exploring Lewis and Clark: Reflections on Men and Wilderness.* New York: Alfred A. Knopf, 2003.

Web Sites

"Lewis and Clark National Historic Trail." *U.S. National Park Service.* http://www.nps.gov/lecl/ (accessed on August 16, 2005).

"Rivers of Words: Exploring with Lewis and Clark." *American Memory, Library of Congress.* http://memory.loc.gov/learn/features/lewisandclark/resources_1.html (accessed on August 16, 2005).

Nelly Custis Lewis

Born March 2, 1779 (Alexandria, Virginia)
Died July 15, 1852 (Shenandoah Valley, Virginia)

First family member

Eleanor Parke Custis and her brother George Washington Parke Custis (1781–1857; see box) were the grandchildren of **Martha Washington** (1732–1802; see entry in volume 2) and the step-grandchildren of the first U.S. president, **George Washington** (1732–1799; served 1789–97; see entry in volume 2). Eleanor, known as Nelly, and little George, known as Wash, became the first children to live in a U.S. presidential mansion.

After Nelly and Wash's father died, George and Martha reached an agreement with the children's mother, Eleanor Calvert Custis (1757–1811), to raise both youngsters as their own. Nelly had just turned ten years old when she and Wash traveled with Martha to New York City, the nation's temporary capital, to join newly inaugurated President Washington. Nelly grew to womanhood during Washington's eight-year presidency. Martha, Nelly, and Wash had to forge their own path, because no guidelines existed on the role of the presidential family.

Nelly was a very intelligent, high-spirited, strong-willed, and personable preteen and teenager. First in New York City

"Granddaughter of Mrs. And adopted daughter of General Washington, reared under the roof of the Father of his Country. This lady was not more remarkable for the beauty of her person, than for the superiority of her mind. She lived to be admired. . . ."

Gravesite inscription of Nelly Custis Lewis

Nelly Custis Lewis. *(The Granger Collection, New York.)*

and then in Philadelphia, where the seat of government was moved in 1790, Nelly thrived. She received an extensive education, which was highly unusual for a girl of the late eighteenth century. New York and Philadelphia also provided an endless array of activities, entertainment, and parties, and Nelly relished every moment. During the 1790s, she became the teenage darling of America. Nelly later referred to this period as her "golden years."

The Washingtons left Philadelphia in March 1797 at the end of George's presidency to resume private life at their plantation, Mount Vernon, south of Alexandria, Virginia. Two years later, Nelly married and soon was caught up in motherhood, giving birth eight times between 1799 and 1813. Nelly would bury seven of her eight children before her own death. Besides motherhood, Nelly's chief role was managing her Virginia plantation house, Woodlawn, where she lived with and dutifully cared for a constantly ailing husband, Lawrence Lewis (1767–1839).

After her early "celebrity" years as America's best-known teenager, Nelly became a dissatisfied plantation matron; she felt trapped in rural Virginia. Nelly's life illustrates how even for the most privileged eighteenth- and nineteenth-century women, opportunities were very limited. The most a well-educated woman could hope for was to show off her skills by running an efficient home and raising many children. During the eighteenth and nineteenth centuries, the lives of women, whether wealthy or poor, were dominated by births and deaths, marriage and duty to husband, rearing and burying their children, nursing family members through illnesses, the rhythms of the farming cycle, and religion. A woman's first and only duty was to her family, whose needs she placed above any personal desires of her own.

Eighteenth-century families were large and compli-cated, often with many half brothers, half sisters, nieces, nephews, cousins, and stepchildren, and often living in one household. Because medicine had not yet advanced, earlier and more frequent deaths were common. Remarriages—and the combining of families of two widowed parents—occurred regularly. Further, people often took in the child-ren of relatives who had died, whether they were orphans or had lost only one parent. When Nelly and Wash remained with their grandparents, the situation was not out of the ordinary.

Sixty years of letters

A full picture of Nelly's life emerges from her nearly sixty years of correspondence with Elizabeth Bordley Gibson (1777–1863), whom she met in Philadelphia when she was twelve years old. Their friendship remained steadfast throughout their lives. Gibson, who lived in

Philadelphia her entire life, kept virtually all the letters Nelly wrote to her between 1794 and 1852. The 189 original letters are housed at the Mount Vernon Library.

Nelly's letters describe her devotion to her grandparents and the closeness of the Washington household. Through Nelly's eyes, readers see George and Martha not as historic founders of the country, but as doting, loving grandparents who worried, gave advice, and, like all grandparents, were eager to see their grandchildren make the most of their lives. For example, in the fall of 1795, Nelly was to leave Martha and George and live with her mother for several months through the winter. Nelly wrote the following words in a letter to Gibson, as reprinted in *Nelly Custis: Child of Mount Vernon*, about her leaving the Washingtons: "I have gone through the greatest trial—this is the first separation for any time since I was two years old. Since my father's death she [Martha] has been even more than a Mother to me, and the President the most affectionate of Fathers. I love them more than any one—You can guess then how severely I must feel this parting, even for a short time." The letters also reflect Nelly's changing life and her views. Together, they are a study of a Southern plantation woman's role and place in society.

Toddler Nelly remains at Mount Vernon

Nelly Custis was born on March 2, 1779, the third child of John Parke Custis (1754–1781), known as Jacky, and his wife Eleanor Calvert Custis. Jacky was Martha Washington's son from her first marriage. She was born on the Abington Plantation in Alexandria, Virginia. Nelly had two older sisters: Elizabeth Parke Custis (1776–1832), known as Eliza and sometimes Betsy, and Martha Parke Custis (1777–1854), known as Patsy. Their mother suffered greatly during her pregnancies (she would experience twenty in her lifetime) and was too ill to care for the infant Nelly. Nelly's grandmother, Martha Washington, took her to Mount Vernon, where she was nursed by the wife of the plantation's overseer (manager). Likewise, when Wash was born in the spring of 1781, he went to live at Mount Vernon while his mother regained her health.

The Custis children had been born during the American Revolution (1775–83), America's war to gain independence from Britain. In the fall of 1781, the British surrendered to the Americans. Jacky Custis, the children's father, accompanied General George Washington, commander of America's Continental Army, to Yorktown, Virginia, where the surrender took place on October 19, 1781. At Yorktown, Jacky came down with camp fever and died in November. Left a widow at the age of twenty-four, Eleanor Custis had four children under the age of five. She was in no condition to care for the four children, so Nelly and Wash remained at Mount Vernon. George and Martha agreed to raise them as their own. Although there was never a formal adoption, the family viewed the arrangement as an adoption. Eliza and Patty remained with their mother. Eleanor, Eliza, and Patty visited Mount Vernon often, and Nelly and Wash knew Eleanor as "mother." They always referred to George and Martha as "grandpapa" and "grandmama."

Early childhood years

From Christmas Eve 1783 until the spring of 1789, George, Martha, Nelly, and Wash lived at Mount Vernon. The family led a busy life amid the constant activities required to run a plantation and entertain a steady stream of important visitors anxious to visit with the famous general.

Martha saw to it that Nelly received an excellent education in her early childhood years. Nelly was tutored privately and learned to read and enjoy poetry and literature. (Only 30 percent of Virginia women of the late eighteenth century could read.) Martha began to teach Nelly how to manage a large household, vital instruction for any young woman who might marry a plantation owner.

Grandpapa becomes first U.S. president

On April 14, 1789, Nelly's grandpapa was informed that electors had unanimously chosen him to be the first president of the United States. George left for New York City on April 16. On May 16, Martha, Nelly, and Wash followed. Neither child had ever traveled more than a few

George Washington Parke Custis

Born in 1781, George Washington "Wash" Parke Custis was the fourth child of John "Jacky" Parke Custis and Eleanor Calvert Custis. Jacky was Martha Washington's son by her first marriage, and Wash was her grandson. When Jacky died suddenly in November 1781, Martha and George Washington took responsibility for raising Wash and his older sister, Nelly Custis.

For the first eight years of his life, Wash lived at Mount Vernon. Then, while his step-grandfather was president of the United States, Wash lived in the presidential mansion, first in New York City and then in Philadelphia. Fussed over and spoiled by Martha, Wash was an inattentive student. President Washington lamented that Wash was only interested in activities that brought him fun and pleasure. In 1795, President Washington enrolled him at Princeton College, but in October 1797, Wash was expelled for misconduct, most likely involving girls. The president battled on to educate Wash, enrolling him at St. John's College in Annapolis, Maryland. However, on August 5, 1798, the seventeen-year-old Wash returned home to Mount Vernon, and attempts to formally educate him ended.

George and Martha did not live to see Wash's many accomplishments. In 1802, Wash began building Arlington House on the old Custis property that he inherited from his natural grandfather, Daniel Parke Custis (1711–1757). The property was located along the Potomac River across from the nation's new capital city, Washington. Wash hoped the mansion would be not only his home but a memorial to his step-grandfather and grandmother.

Wash considered himself keeper of the Washington family tradition, and he filled Arlington House with memorabilia from Mount Vernon. He never tired of showing Arlington and its collections to many prominent visitors. He held events and celebrations to commemorate his family's accomplishments. Wash also wrote *Recollections and*

miles from Mount Vernon. Ten-year-old Nelly was amazed how people cheered for them along the way and how much people loved her grandpapa.

Life for Nelly changed from the slow daily rhythm of plantation activities to the excitement of city events. The presidential home on Cherry Street was the finest in New York. Nelly immediately relished the attention given her as the president's granddaughter. Martha enrolled Nelly in a well-known school run by Isabella Graham at Five Maiden

George Washington Parke Custis. *(© Bettmann/ Corbis.)*

Private Memoirs of Washington, which was published in book form in 1860, three years after his death.

Wash married sixteen-year-old Mary Lee Fitzhugh (1788–1853) in 1804. The couple had four children, but only one survived, Mary Anna Randolph (1808–1873).

Wash tried to manage the estates he inherited, but he never succeeded in making them profitable. Instead, he most enjoyed the arts and became a fine playwright. When Wash was a youngster, Martha and George had taken him and Nelly to many plays in New York City and Philadelphia. Wash and Nelly staged their own plays in the attic of the president's mansion in Philadelphia. These experiences provided the education that stayed with Wash. He wrote several plays: *The Indian Prophecy* (1827), *Pocahontas* (1830), and *The Railroad* (1830). Wash also enjoyed painting and in his later years painted a number of battle scenes from the American Revolution.

In 1831, Wash's daughter married Lieutenant Robert E. Lee (1807–1870) at Arlington. Lee would later lead the Confederate army in the American Civil War (1861–65). Mary Anna and Robert lived at Arlington, and Wash was a loving grandfather to their seven children. Wash died at Arlington after a short illness on October 10, 1857. Arlington House became part of the Arlington National Cemetery.

Lane. Nelly's subjects included reading and writing, spelling and grammar, arithmetic, geography, and French. In addition, Madam Graham's curriculum included sewing, embroidery, drawing, music, and dancing. Nelly excelled in her studies, as she would throughout her school years. Martha gave her private lessons in piano and painting. Martha also instructed Nelly in proper religious observances. Each evening throughout Nelly's teen years, a favorite time was just before bed when she joined her grandmama in her bedchamber for devotions, Bible reading, prayer, and song.

George and Martha Washington are seated at a table as young George and Nelly Custis stand nearby. *(National Portrait Gallery.)*

Move to Philadelphia

Soon, the U.S. Congress decided to move the nation's capital to the city of Philadelphia. It would be the nation's temporary capital through the 1790s. After a fall visit to Mount Vernon, the Washingtons left for Philadelphia on November 22, 1790. Philadelphia was the most exciting city in America. It was full of wealthy, highly educated, sophisticated individuals who were active in the city's social life. Prominent residents held elegant parties and balls. Martha allowed eleven-year-old Nelly to begin attending many parties. Nelly enjoyed being the center of attention. She was a vibrant, high-spirited young girl who instantly became a favorite of Philadelphia society.

George, Martha, Nelly, and Wash enjoyed family outings and activities together. On Saturdays, they usually took a ride around the city in their coach. Nelly generally brought along her pet, a green parrot that she was teaching to sing in French. Martha and Nelly shopped together in Philadelphia's fine shops. All four Washingtons also enjoyed theater and went to plays regularly. On Sunday, they attended Christ Church on Second and Market Streets.

When she was twelve, Nelly met Elizabeth Bordley, the daughter of a wealthy Philadelphian named John Beale Bordley. Elizabeth loved theater as much as Nelly did. The two girls, along with Wash, often spent Saturdays staging plays in the attic of the president's mansion. Nelly and Elizabeth became lifelong friends.

A cherished granddaughter

George and Martha both cherished Nelly. She was a constant joy for them. Nelly made both grandparents laugh with her lively talk and antics. President Washington bought a fine London-made harpsichord (a musical instrument similar to a piano) for Nelly in December 1793. Nelly loved music, but Martha made her practice many long hours, creating some tearful sessions. The practice paid off. Nelly learned to play beautifully and entertained not only the president and first lady but many of their important guests.

A beauty with dark curly hair and large dark eyes, Nelly had become a polished young woman by the age of fifteen. Suitors were plentiful, but Nelly was careful not to commit to any young man. The president had cautioned his grand-daughter to be sure she had knowledge of a man's character before falling in love. Nelly adhered to her grandpapa's advice.

Return to private life

George, Martha, Nelly, and Wash returned permanently to Mount Vernon in March 1797 at the end of Washington's second term. Just before her eighteenth birthday, Nelly tearfully said goodbye to her close friend Elizabeth Bordley Gibson, gathered her parrot and dog, Frisk, and joined the Washingtons for their journey home.

Nelly took the same upstairs corner room she had occupied as a child and was pleased to settle back into Mount Vernon with her grandparents. She helped Martha manage the house; constant companions, grandmother and granddaughter spent many happy hours together. The usual stream of visitors came to Mount Vernon, and Nelly delighted all by playing her harpsichord in the evening.

Although a number of would-be suitors came to Mount Vernon hoping to court Nelly, she remained determined to give her affections to no one but her grandparents. She playfully began signing her letters to Gibson as "E. P. Custis Spinster for life." A spinster is a woman who never marries.

Marriage, birth, death

Nelly did not remain true to spinsterhood for long. In the winter of 1797–98, George brought his nephew, Lawrence Lewis, to Mount Vernon to help entertain the many guests who came to visit. Lewis was twelve years older than Nelly and very reserved. However, he was captivated by Nelly's charm, and they soon fell in love. In Lewis, Nelly saw a man who would not take her away from her grandparents. He had no desire to move from rural Virginia. They married by candlelight at Mount Vernon on February 22, 1799, George's sixty-seventh birthday.

Nelly and Lawrence's first child, Frances Parke Lewis, was born at Mount Vernon on November 27, 1799. Only three weeks later, on the evening of December 14, 1799, Nelly's beloved grandpapa died suddenly from an infected throat. When the former president died, Nelly ceased writing her letters to Gibson for a long time.

Nelly watched her once happy existence disintegrate around her. Martha passed away a few years later on May 22, 1802. Martha had lived long enough to know her second great-grandchild, Martha Betty, born to Nelly and Lawrence in 1801. At the time of her grandmother's death, both of Nelly's daughters had the measles. Frances recovered, but one-year-old Martha Betty died in June. Nelly gave birth to her first son, Lawrence Fielding, in 1802, but he died immediately after his birth.

Woodlawn

Nelly resumed writing to Gibson in December 1804. By then, the Lewises had moved into the not-yet-finished Woodlawn Plantation. They were constructing their beautiful redbrick home on acreage George had given Nelly; the land was adjacent to Mount Vernon. Nelly ran Woodlawn with the good management skills Martha had taught her. However, Lawrence did not have the motivation or energy that Nelly had expected in a husband. He planted the land because it was expected but made no effort to profitably manage and develop the plantation. As a result, the Lewises were short of money most of their married life. Lawrence also suffered from very poor health and would spend months at a time in bed. Nelly dutifully nursed him but looked with longing to her past, when she had happily lived with George and Martha.

Nelly's first child born at Woodlawn was Lorenzo (1803–1847), who arrived on November 13, 1803. Lorenzo was the only one of Nelly's sons who would live into adulthood. Between Lorenzo's birth and 1813, Nelly had four more children. Eleanor Agnes Freire (1805–1820) died suddenly while at school in Philadelphia in 1820. Fielding Augustine (1807–1809) lived one year and seven months. George Washington Custis (1810–1811) lived only one year and nine months. Nelly and Lawrence's last child, Mary Eliza Angela (1813–1839), lived into adulthood but died at the age of twenty-six.

Because of Lawrence's chronic bad health, Nelly made almost all the child-rearing decisions for their family. Like other nineteenth-century mothers, Nelly found her greatest joy and comfort in her children. She existed now only to care for her surviving children: Frances Parke, Lorenzo, Eleanor Agnes, and Mary Eliza Angela. She did enjoy her housekeeping duties and loved to read biographies and books on history and travel.

Frances Parke married army officer Lieutenant Edward George Washington Butler at Woodlawn in 1826 and eventually settled on a sugarcane plantation in Iberville Parish, Louisiana. For the rest of her life, Nelly hated the hot-tempered and abusive Butler. In 1827, Lorenzo married Esther Maria Coxe, the kind and loving daughter of a Philadelphia doctor. They settled on Audley Plantation in the Shenandoah Valley of Virginia. Mary Eliza Angela married Charles Magill Conrad, a New Orleans lawyer and son of a wealthy Louisiana planter, in 1835. She died shortly after giving birth in 1839. Nelly's husband also died in 1839, and she went to live with Lorenzo and Esther.

A grandmother

Nelly became a doting grandmother to Lorenzo and Esther's six sons, all of whom lived to adulthood. Likewise, she dearly loved the two Conrad boys, who visited often, and the three Butler children who came east for schooling. Although Nelly's last years at Audley Plantation were generally happy, they were saddened by the sale of Woodlawn in 1846, the death of Lorenzo in 1847, and the inability of Frances Parke, her only living child, to visit from distant Louisiana.

Nelly continued to correspond with Elizabeth Bordley Gibson even in old age. Nelly suffered a stroke in 1850 but was able to continue writing, reading, and enjoying guests. Carefully cared for by Esther, she often reminisced about her "golden years." Nelly enjoyed political discussion and believed only two presidents had been good successors to President Washington: **Andrew Jackson** (1767–1845; served 1829–37; see entry in volume 1) and Zachary Taylor (1784–1850; served 1849–50). Nelly had visited the White House for two weeks in 1849 as a guest of President Taylor and his wife.

Nelly died at Audley Plantation on July 15, 1852. Her body was taken to Mount Vernon to be buried near the Washingtons. She was at last reunited with her grandmama and grandpapa.

For More Information

Books

Brady, Patricia, ed. *George Washington's Beautiful Nelly: The Letters of Eleanor Parke Custis Lewis to Elizabeth Bordley Gibson, 1794–1851.* Columbia: University of South Carolina Press, 1991.

Bryan, Helen. *Martha Washington: First Lady of Liberty.* New York: Wiley, 2002.

Ribblett, David L. *Nelly Custis: Child of Mount Vernon.* Mount Vernon, VA: Mount Vernon Ladies' Association, 1993.

Schmit, Patricia B. *Nelly Custis Lewis's Housekeeping Book.* New Orleans, LA: The Historic New Orleans Collection, 1982.

Web Sites

George Washington's Mt. Vernon Estates and Gardens. http://www.mountvernon.org/ (accessed on August 15, 2005).

Little Turtle

Born 1752 (Whitley County, Indiana)
Died July 14, 1812 (Fort Wayne, Indiana)

Miami tribal leader

Little Turtle was a distinguished war chief of the Miami tribe of Native Americans in the Great Lakes region in the late eighteenth century. He was one of the most successful woodland military commanders of his time and led an intertribal force to victory against two American frontier armies in 1790 and 1791. The battle known as St. Clair's Defeat marked the largest defeat of a U.S. Army force during a single battle in all of the U.S.–Native American wars. The loss exceeded any inflicted on the United States by the British in a single battle during the American Revolution (1775–83).

Little Turtle enjoyed this leading role in Native American resistance against American settlement of tribal lands until the superior forces of General **Anthony Wayne** (1745–1796; see entry in volume 2) triumphed in the Battle of Fallen Timbers in 1794. Little Turtle then signed the Treaty of Greenville in 1795, establishing a temporary peace in the region. He spent the rest of his life negotiating land cessions (giving up land by treaty) to the United States in the Northwest Territory. The Northwest Territory included

Little Turtle. *(The Granger Collection, New York.)*

the future states of Ohio, Illinois, Indiana, Michigan, Wisconsin, and part of Minnesota. Known as a skilled speaker, Little Turtle worked to keep his tribe at peace while he served as an ambassador of his people to the new U.S. government.

A distinguished heritage

Little Turtle was born along the Eel River, about 20 miles northwest of Fort Wayne in Whitley County, Indiana, around 1752. His Native American name was Mishikinakwa (many spelling variations exist for this name), which means "The Turtle." He was called Little Turtle to distinguish him from his father, also called Mishikinakwa. To the Algonquian tribe, a group that included the Miami tribe, the turtle symbolized the earth. The Miami signed documents, agreements, and treaties by drawing a picture or a symbol rather than signing a name. Little Turtle was an Atchatchakangouen Miami, the leading division of the Miami tribe.

Not much is known about Little Turtle's mother, but she was probably a member of the Mahican tribe. His father was a respected war chief among the Miami tribe. He achieved his position through his battle victories against the Iroquois. In 1748, the elder Mishikinakwa traveled to Lancaster, Pennsylvania. He was the first Miami to meet with European immigrants and he signed a pact with the English called the Treaty of Lancaster. His family's reputation and connections would help Little Turtle in his rise to leadership, but he had to earn his own position within the tribe through merit.

On June 21, 1762, a raiding party of Chippewa and Ottawas assisted by the French launched a surprise assault on Little Turtle's village. The Miami chief was killed, but Little Turtle showed great bravery during the battle and gained respect among his tribe. The attack left him with a scar along his lower right jaw, from his chin almost to his ear. This was the result of a slashing tomahawk wielded by a French soldier.

Little Turtle would come to prominence as a war chief in 1780 during the American Revolution (1775–83). Little Turtle and the Miami allied with the British and successfully defeated a French detachment led by Augustin Mottin de La Balme (1740–1780). La Balme's forces threatened Little Turtle's village on their march to attack the British post of Detroit. Because they were in Little Turtle's territory, he was put in charge of the Native American attack and proved himself an able commander. By 1790, Little Turtle was the chief military leader of the Miami and principal war chief of the allied tribes, which included the Shawnee, Delaware, Wyandot, and others. This confederacy of tribes in the Ohio River valley shared close ties because of their mutual defensive and economic needs.

Little Turtle's victories

In a 1787 treaty, the hunting grounds of the Miami and their allies had been guaranteed in perpetuity (without end) by the U.S. Congress. Despite this promise, white settlers continued to overflow onto tribal lands. The Native Americans responded with raids and ambushes, which became increasingly violent. Greatly concerned over maintaining control over the region, President **George Washington** (1732–1799; served 1789–97; see entry in volume 2) ordered an army into the Northwest Territory to end the Native American attacks.

In October 1790, General Josiah Harmar (1753–1813) led his force of almost fifteen hundred men toward present-day Fort Wayne. He intended to attack the concentration of tribes gathered there and destroy their villages. The frontier army had only three hundred regular soldiers; the remainder consisted of poorly trained militiamen from Pennsylvania, Virginia, and Kentucky. Some of the backwoodsmen had equally primitive weapons and, therefore, no advantage over the Native Americans. On October 18 and again on October 22, Little Turtle led his alliance of Native American tribes into battle along the Maumee River against Harmar's forces. His style of woodland fighting resulted in extensive U.S. casualties and a full retreat by Harmar's army, who barely saved themselves from a disaster. The defeat stunned the army and heightened the tensions between white settlers and Native Americans.

General Arthur St. Clair (1736–1818) was then given command of the army's offensive, and he gathered a force of two thousand men during the summer of 1791. They advanced toward the Maumee River and built Fort Hamilton and Fort Jefferson along the way for added security. St. Clair's army was plagued by problems from the start. Their progress was hampered by the weight of eight field artillery pieces as well as a large group of camp followers. This group included the soldiers' wives and children, along with an assortment of carts and pack animals. St. Clair's forces experienced cold, snowy weather; morale was low, and many of the troops deserted the army.

Little Turtle's Native American scouts, including the young Shawnee warrior **Tecumseh** (1768–1813; see entry in volume 2), kept him informed daily of the army's movements.

An account of the defeat of the American army under the command of General Arthur St. Clair to Native Americans on November 4, 1791. *(The Granger Collection, New York.)*

The tribes obtained support from several other tribes in the area and were well supplied with guns and ammunition by British traders. On November 4, 1791, the multitribal force under Little Turtle surprised St. Clair near the Wabash River. After three hours of battle, the U.S. forces experienced an overwhelming loss—half of the troops were killed or wounded. St. Clair's defeat was the single greatest U.S. setback in all of the Native American wars.

Defeat at the Battle of Fallen Timbers

St. Clair's defeat electrified the frontier. Some in the Native American confederation believed that they could now win the battle for their land. Even British diplomats began to anticipate that the United States might have to yield ground. There was talk of creating a Native American buffer state in the Northwest Territory that would separate the British and American possessions. But President Washington's administration was determined to hold the Northwest Territory, and they moved forward despite criticism from various sides. Washington's political enemies were opposed to strengthening the military, because they did not believe the Constitution gave the president the power to do so. Easterners also strongly criticized the war against the Native Americans, regarding Washington's military action as expensive and unjust.

Washington ordered a third army into the field. This one was three thousand strong and led by General "Mad Anthony" Wayne, a hero of the American Revolution. Wayne ordered the construction of a series of forts to protect his army and store their supplies. The forts served as staging areas for future attacks against the Native Americans. While Wayne organized his forces and gathered the supplies needed for battle, Little Turtle began lobbying for peace. He approached the Native American confederacy of tribes with a warning about the new American commander's capabilities. Little Turtle wanted to negotiate for peace while the Native Americans were still in a position of strength following their victories. He did not want to wait until utter defeat, knowing that they would then surely lose everything.

Little Turtle had a healthy respect for Wayne and refused to take the primary leadership role with the Native Americans against him. He was relieved of command and replaced by the Shawnee leader, Blue Jacket (c. 1745–c. 1810). The two chiefs disagreed about the best way to oppose Wayne's army. Blue Jacket's plan was adopted, but Little Turtle agreed to lead a small party of Miami into battle. As a brave of distinction, the Shawnee Tecumseh took command of a party of his tribe in the engagement as well. By August 1795, Wayne was prepared to strike and moved toward the Maumee River. The Native Americans prepared to attack him at an area known as Fallen Timbers, so named because a big storm, possibly including a tornado, had knocked down many trees there.

On August 20, 1794, the two sides met in the Battle of Fallen Timbers. This time the Native Americans suffered hundreds of casualties, while the whites had only a few. The Native Americans had believed that the British would protect them in their retreat after the battle, but they found the gates shut at nearby Fort Miami. The fleeing warriors were killed, and the U.S. soldiers then marched through Native American country, destroying villages, trading posts, farms, and crops in a swath 10 miles wide.

The Treaty of Greenville

After their defeat at the Battle of Fallen Timbers in August 1794, the Native Americans realized that the Americans were now the dominant force in their country. The time to talk peace had arrived. This was especially true after November 19, 1794, when the United States signed the Jay Treaty with the British. This pact gave American authorities control of all military posts held by the British on the American side of the Great Lakes by the year 1796.

On August 3, 1795, almost a full year after the Native Americans' defeat at Fallen Timbers, General Wayne called a general council with Native American tribes of the Old Northwest of the Ohio River. They met at Fort Greenville in present-day Ohio and laid the foundation of a general peace. The majority of Native Americans were tired of war and boundary disputes and being caught between the two opposing white powers. The chiefs of the allied tribes signed the Treaty of Greenville with the belief that they could now return to hunting and fishing in their traditional territories, enjoy a peaceful trade, and raise their crops and families in peace. Little Turtle and the other Native Americans gave up most of their land north of the Ohio River in exchange for a guarantee of land farther west.

Little Turtle was one of the last to put his name to the treaty, declaring he would be the last to break it. He never fought again. Little Turtle continued his policy of cooperation with the United States and became a great advocate for peace. Little Turtle promoted a farming lifestyle among his people and strongly urged abstinence from alcohol. On one trip to Philadelphia, Pennsylvania, he met President Washington during the last days of his presidency. Washington presented Little Turtle with a sword and gun and arranged to have his official portrait painted.

After 1800, great sections of land were steadily ceded to the United States by Native American tribes. As Little Turtle and other Native American leaders signed away their rights to tribal lands, more and more white settlers pushed westward into traditional Native American territory. Large numbers of Native Americans were being pushed off their land. Not all Native Americans agreed with the Treaty of Greenville or with the authority of individual Native Americans and tribes to sell their land without the approval of others. Some Native Americans began to talk of revenge and recovery of the lost lands. Little Turtle and Blue Jacket were still the leading chiefs among the northwestern tribes. Little Turtle was committed to peace, but Blue Jacket favored Tecumseh's plan of uniting all the tribes in one confederacy and fighting back.

Little Turtle was of the opinion that the Native American tribes were no longer a match for America's military strength. He argued that without considerable aid from Britain, the Native Americans were likely to lose even more of their lands if they took the offensive. Little Turtle opposed Tecumseh's plan because he considered it dishonorable in view of the Treaty of Greenville. Despite repeated efforts by Tecumseh to enlist his support, Little Turtle remained an advocate of peace. His counsels kept the majority of Miami from actively joining Tecumseh. Nonetheless, Tecumseh diligently pursued his plan of uniting the tribes and was encouraged and supported by British agents. They warned the Native Americans that to make peace with the United States would mean starvation, poverty, and removal from their land. The resulting tensions affected the course of Native American relations with the United States and Britain on the eve of the War of 1812 (1812–15). By 1812, President **James Madison** (1751–1836; served 1809–17; see entry in volume 2) could no longer tolerate Britain's support of Native American resistance. America had several other grievances against the British, and Madison decided it was time to act. He asked Congress to declare war against Britain.

A bitter end

With the declaration of war, the Native Americans faced familiar alternatives. They could ally with the British, who had deserted them in the past, or give aid to the United States, a nation that seemed intent on consuming their lands. At this critical time in history, Little Turtle died. The Miami tribe lost the chief who had directed their destiny for decades. His loss was mourned by all, including Tecumseh. Little Turtle's death occurred on July 14, 1812, at the Fort Wayne home of his son-in-law, William Wells (see box); the cause of death was gout (a disease of the joints). Little Turtle was buried with full military honors by the American government. Buried with him were several of his prized possessions, including the sword given to him by President Washington.

Tecumseh was soon killed by American forces in October 1813. Although several war chiefs tried, none could match Little Turtle's stature after the War of 1812. In 1818, the United States forced the Miami tribe to give up their last lands in Ohio. Many

William Wells

Little Turtle married twice in his life, but the names of his wives and the marriage dates are unknown. He had four children with his first wife and one child with his second. Little Turtle also adopted a young, redheaded white youth who had been captured by the Miami in 1784. His birth name was William Wells (1770–1812), but his Native American name was Apekonit. The custom of adopting captives was not unusual, and those adopted were most often treated like family. Wells spent several years among the Miami tribe as one of their warriors and led a group of Miami in the battle against U.S. forces commanded by General Arthur St. Clair. Wells married Little Turtle's daughter, Wanagapeth, which means "A Sweet Breeze."

In June 1793, Wells asked to return to the people of his birth, and Little Turtle reluctantly approved of the reunion. Wells offered himself to the U.S. government as an interpreter and expert on the Miami tribe and other tribes with whom he was familiar. He became the U.S. Indian agent for the region at Fort Wayne. His orders were to issue payments promised by treaties, promote "civilization" among the Native Americans, and generally further American interests in the Northwest Territory. He was given a large farm in the area, and his wife came to live with him there. In 1797, Wells and Little Turtle traveled to Philadelphia to meet President **John Adams** (1735–1826; served 1797–1801; see entry in volume 1). Shortly after Little Turtle's death in 1812, Wells died while defending a Kentucky relative at Fort Dearborn (present-day Chicago, Illinois).

settled in Indiana, but in the late 1820s they were moved yet again, this time to Kansas.

For More Information

Books

Anson, Bert. *The Miami Indians*. Norman: University of Oklahoma Press, 1970.

Carter, Harvey L. *The Life and Times of Little Turtle: First Sagamore of the Wabash*. Chicago: University of Illinois Press, 1987.

Johansen, Bruce E. *Shapers of the Great Debate on Native Americans— Land, Spirit, and Power: A Biographical Dictionary*. Westport, CT: Greenwood Press, 2000.

Johansen, Bruce E., and Donald A. Grinde Jr. *The Encyclopedia of Native American Biography*. New York: Henry Holt, 1997.

Web Sites

"Little Turtle." *Ohio History Central.* http://www.ohiohistorycentral.org/ohc/h/peo/lt.shtml (accessed on August 16, 2005).

"Little Turtle (Miami)." *Shelby County Ohio Historical Society.* http://www.shelbycountyhistory.org/schs/indians/chflittleturtle.htm (accessed on August 16, 2005).

Dolley Madison

Born May 20, 1768 (Guilford County, North Carolina)
Died July 12, 1849 (Washington, D.C.)

First lady, hostess

Dolley Madison was the wife of the fourth president of the United States, **James Madison** (1751–1836; served 1809–17; see entry in volume 2). As the nation's official hostess, she set entertainment standards that were copied by future first ladies for decades. Known for her genuine warmth, kindness, and elegant style, she was at the center of the Washington, D.C., social circle for years. With purpose and charm, she hosted social functions that brought together politicians and diplomats with widely differing views. Her presence and conversation skills opened discussions between individuals who otherwise may have never spoken to one another. The American public adored Dolley. Through forty-two years of marriage, the Madisons were seldom apart for more than a few days. Dolley sustained her husband through his time in public office. Her loyalty never wavered, and her cheerfulness rarely failed.

Young Dolley

Dolley Payne was born on May 20, 1768, in a two-room log house in Guilford County, North Carolina. She was the third of eight children born to John and Mary Coles Payne. Mary, often

Dolley Madison. *(National Archives and Records Administration.)*

called Molly, was from a well-known Virginia Quaker family. John's prominent Virginia family were members of the Anglican Church, also known as the Church of England. This was the official church of Britain and of Virginia. The Anglican Church in America changed its name to the Episcopal Church. Quakers had split from the Church of England in the 1640s and began settling in America in 1681. The Quaker community as a whole is known as the Society of Friends.

When John and Mary married, John converted to the Quaker faith. John's family was not happy to see him join the Quakers, and their feelings about the matter are probably what caused him to move to frontier land in North Carolina in 1765. Only ten months after Dolley's birth, the family moved back to Virginia, settling at Mary's old home at Coles Hill near Hanover, Virginia. When Dolley was ten years old, the family moved to a large tobacco plantation, Scotchtown, 10 miles from Coles Hill. Virginia statesman Patrick Henry (1736–1799), a cousin of Mary Payne, had owned the property from 1771 to 1778. Dolley lived at Scotchtown for about five years during the American Revolution (1775–83) and fondly recalled her days there. The Paynes owned slaves, but the Quaker faith was against slavery. Adhering to Quaker beliefs, John freed his slaves and moved his family to Philadelphia in 1783. There, he joined the large Society of Friends community and set up a business. The family attended the Pine Street Meeting House, still in existence in the twenty-first century.

Dolley was educated in strict Quaker tradition. Her lessons included reading, writing, and arithmetic. Her reading did not include literature or poetry; instead, she studied passages from the Quaker Book of Discipline. Dolley dressed in plain gray cloth, wearing skirts that extended down to her ankles. She was not allowed to wear any adornments such as jewelry.

Marriage and motherhood

John's business did not prosper, and the Paynes found themselves moving from house to house in a state of near poverty. John went bankrupt in 1789 and was ousted from the Quaker community. However, John had arranged a marriage between Dolley and a prosperous young lawyer, John Todd Jr., also a Quaker. Dolley and Todd wed in 1790 and purchased a fine brick home at Fourth and Walnut Streets in Philadelphia. Their first son, John Payne Todd, was born in February 1792, shortly before the death of Dolley's father. A second son, William Temple Todd, was born in the summer of 1793. Dolley's eleven-year-old sister, Anna, came to live with the Todd family so that Mary Payne could give adequate care to her other, younger children. Anna would live with Dolley until adulthood.

Dolley's mother had started a boardinghouse to support herself and her children still living at home. Philadelphia was the temporary capital of the United States between 1790 and 1800, and the boardinghouse was popular with senators, including U.S. senator **Aaron Burr** (1756–1836; see entry in volume 1) from New York.

Tragedy struck the Todd family in the fall of 1793. A yellow fever epidemic swept through Philadelphia, killing Dolley's in-laws, her husband, and her infant son, William. Dolley fell ill too, but she recovered. Her year-and-a-half-old son, John, became the center of Dolley's life. She overly indulged young John, catering to his every wish.

The "great little Madison"

Dolley inherited her husband's estate, so her finances were in good condition. The twenty-five-year-old widow had matured into a real beauty, and she turned a considerable number of heads as she strolled with little John Payne along Philadelphia's streets. In the spring of 1794, Senator Burr contacted Dolley and informed her that James Madison, a member of the U.S. House of Representatives, wished an introduction. Dolley was fully aware of the intellect of Madison and knew that he had been the primary author of the U.S. Constitution, written in Philadelphia in 1787. As noted in *The Madisons: A Biography,* Dolley quickly wrote the now famous note to her best friend, Eliza Collins, that described Madison as "the great little Madison." Instead of dull Quaker cloth, Dolley chose a purple dress for the meeting.

When they met, Dolley immediately realized that though the forty-three-year-old Madison was a man small in stature, his character towered over that of other men. Much to the delight of his family and friends, who thought he was a confirmed bachelor, Madison fell in love and within months proposed to Dolley. Although she greatly admired Madison, Dolley was concerned that he was not a Quaker but an Episcopalian. Nevertheless, she accepted his proposal.

Dolley and James wed on September 15, 1794, at the home of Dolley's sister, Lucy Payne Washington, at Harewood in present-day West Virginia. (At age fifteen, Lucy had married George Steptoe Washington, a nephew of the nation's first president, George Washington.) Just as Dolley had expected, the Pine Street Meeting House expelled her from the Quaker community; this was their custom when a member married outside the Society of Friends. However, by this time Dolley not only admired the "great little Madison" but had fallen deeply in love.

Out from under the strict Quaker restrictions on clothing, Dolley began to dress with more flair. By 1795, she was wearing necklaces and increasingly fashionable gowns. James continued serving in the House, and the Madisons lived in Philadelphia for the next few years. Dolley discovered that she greatly enjoyed the social scene. Her energetic, fun-loving ways delighted all.

Three years at Montpelier

During the presidency of **John Adams** (1735–1826; served 1797–1801; see entry in volume 1), the Madisons lived at Montpelier, James's estate in Virginia. The estate of former secretary of state **Thomas Jefferson** (1743–1826), Monticello, was 30 miles from Montpelier. Jefferson and the Madisons became the closest of friends.

Dolley loved the property at Montpelier as much as James did. Her young son, John Payne, whom they generally called Payne, relished his life at Montpelier, especially Christmas. Quakers shunned the holiday, but the Madisons celebrated with food and drink. Their home was decorated with the traditional cedar greenery, holly, and candles. Christmas trees were not yet used in American homes. The only sadness in the Madisons' life was their apparent inability to have children of their own.

To Washington, D.C.

When Jefferson was inaugurated as the third president of the United States on March 4, 1801, he chose his friend and confidant James Madison as his secretary of state. From March 1801 until March 1809, Madison served as Jefferson's right-hand man. Dolley played a key role, too. Jefferson was a widower (his wife had died in 1782), so Dolley took on the role of official hostess at the President's House. She was often assisted by her sister Anna and by Jefferson's grown daughters, Patsy and Polly.

Federal City, as Washington, D.C., was often called, had a small but vibrant social scene, and Dolley was at the center. She charmed people with her lively manner and friendliness. While James approached strangers with caution, Dolley greeted all as if they were old friends. In public, Dolley had exchanged her dull Quaker dresses for beautiful French gowns and turban headdresses.

Invitations to the Madisons' home were prized. An evening included superb food, drink, lively conversations, and a game of backgammon. Dolley had a talent for putting guests at ease, including gatherings of people with strongly differing political views. She often used this talent to glean political information that might be helpful to her husband.

By the early 1800s, Dolley had become engrossed in James's political interests and had an excellent understanding of political issues. The Madisons freely conversed and confided in each other about political matters. However, unlike **Abigail Adams** (1744–1818; see entry in volume 1), wife of the second U.S. president, John Adams, Dolley kept both her political philosophies and opinions private, sharing them only with her husband and closest confidants, including Jefferson.

Wife of the president

James Madison succeeded Jefferson as president on March 4, 1809. At the inauguration, Dolley wore a glamorous champagne-colored gown and a purple velvet bonnet with white plumes. Dolley's years as hostess for Jefferson had prepared her well for her role as the president's wife. Dolley took charge of the Madisons' social life, planning official dinners and deciding what invitations to accept or reject. She set the standard for presidential entertaining for decades to come.

Dolley held Wednesday receptions called "levees" or "drawing rooms." She could skillfully entertain a diverse group of people—from diplomats to everyday citizens—in one room, keeping the peace and having a friendly word for all attendees. Dolley managed to smooth over political differences and left all guests eager for a return visit.

Benjamin Henry Latrobe (1764–1820)

Benjamin Henry Latrobe, born in England and educated in both England and Germany, immigrated to America in late 1795. Latrobe was the first formally educated architect to practice and teach in the United States. When he first came to America, he worked as an architect, mapper, and surveyor for three years in Virginia and designed the Virginia State Penitentiary. Moving to the cosmopolitan city of Philadelphia, he introduced classical Greek Revival architectural elements to America when he designed the Bank of Pennsylvania. He then designed and developed the Philadelphia Waterworks system, which included a steam engine to raise the water level of the Schuylkill River. In 1799, Latrobe was elected to the prestigious American Philosophical Society, founded by American statesman **Benjamin Franklin** (1706–1790; see entry in volume 1) to promote scholarly advances in the sciences and arts.

In 1802, President Thomas Jefferson engaged Latrobe to help design dry docks for the U.S. Navy in Washington, D.C. The next year, Jefferson appointed him as surveyor of public buildings in the United States. For the next nine years, Latrobe directed construction of the south wing of the U.S. Capitol and influenced the Capitol's design at every opportunity. He aided Jefferson in continuing to execute the original plans for the President's House, which was not yet finished when President Adams moved in in December 1800, only a few months before the end of his term. Latrobe added porches to the east and west ends. A few years later, Latrobe and Dolley Madison worked together to elegantly redecorate the President's House. Latrobe designed the U.S. Customs House in New Orleans in 1809 and St. John's Church on Lafayette Square in Washington, D.C., in 1815. He also contributed to the design of the University of Virginia.

Between 1815 and 1817, Latrobe helped in the reconstruction of Washington's public

Often when Dolley attended the theater, her dress, jewels, and hairstyle stole the show, apparently creating more excitement than the appearance of the actresses. At forty-one, she was a fresh spirit, one who truly enjoyed living. Americans admired and idolized her.

Dolley oversaw the first redecoration of the President's House. Once Jefferson moved his furniture back to Monticello, Dolley worked closely with architect-designer Benjamin Henry Latrobe (1764–1820; see box) to refurbish the mansion. With good taste and enthusiasm, Dolley helped Latrobe shape the decor.

resigned amid disagreements over design changes and costs. Latrobe was overseeing construction of the New Orleans Waterworks when he died of yellow fever in 1820.

The Baltimore Cathedral, officially known as the Basilica of the National Shrine of the Assumption of the Blessed Virgin Mary, is considered Latrobe's masterpiece. Latrobe designed the Basilica in consultation with President Jefferson and Father **John Carroll** (1735–1815; see entry in volume 1), the first U.S. Catholic bishop. The cornerstone was laid in 1806, but construction was delayed during the War of 1812. Completed in 1821, one year after Latrobe's death, the Basilica was the first Catholic cathedral in the United States and is considered a symbol of religious freedom in America. In the twenty-first century, the Basilica is recognized as one of the most beautiful churches in the United States.

The Basilica of the Assumption of the Blessed Virgin Mary, the oldest cathedral in the United States. Located in Baltimore, Maryland, it was designed by Benjamin Henry Latrobe. (© AP/Wide World Photos.)

buildings including the Capitol, which had been destroyed during the War of 1812. He

War of 1812

When the United States launched the War of 1812 (1812–15) against Britain, Dolley and James waited together in agonizing suspense to hear of military encounters, successes or failures. The battle came directly to Washington, D.C., in August 1814. While President Madison fled the city to command troops, Dolley waited until the last minute to evacuate. She courageously gathered and successfully moved out of the city vital government papers and some of the young nation's few treasures, such as silverware, eagle ornaments from the East Room, and a full-length portrait of George

First lady Dolley Madison rescues the Gilbert Stuart portrait of President George Washington from the White House, before British troops set fire to the building. (© Hulton Archive/Getty Images.)

Washington painted by Gilbert Stuart (1755–1828). (In the twenty-first century, the portrait hangs in the mansion's East Room.) To transport the heavy painting, Dolley had the gardener, Tom Magraw, who remained at the mansion to help her, break the glass and remove the canvas from the frame. The British burned the mansion the night of August 24, 1814. After Dolley evacuated, she did not meet up with James for thirty-six hours.

Within a few days, the president and first lady sadly viewed the destruction of Washington's public buildings, including the burned-out shells of the Capitol and

President's House. Immediately following the invasion of Washington, the British turned toward nearby Baltimore, but American troops at Fort McHenry, at the entrance to Baltimore's port, fought back, causing the British to retreat. Then in September, U.S. commodore Thomas Macdonough (1783–1825) took his small fleet of four ships and turned back a British advance that was intended to capture New York City. Dolley, the president, and the rest of America rejoiced. Peace would follow within a few months.

Peace restored

Dolley and James moved their residence to a beautiful and unusual building, the Octagon House, two blocks west of the President's House. When the news of a decisive American victory at New Orleans and the signing of the peace treaty reached Washington, D.C., in January 1815, the Octagon House overflowed with celebrants. As usual, Dolley led the festivities.

After a brief trip to Montpelier in the spring of 1815, the Madisons returned to Washington and took up residence at the Seven Buildings, from which they could look out on the shell of the President's House. The blackened sandstone walls were painted white, and from that time on, the home of the president was called the White House. The Octagon House still stands in Washington in the twenty-first century, but the Seven Buildings, a complex of buildings, does not. Dolley began her Wednesday night receptions again, and the mood in Washington was joyous. Peace had arrived, respect for America had been won, and all looked to the future. The rebuilding of Washington had begun.

Worrisome Payne

Payne, Dolley's son from her first marriage, infused some worry into the Madisons' otherwise happy life. He had finished at Baltimore's St. Mary's Academy in 1812. In the spring of 1813, the Madisons sent him to France as one of three secretaries for the U.S. peace delegation attempting to negotiate an end to the War of 1812. Payne was treated like royalty because he was the president's stepson, and he took full advantage of the situation. He stayed in Paris long after the peace treaty was signed, gambling and freely spending Madison's money. He ran up huge debts that Madison had to cover.

Full of stories of his Paris adventure, Payne returned to Washington and to his parents in 1815. He was tall, handsome, and had a European elegance about him. He was an intriguing storyteller and conversationalist. Dolley and James hoped the young man would soon settle into a career, perhaps as a diplomat. They also hoped he would marry and present them with grandchildren.

Instead, Payne became quite the man-about-town. He danced, played cards, drank a considerable amount in taverns, hunted, rode on horseback over Maryland and Virginia, and showed not the slightest inclination to set any long-term goals. Dolley loved his company and assumed he would find himself eventually, but James was worried.

Glittering social season

In the winter of 1815–16, Dolley directed the most glittering social season Washington, D.C., had ever seen. At forty-seven, she was more attractive than ever, and she dressed in beautiful colors. She loved all shades of pink, but white was also a favorite. Then in early 1816, she appeared at a ball in a black velvet gown trimmed in gold; she wore a gold lace turban on her head. Everyone scrambled to get a glimpse of her. Dolley also entertained an adoring public with her beautiful bird, a macaw from Brazil. Every day, people gathered at a certain hour to watch Dolley at a corner of the house where she stroked and conversed with the talkative bird.

For every hour Dolley spent entertaining in glamorous style, she spent many more taking care of household duties and working with her hands. She would dress in her plain Quaker garb and cook, embroider, and sew; she even dusted the house's treasures. She also worked on a project to establish an orphanage in Washington and spent the winter hours sewing clothes for the children.

Retirement to Montpelier

On March 4, 1817, **James Monroe** (1758–1831; served 1817–25; see entry in volume 2) was inaugurated as the fifth U.S. president. James and Dolley Madison attended the inauguration and the ball just long enough to say their goodbyes. Within a few weeks James, Dolley, and the pet macaw arrived at Montpelier. Nelly Madison, James's energetic eighty-five-year-old mother who lived at Montpelier, greeted them.

Once at home the Madisons knew they would need to cut back on expenses. They would no longer draw James's $25,000 annual salary, but living on a smaller budget proved difficult. There was a steady stream of visitors to entertain. Guests enjoyed the Madisons so much that they stayed and stayed. At Christmas, the home was always filled with candlelight, holly, cedar, and many family and guests. Montpelier's Christmas eggnog was a popular drink.

Also at Montpelier were over a hundred slaves to feed and clothe. The Madisons by then believed slavery was an evil but did not know how to eliminate it. The slaves were still needed for crop production. Montpelier's slaves were treated in an exemplary manner. They lived in a shaded area of the plantation known as Walnut Grove. They were well fed, decently clothed, and not overworked, and their health needs were taken care of by the Madisons. The slaves were treated as humans, not property. When the Madison nieces and nephews would walk down to Walnut Grove with a special food treat to share, they usually returned with a squash or another vegetable that the slaves had grown in their gardens.

Since the Madisons never had children of their own, they enjoyed their many nieces and nephews. Anna had married U.S. representative Richard Cutts (1771–1845) of Massachusetts in the Madisons' Washington home in 1804, and the couple had six children. Dolley's brother John Payne and his wife, Clary, had four children. Their daughter Anne Payne became like a daughter to Dolley as the Madisons grew older. Dolley's sister, Lucy Washington, had three children. Various combinations of nieces and nephews were always racing through the halls of Montpelier. Dolley's macaw was allowed to fly about the house in the day. The children would run with real or pretend fear if someone yelled "Polly's coming!"

In retirement Dolley helped James organize presidential correspondence and notes. James spent long hours preparing his notes on the 1787 Constitutional Convention. He intended to allow the sale of these notes at his death to help sustain Dolley economically. Madison managed the farm lands at Montpelier. Despite droughts, new plant pests, the financial ups and downs of the nation, and decreasing real estate values in Virginia, Madison's thrift allowed the plantation to turn profits; most of his neighbors struggled just to break even. If it had not been for Payne's irresponsible spendthrift ways, the Madisons would have been economically comfortable.

A compulsive gambler, Payne drifted from city to city through the 1820s, running up debt. He landed in debtors' prison in Philadelphia in both 1829 and 1830. Between 1813 and 1836, Madison covered about $40,000 of Payne's debt, the equivalent of at least a million dollars in the twenty-first century. Madison kept most of the debt payments secret from Dolley, who still loved Payne dearly and still hoped he would straighten out.

The Madisons enjoyed visiting with their best friend, Thomas Jefferson, at nearby Monticello. Together, Jefferson and Madison developed plans for a new university, the University of Virginia. Dolley was in the audience at its opening ceremonies on March 7, 1825.

In 1826, Jefferson died, and the Madisons sorely missed him. Nelly Madison, James's mother, died on February 11, 1829, at ninety-seven years of age. James and Dolley had to get used to Monticello without Jefferson and Montpelier without Nelly. Later in 1829, they were temporarily distracted from their worries when Madison was elected to the Virginia Revisionary Convention to revise the Virginia constitution. The convention took place in Richmond, the state capital. Dolley enjoyed seeing the sights there and being back in the social whirl. Both Madisons were vigorous, cheerful, and entertaining—James had long ago given up his stiff demeanor.

By the early 1830s, Madison's health began failing. He suffered from increasingly crippling arthritis. Dolley stayed by his side constantly, writing notes he dictated when his fingers could no longer hold a pen. Dolley's beloved sister Anna died in 1832. On June 28, 1836, former president Madison passed away.

Return to Washington, D.C.

After James's death, Dolley spent more and more time at her house in Washington on Lafayette Square. She received $30,000 from Congress for the sale of Madison's Constitutional

Convention papers, but Payne managed to squander most of it. In 1844, she sold the last of the property at Montpelier and lived in Washington permanently. Her niece, Anne Payne, was her constant companion. In 1846, she and Anne were baptized at St. John's Church, an Episcopalian church on Lafayette Square near her house and across the square from the White House. St. John's continued as an active parish into the twenty-first century.

Much of Dolley's fun-loving spirit returned, after the deaths of her sister and husband, and she was an honored part of Washington society. She frequently was a guest at the White House, and first ladies asked her advice on matters related to the White House. She attended the dedication of the Washington Monument in 1848. That year, Congress purchased the rest of James's writings for $25,000 and set up a trust for Dolley to keep the money out of Payne's hands.

Dolley Madison died in Washington on July 12, 1849, at the age of eighty-one. Her funeral, held at St. John's, was attended by every major government official in Washington—the president, congressmen, judges, and military officials—and many private citizens.

For More Information

Books

Anthony, Katharine. *Dolly Madison: Her Life and Times.* Garden City, NY: Doubleday, 1949.

Flanagan, Alice K. *Dolley Payne Todd Madison, 1768–1849.* Children's Press, 1997.

Madison, Dolly. *Memoirs and Letters of Dolly Madison.* Boston: Houghton, Mifflin, and Company, 1886.

Moore, Virginia. *The Madisons: A Biography.* New York: McGraw-Hill, 1979.

Web Sites

"Dolley Payne Todd Madison." *The White House.* http://www.whitehouse.gov/history/firstladies/dm4.html (accessed on August 16, 2005).

University of Virginia. *The Dolley Madison Project.* http://moderntimes.vcdh.virginia.edu/madison/index.html (accessed on August 16, 2005).

James Madison

Born March 16, 1751 (Port Conway, Virginia)
Died June 28, 1836 (Montpelier, Virginia)

U.S. president, secretary of state

"The advice nearest to my heart and deepest in my convictions is that the Union of the States be cherished and perpetuated."

Between 1780 and 1817, James Madison's overriding goal was the success of American independence. Madison directed key aspects of the formation of the new nation. At the age of twenty-nine, he produced a plan for ceding (giving up) Virginia's western land claims, a plan that prompted the successful ratification (approval) of the nation's first constitution, the Articles of Confederation. When barely thirty-five, Madison worked with the Virginia legislature to pass a document written by his friend **Thomas Jefferson** (1743–1826; see entry in volume 1) that provided a basis for religious freedom in America. At thirty-six, he was the chief author of the U.S. Constitution, which was adopted by the states in 1788. A year later, he pulled together suggestions by the states for additions to the Constitution; these additions became the Bill of Rights. For eight years, from 1801 to 1809, he served under President Jefferson as secretary of state. From 1809 until 1817, Madison served as the nation's fourth president. He retired feeling convinced that American independence was secured.

James Madison. (© Corbis.)

Young Madison

Born on March 16, 1751, to James Madison Sr. (1723–1801) and Nelly Conway Madison (1732–1829), James was the first of eleven children. He grew up on a prosperous tobacco plantation in Virginia called Montpelier, which was home to over one hundred slaves.

James's early education with tutor Donald Robertson between 1762 and 1767 instilled in him a love of learning. His second teacher, the Reverend Thomas Martin, was a graduate of Princeton, then called the Presbyterian College of New Jersey.

Most likely at Martin's urging, young Madison decided to attend Princeton rather than the College of William and Mary in Williamsburg, where most sons of wealthy Virginians were educated.

Madison left for Princeton in 1769. Intent on his studies, he graduated in only two and a half years at the age of twenty. His rigorous regimen of study, which was self-imposed, left him exhausted. He recovered at Montpelier while helping his father manage the property. However, Madison's first interest was reading and learning all he could. Madison Sr. allowed his son to order books on many subjects—philosophy, law, economics, sciences, literature, history, and politics. Madison could competently read books written in French, Greek, Italian, Latin, Spanish, and Hebrew.

Public life begins

Madison's life took a new meaning when the first shots of the American Revolution (1775–83) were fired at Lexington and Concord, Massachusetts. Madison wholeheartedly embraced separation from Britain and creation of a republican form of government, one run for and by the people. Orange County voters elected him as a delegate to the Virginia Constitutional Convention of 1776 in Williamsburg. On June 7, 1776, the convention delegates adopted the Declaration of Rights and a constitution written by a fellow delegate, George Mason (1725–1792).

Twenty-five-year-old Madison made a favorable and lasting impression on the other Virginia delegates. His next official duty was to serve on Virginia's Privy Council or Council of State. The council aided Governor Patrick Henry (1736–1799) in carrying out his duties. In 1777, those duties generally had to do with the war effort and included recruiting soldiers and ordering supplies. Madison kept a close watch on the war's progress. He had become a revolutionary through and through, and from this time on, his whole life was dedicated to the success of the American Revolution.

In June 1778, the General Assembly of Virginia chose Madison as a delegate to the Continental Congress meeting in Philadelphia. Madison declined, saying he preferred serving on the Council of State. In 1779, Thomas Jefferson succeeded Henry as governor, so for the first of many occasions, Madison

James Madison and the Library of Congress

James Madison was a bibliophile, a lover of books. He began his library at his home in Montpelier, Orange County, Virginia. His father allowed James to purchase books on any topic that he found interesting. James was interested in most subjects—philosophy, law, economics, sciences, literature, history, and politics. He could also read in six languages—French, Greek, Italian, Latin, Spanish, and Hebrew—so his library was not confined to books written in English. By the time Madison retired to Montpelier in 1817, his library contained several thousand books, less than one-third in English.

When Madison was a Virginia delegate to the Continental Congress in 1783, he naturally volunteered to serve on a committee called the Committee on Books. Congress hoped to start a library for congressional research and asked the committee to look into the idea. Madison made a list of three hundred titles that should be purchased for such a library. The titles included books on law, politics, history, geography, war, language, and subjects related to the United States. The three hundred titles represented about thirteen hundred volumes. The list, in Madison's handwriting and dated January 24, 1783, is still preserved at the modern Library of Congress. Unfortunately in 1783, Congress had no funds for a library, so the list was never used.

In 1800, Congress passed an act signed by President John Adams that established the Library of Congress. It was first housed in one room in the first and only completed wing of the U.S. Capitol in Washington, D.C. Congress appropriated $5,000 to buy books. Between 1801 and 1814, the library's collections grew rapidly under the presidencies of Thomas Jefferson, another bibliophile, and Madison. During the War of 1812, British troops almost completely destroyed the collection when they marched on Washington and set fire to all the government buildings. Immediately, President Madison signed an act of Congress to buy Jefferson's private library of 6,487 books to replace the collections lost in the fire. Thereafter, the library continued to grow.

In 1897, the library moved into an elaborate sandstone building just east of the Capitol. A second library building was completed in 1938. In 1980, the third building, the largest library building in the world, was completed and named the James Madison Memorial Building. The 1897 structure was renamed the Thomas Jefferson Building, and the 1938 building was renamed the John Adams Building in honor of the nation's second president. These three buildings make up the Library of Congress, the world's largest library. They house 130 million items— books and other printed material, recordings, photographs, maps, and manuscripts—that are available for use by Congress and the American people.

served under Jefferson. Madison immediately liked the personable Jefferson and enjoyed conversing with him. Likewise, Jefferson took note of Madison's intellect, energy, and commitment to the cause of American independence. Jefferson and

Madison began what would be almost fifty years of cooperation and friendship. However, Madison's time under Jefferson ended when the Virginia General Assembly insisted that Madison join the state's delegation at the Continental Congress.

Serving in the Continental Congress

Madison arrived in Philadelphia in March 1780 to begin his service in the Virginia delegation at the Continental Congress. Madison's two primary accomplishments during his almost three-year stay in Congress involved the cession of western claims by states and fierce support for U.S. navigation rights on the Mississippi River.

When Madison took his seat in Congress, the ratification process of the Articles of Confederation was stalled. The chief obstacle to approval was disagreement among the states over ownership and use of western lands, which at that time meant the region between the Appalachian Mountains and the Mississippi River.

Madison came up with an idea about how to resolve the issue of western land use. By January 1781, he produced a plan for cession of Virginia's western claims; the document was called "Virginia's Cession of Western Lands to the United States." The plan suggested that Virginia give up its western land claims to Congress so that the land could be used for the common good of all the states. It also provided a cession model for the six other states holding western claims. Several years of negotiation between Congress and Virginia followed ·before the plan was agreed to. Nevertheless, the other states realized in 1781 that if Virginia, America's most influential state, was willing to cede its claims, the rest of the states holding claims should do likewise. When Madison submitted his proposal, Maryland was the only state still holding back its approval of the Articles of Confederation. Once they were convinced that all the states holding claims would give up their lands, Maryland's delegates signed the Articles on March 1, 1781, and the nation's first constitution was officially in force.

The second issue that consumed a large part of Madison's time was navigation rights on the Mississippi River. Pioneers in the Ohio River valley and those settled in western areas bordering the Mississippi, such as Kentucky, needed to send their goods to market down the Mississippi and through the port of New Orleans to the east coast and Europe. Spain held claim to the Mississippi and to New Orleans and harassed American boatmen, occasionally closing the port at New Orleans. Madison fiercely defended U.S. rights on the Mississippi, and eventually U.S. navigation claims were secured.

Aside from congressional matters, Madison found time in 1783 to court and propose marriage to sixteen-year-old Catherine Floyd, the daughter of Continental congressman William Floyd (1734–1821) of New York. However, within the year, Catherine broke off the engagement. A disappointed Madison wrote to his friend Jefferson to tell him of this woeful love affair.

Return to Virginia

At the end of his term in late 1783, Madison returned to Montpelier and tried to interest himself in plantation management and perhaps training to become a lawyer. Neither subject held his attention, and he felt rescued when in April 1784 Orange County elected him to the Virginia House of Delegates. For the next three years, Madison attended legislative sessions in the House of Delegates in the fall and winter. His major accomplishment was successfully shepherding the Virginia Statute of Religious Freedom through the Virginia legislature. Religious freedom was a hotly debated topic in the states. The statute, written by Jefferson with Madison's help, stated that an individual was free to decide all religious matters for himself—religious freedom was a natural right. Historians recognize the document as the most important step toward religious freedom in America.

In the spring and summer, when the House of Delegates was not in session, Madison spent time at Montpelier and also traveled to the growing northern cities, especially Philadelphia and New York. Besides spending long hours in the cities' bookstores, he listened to people talk about their growing disenchantment with the Articles, which were proving too weak to hold the states in line. The Articles contained no plan for a national executive (president) or national court system, no way to tax the people to raise needed funds, and no way to regulate foreign trade alliances.

States in competitive turmoil

By 1786, the cooperation that had existed between the states during the Revolution had given way to mistrust, jealousy, and conflict. Each state issued its own currency and squabbled over its worth. States imposed taxes on each other. They made trade agreements with foreign nations to gain the upper hand over their neighboring states. The confused, deteriorating trade conditions made it difficult for Virginia planters to sell and export their products and to obtain loans to expand. In addition to economic turmoil over trade issues, the states were increasing taxes to pay for their war debts. Businessmen often passed on these taxes to farmers in the form of higher priced goods. Farmers had little money to pay for goods in the first place. Taking matters into their own hands, in August 1786 some Massachusetts farmers protested in the streets, and by spring of 1787 they were closing down state courts before being stopped by the Massachusetts militia. The protest was known as Shays's Rebellion.

Madison looked at the financial and trade problems with real misgivings. Fellow Virginian **George Washington** (1732–1799; see entry in volume 2), who had commanded the Continental Army during the Revolution, wrote to Madison that he feared a collapse of the union and all that had been won in the war might be lost. Madison also received letters from Jefferson, who was serving as minister to France. Jefferson said that European officials thought the young nation would soon collapse. Madison shuddered to think of such a possibility.

Making a start at state cooperation, a concerned Madison, together with Washington and **Edmund Randolph** (1753–1813; see entry in volume 2), called a meeting between Virginia and Maryland in the spring of 1785. The purpose of the meeting was to discuss commercial uses of the Potomac River, which flowed between the two states. The meeting, held at Mount Vernon, was successful, and the two states made plans to meet again. By the summer of 1786, the plans had grown to include all the states; the meeting was scheduled to begin in September in Annapolis, Maryland. Only five states—Virginia, Delaware, Pennsylvania, New York, and New Jersey—showed up, but they made a momentous decision. Led by Madison and **Alexander Hamilton** (1755–1804; see entry in volume 1), a brilliant young lawyer from New York, the states in attendance decided to call for a general meeting of all states to consider changing and strengthening the Articles of Confederation.

Constitutional Convention of 1787

Declining national economic conditions and the fear of another incident similar to Shays's Rebellion gave the states a strong incentive to attend the proposed meeting; it was clear that the Articles were not adequately serving the nation or the individual states. Seven state legislatures immediately authorized delegates. The Continental Congress, now meeting in New York City, put out an official call for the states to meet the second Monday in May 1787 in Philadelphia. Although not called such at the time, this meeting would become the Constitutional Convention of 1787. All states except Rhode Island attended.

During the winter of 1786–87, Madison prepared extensively for the meetings. He read all he could gather about different government systems both modern and ancient; he studied ideas about what a government should be and how it could be put together. Madison wrote to Jefferson in France for books about European political histories. Jefferson responded by sending him one hundred volumes. Through his studies, Madison became convinced that it was useless to merely fix the Articles. Instead, Madison would propose that a new constitution be written to create a new structure of government.

Virginia Plan

The Philadelphia convention was scheduled to begin on May 14, but because of heavy rain and extremely muddy roads, many delegates arrived late, and the convention did not begin until May 25. Madison had arrived early on May 3. Governor Randolph had also arrived early. While waiting for more delegates to arrive, Madison took advantage of the time to craft the Virginia Plan, his plan for a new frame of government.

When the convention finally got under way on May 25, 1787, the delegates chose General George Washington to preside as president of the convention. Major William Jackson (1759–1828) was designated secretary for the convention but did not carefully record the proceedings. If it had not been for Madison, little detail would be known about the creation of the U.S. Constitution. Madison chose a seat up front close to

Washington and took comprehensive notes on everything that was said. He would not miss even one hour of the entire four-month convention and addressed the convention 161 times.

Although not authorized by Congress to do so, the convention quickly moved to throw out the Articles and devise a new form of government; in other words, they decided to write an entirely new national constitution. The Virginia delegation took a leadership role from the start. Governor Randolph read the Virginia Plan on May 29 and 30, though everyone present knew that Madison was the author of the plan. Historians assume Madison believed Randolph's tall stature would create a more commanding presence as he read. Madison stood only 5 feet 4 inches tall and did not present an imposing figure.

The Virginia Plan called for replacing the single-house Continental Congress with a powerful two-house legislature; it also proposed the addition of a president or executive, a national court system, and a system of checks and balances, measures to keep the three branches of government balanced in their powers. Although the original details of the plan were significantly altered through debate and compromise, the basic ideas proposed by Madison stood. Madison played a dominant role in deliberations, and history remembers him as the "Father of the Constitution."

Federalist Papers and ratification

The new constitution was sent to the states for ratification in September 1787. People who favored ratification were called Federalists; they supported a strong central or federal government. Those who opposed ratification were called Anti-Federalists. Madison teamed with Alexander Hamilton and statesman John Jay (1745–1829) of New York to anonymously write essays explaining why the Constitution should be ratified. The essays, called the *Federalist Papers,* were published in newspapers throughout the states. In total, the three men wrote eighty-five essays presenting the Federalist position. Madison authored twenty-nine of the essays, including the most famous, *Federalist Paper, Number 10.* His essays are considered the most important original analysis of the U.S. system of government ever written.

Only nine states needed to approve the Constitution to put it into effect, but by the end of July 1788, eleven had ratified and the Constitution became the law of the land. Only North Carolina and Rhode Island had not yet ratified. The chief obstacle to ratification had been the lack of a bill of rights, a basic set of individual liberties that could never be taken away. During the ratification debates, various states had sent to Congress their requests for changes or additions to the Constitution; these were called amendments. Madison, who was now serving in the House of Representatives, combined the many recommendations into a concise list of twelve amendments. By December 15, 1791, the states had ratified ten of the twelve amendments. Those ten became the Bill of Rights.

Political parties develop

Madison understood the intent of the Constitution better than anyone in the country, and he advised George Washington, the nation's first president, on what it allowed. Madison also played an active role in helping Washington choose a permanent site for the U.S. capital, on the Potomac River between Maryland and Virginia. Washington called on Madison to write his speeches. When Washington considered stepping down from the presidency in 1792, Madison prepared a farewell speech. Washington did not step down, instead choosing to serve out the remainder of his second term in 1797, but parts of his famous *Farewell Address,* a published statement that announced his retirement, were written by Madison in 1792.

During Washington's second term, Madison and Washington parted ways over constitutional issues. Washington looked more and more to Secretary of the Treasury Alexander Hamilton for direction in solving the nation's financial difficulties. Hamilton supported establishment of a national bank. He also wanted to build up the nation's navy and commercial shipping fleet. Bankers and merchants favored this approach. Madison opposed establishment of a national bank because it was not called for in the Constitution. Madison and Jefferson, longtime friends who shared similar political views, opposed the national bank, intended to keep taxes low, and had no desire to build up the navy. Farmers tended to side with Madison and Jefferson. Two political parties emerged.

Washington, Hamilton, and **John Adams** (1735–1826; see entry in volume 1), Washington's vice president, along with many bankers and merchants, became known as Federalists.

Madison and Jefferson, and like-minded farmers, were called Republicans (or later, Democratic-Republicans). The Republicans of the 1790s were entirely different from the modern Republican Party, which formed in the mid-1850s.

After two terms as president, Washington decided not to run again. At the time, ordinary citizens did not vote directly in presidential elections. Instead, electors chosen from each state cast votes for president. Whoever got the most votes was president, and whoever got the second most was vice president. In the 1796 election, the Federalist candidate, John Adams, received the most votes, seventy-one, and the Democratic-Republican candidate, Thomas Jefferson, came in second with sixty-eight. So in 1796, the nation had a president and vice president aligned with different political parties. Madison was offered a diplomatic mission to France, which he declined.

Dolley and solidifying beliefs

Madison went home to Montpelier in early 1797 to be with his wife, **Dolley Madison** (1768–1849; see entry in volume 2). Dolley and Madison had married in September 1794 after only a few months of courtship. Dolley grew up in Virginia and Philadelphia. She first married lawyer John Todd, but he died in the 1793 yellow fever epidemic. Dolley's energy would help sustain Madison through the rest of his public career. They remained at Montpelier until 1801.

Madison and Jefferson wrote to each other frequently and together solidified their ideas about how the U.S. republic should operate. Madison and Jefferson championed the common people, believing that they could make good decisions on political issues and cast thoughtful votes. They also believed that the rights and liberties of all people, not just the majority, had to be protected. Increasing numbers of Americans and newly arrived immigrants joined the Democratic-Republican side.

Federalists, on the other hand, tended to believe that the country would be run best by wealthy, highly educated men. Federalists began to see their numbers declining. Many newspapers, favoring the Democratic-Republican view, criticized President Adams, a Federalist, and the Federalist-controlled Congress. Congress lashed back by passing the Alien and Sedition Laws.

Alien and Sedition Laws

The Alien and Sedition Laws clearly infringed on civil rights (the basic rights that belong to individuals by virtue of their citizenship). The Alien Laws made it more difficult for immigrants to become U.S. citizens and allowed the president to expel or imprison an alien without giving a specific reason. An alien is a person who holds citizenship in one country but resides in a different country. The Sedition Act provided heavy fines and imprisonment for anyone writing, publishing, or speaking in a manner considered critical of the government or its officials. Ultimately, the Alien Laws were never used, but a number of newspapermen were charged under the Sedition Act.

Virginia and Kentucky Resolutions

In 1798 and 1799, Democratic-Republicans fought hard against the Alien and Sedition Laws. Madison and Jefferson anonymously wrote resolutions denouncing the Alien and Sedition Laws as unconstitutional, meaning that the laws went against the intent of the Constitution. Jefferson wrote the Kentucky Resolution, which Kentucky's legislature passed. Madison wrote the Virginia Resolution, which Virginia's General Assembly passed. The resolutions declared the Alien and Sedition Laws to be null and void, in essence saying states had the right to declare laws passed by Congress unconstitutional. Jefferson and Madison were soon disappointed, however, because no other states agreed that it was within state power to decide the constitutionality of congressional laws. The debates over Madison and Jefferson's resolutions led the Supreme Court in 1803 to adopt the role of ruling on the constitutionality of laws passed by Congress. The Constitution did not specifically say the Supreme Court had or did not have such power.

Although most states failed to adopt the resolutions, the debate focused opposition against the Federalist-written Alien and Sedition Laws. The laws proved disastrous for the Federalists in the presidential election of 1800. Democratic-Republicans won the election, and Jefferson became the nation's third president. He appointed Madison as his secretary of state.

Secretary of state

Madison served as Jefferson's secretary of state, his right-hand man, for the entire Jefferson presidency, from March 1801 until March 1809. Madison's wife, Dolley, also played a key role. Because Jefferson was a widower, Dolley took on the duties of official hostess at presidential social functions.

President Jefferson and Madison set about dismantling some Federalist policies that they found unacceptable. The hated Alien and Sedition Laws expired in 1801, and Congress, now controlled by Democratic-Republicans, failed to renew them. Both the president and Madison were determined to reduce the national debt, and they were successful. By the time Madison took over the presidency in 1809, the debt had been reduced from $83 million in 1801 to $57 million. With no war threatening, they reduced the navy and army that Presidents Washington and Adams had built up. At the urging of Secretary of the Treasury **Albert Gallatin** (1761–1849; see entry in volume 1), a wizard with figures and finance, Jefferson and Madison kept the Federalist-established national bank.

Undoubtedly the most important happening during Madison's first four years as secretary of state was the purchase of Louisiana from France, a land deal that doubled the size of the United States. Louisiana referred to an immense region west of the Mississippi River from New Orleans north to Canada and west to the Rocky Mountains. Jefferson was easily reelected in November 1804, and Madison remained at his side as secretary of state.

As soon as Jefferson's second term began, war between Britain and France erupted after a few years of peace between the two old enemies. Jefferson and Madison held to a policy of neutrality, not favoring either side. They insisted neutrality gave the United States the right to continue freely trading with any foreign country as long as the trade did not involve war materials. Neither Britain nor France recognized such a right, and both warring countries seized American merchant ships when they had the opportunity to do so. Britain seized sailors from these ships as well, an action called impressment. British seamen would board American ships, seize crew members, and force them to work on British ships.

Jefferson decided to try to force Britain and France to stop their seizure of American ships by passing the Embargo Act. Madison agreed with the move, as he firmly believed in using economic controls or sanctions on other countries. Besides, they had reduced the U.S. Navy to only four ships, so going to war was not an option. The Embargo Act, passed on December 22, 1807, banned all U.S. merchant ships from sailing to foreign ports. It also prohibited foreign ships from carrying American goods away from U.S. ports. Jefferson and Madison believed that Britain and France relied on American goods and that they would agree to halt seizure of American ships so trade with America could resume.

The act backfired, crippling the U.S. economy rather than Britain and France. Exports (goods leaving the country) and imports (goods coming into the country) plummeted. Mid-Atlantic farmers saw wheat prices fall from $2 to 75 cents a bushel. Southern farmers saw tobacco and cotton stack up on wharves because there were no buyers. New Englanders, who relied most heavily on international shipping from their ports, felt great resentment over the Embargo Act.

Although the Embargo Act increased public support for the Federalist Party, the Democratic-Republican base was still widespread among ordinary Americans. Jefferson's exceptional ability to relate to the public outweighed his problems as president. Knowing Madison would most likely become the next president, Jefferson was ready to retire to his Virginia home at Monticello. Madison, the Democratic-Republican candidate for president in 1808, received 122 electoral votes, while Charles Cotesworth Pinckney (1746–1825), the Federalist candidate, received 47 votes.

President

President Madison inherited from Jefferson a country with major economic woes, primarily because of the Embargo Act. To make matters worse, the nation was creeping toward another war with European powers. Just before Madison took office in early 1809, Congress replaced the Embargo Act with the Intercourse Act, which restricted trade with Britain and France, but not other countries. Again, instead of easing trade restrictions on the United States to revive trade, Britain and France stubbornly continued seizing American ships and further closing ports to U.S. trade.

Out of desperation, Congress passed Macon's Bill No. 2 in May 1810. It temporarily lifted all trade restrictions against Britain and France, but promised to keep the restrictions lifted against whichever country lifted their restrictions against the United States while reimposing restrictions against the other country. In essence, the United States promised to economically assist whichever country quit harassing U.S. ships first. French leader Napoléon Bonaparte (1769–1821) announced he would repeal the French restrictions. Eager for any kind of resolution, Madison in November 1810 announced that France had complied with Macon's Bill and that the United States would therefore place restrictions on British trade once again. Trade with France resumed, while the United States and Britain grew further apart.

The midterm congressional elections in the fall of 1810 brought major changes to Congress. The government's failure to stop British seizures of American ships and sailors was a major source of public disgust. The country elected a group of twenty to thirty congressmen, primarily from the South and West and all Democratic-Republicans, who were eager to go to war with Britain to reclaim American honor. These congressmen became known as war hawks. Meanwhile, the Federalists, who were concentrated in the New England region, demanded that Madison resume trade with Britain and not go to war. New England merchants and manufacturers needed to ship their products to Britain. Madison himself wanted to avoid a declaration of war and was dismayed over the split in the nation.

The conflict with Britain over seizures of American ships and sailors continued in the spring of 1811. The war hawks wanted the U.S. Navy to begin escorting American merchant ships across the Atlantic. In May, a British warship approached an American merchant ship escorted by the U.S.S. *President*. The *President* fired on the British ship, killing several crewmen. War seemed close at hand.

War of 1812

With not even the slightest hint from Britain that it might halt the seizures and restrictions on U.S. trade, Madison felt he had no choice but to take the nation to war. In early June 1812, he delivered a war message to Congress. On June 18, Congress declared war against Britain. All Federalists in Congress voted against the war, but most Democratic-Republicans supported Madison's decision, with the exception of fourteen Democratic-Republicans from the North.

The British had actually been suffering a great deal from not being able to trade with America; therefore, on June 23, 1812, Britain revoked its restrictions on U.S. trade. However, the news took weeks to cross the Atlantic, and no one in America knew of Britain's decision before war was already declared.

The United States was ill prepared for war. During Jefferson's administration, the army and navy had been slashed. There was little money to rebuild them. Most of America's military officers were aging veterans of the American Revolution. Congress decided that state militias would fight the war. By the end of 1812, "Mr. Madison's War," as it was called, was not going well. Aside from some amazing U.S. victories on the Great Lakes and on the high seas, carried out by two U.S. ships, the *Constellation* and the *Constitution,* Britain had the upper hand. Nevertheless, in November 1812, Madison was reelected to a second term.

The low point of the war came in August 1814. The British landed in Chesapeake Bay and marched down the streets of Washington, D.C., burning every public building, including the Capitol and the President's House. Dolley Madison's courageous attempts to save a few American treasures, such as a portrait of George Washington, became legendary. The British next turned on Baltimore and bombarded Fort McHenry. After a long night, the fort held, and Americans rejoiced.

In September 1814, Americans had another victory to celebrate. A small fleet of four ships commanded by thirty-year-old U.S. commodore Thomas Macdonough (1783–1825) turned back a British advance on Lake Champlain in northern New York state. Macdonough's heroic efforts probably saved New York City.

A weary Madison had sent five diplomats to Ghent, Belgium, to begin negotiations with Britain to end the war. The group was led by John Quincy Adams (1767–1848), son of the second U.S. president, John Adams. John Quincy Adams would later become the sixth U.S. president. In the fall of 1814, news of the failed British invasions and the destruction in Washington, D.C., subdued the mood on

A BOXING MATCH, or Another Bloody Nose for JOHN BULL.

Despite some naval successes against Britain (as illustrated here, with President James Madison punching Britain's King George III), the United States was ill prepared for the War of 1812. *(© Hulton Archive/Getty Images.)*

both sides of the negotiating table in Ghent. Demands stopped, and the Treaty of Ghent was signed on December 24, 1814. News that General **Andrew Jackson** (1767–1845; see entry in volume 1) had defeated some eight thousand British troops at New Orleans on January 8, 1815, reached Washington, D.C., about the same time as the news of the peace treaty. Some Americans mistakenly thought the victory at New Orleans had spurred the treaty signing. Although the war had essentially ended in a draw, Americans praised Madison for not giving in. Madison and his fellow Americans were eager to move forward to a time of peace and rebuild the Capitol and the economy.

Contented

Madison completed his final two years in Washington in a time of peace and prosperity. Trade with European nations normalized for both New England merchants and American farmers. Madison worked closely with his secretary of state, **James Monroe** (1758–1831; see entry in volume 2), hoping that Monroe would become the fifth president. In November 1816, Monroe was the third Democratic-Republican to be elected president.

The Madisons packed and returned to Montpelier at the end of March 1817. They hosted many guests in their home. They also spent hours arranging old saved correspondence and writing new letters. Madison rode around his property, taking a greater interest in agriculture than ever before.

Madison visited Jefferson at Monticello as often as he could. When Jefferson died in 1826, Madison succeeded him as head of the University of Virginia, which was founded by Jefferson. Madison also served as president of the American Colonization Society, which advocated sending slaves to Africa to set up their own colony. Disturbed by the increasing unrest over the issue of slavery, he hoped this might be a good solution. Despite the slavery matter, Madison believed the American Revolution, which had begun in 1775, had at last been won. Madison dictated his last public message, "Advice to My Country," to Dolley. He died on June 28, 1836.

For More Information

Books

Brant, Irving. *James Madison.* Indianapolis: Bobbs-Merrill, 1941-61.

Rakove, Jack N. *James Madison and the Creation of the American Republic.* Glenview, IL: Scott, Foresman/Little, Brown Higher Education, 1990. Reprint, New York: Longman, 2002.

Rutland, Robert A. *James Madison and the Search for Nationhood.* Washington, DC: Library of Congress, 1981.

Rutland, Robert A. *James Madison: The Founding Father.* New York: Macmillan, 1987. Reprint, Columbia: University of Missouri Press, 1997.

Rutland, Robert A., ed. *James Madison and the American Nation, 1751–1836: An Encyclopedia.* New York: Simon & Schuster, 1994.

Wills, Garry. *James Madison.* New York: Times Books, 2002.

Web Sites

"First Invasion: The War of 1812." *The History Channel.* http://www.historychannel.com/1812/ (accessed on August 17, 2005).

The James Madison Center. http://www.jmu.edu/madison/center/home.htm (accessed on August 17, 2005).

James Madison's Montpelier. http://www.montpelier.org/ (accessed on August 17, 2005).

John Marshall

Born September 24, 1755 (Germantown, Virginia)
Died July 6, 1835 (Philadelphia, Pennsylvania)

Chief justice of the U.S. Supreme Court

John Marshall grew up as a Virginia gentleman who was accepted into the most famous group of national leaders this nation ever produced. His fellow Virginian revolutionaries included **George Washington** (1732–1799; see entry in volume 2), **Thomas Jefferson** (1743–1826; see entry in volume 1), **James Madison** (1751–1836; see entry in volume 2), and **Edmund Randolph** (1753–1813; see entry in volume 2). In January 1801, the U.S. Senate approved Marshall as chief justice of the Supreme Court. At the time, it was a weak federal position. Over the next thirty-four years, however, Marshall made it into one of the most powerful positions in the national government.

In his court position, Marshall assumed the role of chief defender of the U.S. Constitution. He also resolved numerous conflicts between state and federal governments. Marshall took part in over one thousand court decisions, writing the court's opinion on approximately half of them. His defense and interpretation of the Constitution laid the foundation for a strong nation. His decisions also created the legal field of constitutional law as it would be practiced for the next two centuries.

"An act of the legislature, repugnant to the Constitution, is void. This theory is essentially attached to a written constitution, and is consequently to be considered, by this Court, as one of the fundamental principles of our society."

John Marshall.

Marshall treated the Constitution as a law made by the people through their representatives at the Constitutional Convention. Marshall did not consider it an agreement among states as others at the time did. Therefore, the Constitution assumed a supreme role in American law. Marshall also supported a broad interpretation of the Constitution that claimed the existence of implied (unwritten) powers possessed by the Supreme Court to carry out the responsibilities specifically assigned to the government. In the early 1790s, Federalist **Alexander Hamilton** (1755–1804; see entry in volume 1) believed these implied powers existed when Hamilton supported the establishment of the National Bank of the United States over James Madison's objections that it was unconstitutional. By protecting contracts, including corporate charters, from state law restrictions, Marshall's Supreme Court decisions also played a major role in stabilizing U.S. finances.

Through his force of personality, Marshall made the federal judiciary a major branch of government as anticipated in the Constitution. The Supreme Court became equal in power, influence, and prestige to the president and Congress of the United States. He shaped what many still considered a federation of states into a more unified nation.

Youth on the frontier

The oldest of fifteen children, John Marshall was born to Thomas and Mary Marshall in September 1755 on a plantation near Germantown, Virginia. His father rose up in society from a common background while his mother was from the wealthy Randolph family of Virginia. Marshall grew up in the foothills of the Blue Ridge Mountains on the Virginia frontier, which in 1759 became Fauquier County. His father was successful in land speculation, making him one of the wealthiest Virginians in Fauquier County. John would later become a successful land speculator himself. Land speculation is the buying of undeveloped frontier land cheaply with the intent of later reselling it to settlers at a higher price, making a profit. It was a common means of gaining wealth in the early American period.

Marshall received a limited formal education as a youth, but his family paid close attention to world affairs and valued education. His father served in Virginia's House of Burgesses (the colonial legislature) and brought John books on politics. Marshall was also tutored in the literary classics and Latin. However, young Marshall's formal schooling was cut short after only two years when the American Revolutionary War (1775–83) broke out. Nonetheless, throughout his life, Marshall drew on the intellectual influences of his childhood and combined them with the skills of a frontiersman in creating a rugged, self-reliant person.

Legal scholar George Wythe. Future Supreme Court chief justice John Marshall attended a series of Wythe's lectures. *(Library of Congress.)*

Revolutionary War

With the outbreak of the war in 1775, Marshall became an officer in the Virginia militia with his father. He then became an officer in the regular Continental Army in 1776 and served under General Washington for the next three years. He fought in many important battles, including engagements at Brandywine, Germantown, Stony Point, and Monmouth. He also wintered with General Washington and his troops at Valley Forge in 1777-78.

Marshall also served as a judge in the military justice system for the Continental Army. It was his first experience in the administration of justice. While still in the army, in 1780, Marshall had the opportunity to attend a series of lectures on law by the prominent legal scholar George Wythe (1726–1806) at William and Mary College in Williamsburg, Virginia. Wythe also instructed Jefferson and later **Henry Clay** (1777–1852; see entry in volume 1) in law. Deciding on a law career, Marshall gained his license to practice law in August 1780, and he left military service the following year in 1781.

While attending Wythe's classes in Williamsburg, Marshall met Mary Ambler, known as "Polly." Her father was the state treasurer of Virginia. After three years of courtship, they married in January 1783 and settled in Richmond, Virginia, where Marshall's law practice grew rapidly. They had ten children, but Polly suffered a mental breakdown when she had a miscarriage. Though she was left partly an invalid, Marshall cared for her, and their special strong relationship persisted throughout their marriage.

Virginia's top lawyer

In his law practice, Marshall showed a strong gift for oratory, a charismatic personality, and the ability to think quickly. These qualities led to his fast rise in Virginia's legal profession and in politics. Marshall was elected to the Virginia House of Delegates from 1782 to 1784, 1787 to 1791, and 1795 to 1797. In June 1788, Marshall was a delegate to the Virginia convention for ratifying the new U.S. Constitution and supported the constitution's adoption. Not surprisingly, the section of the constitution that he most strongly supported concerned the creation of the new federal judiciary.

In the process of forming the new government in 1789, the newly elected President Washington offered Marshall the position of U.S. attorney in Virginia. However, Marshall chose to remain in the Virginia legislature. As political parties formed through the 1790s, Marshall became a leading Federalist in Virginia. Federalists supported the need for a strong central government.

Marshall continued to rise in national prominence through the 1790s. Aligning himself with President Washington and Treasury Secretary Hamilton, the recognized national leader of the Federalist Party, Marshall actively supported the unpopular Jay Treaty (a settlement with Britain) in 1795. Marshall even presented one case concerning a land dispute before the U.S. Supreme Court in 1796. In his courtroom pleas, he argued for a strong national government. The Federalist Party encouraged him to run for Congress, but he refused that as well. His law practice was doing too well. He remained a strong supporter of President Washington as controversies over foreign and economic policy grew through the mid-1790s, and he rallied Virginia leaders behind the Jay Treaty with Britain in 1795.

Public service

Despite his rise in politics, Marshall carefully selected the public posts he assumed. President Washington offered him the attorney general position and a seat on the U.S. Supreme Court, but he declined both. In 1797, President **John Adams** (1735–1826; served 1797–1801; see entry in volume 1) sent

Marshall with other U.S. diplomats to France to negotiate a treaty. They were to resolve growing disputes between the two nations; causes for the disputes included France's raid of many U.S. merchant ships engaged in war against Britain. When French officials tried to bribe the U.S. delegation before they allowed a meeting with the French foreign minister Charles-Maurice de Talleyrand-Périgord (1754–1838), Marshall and the others protested and left. They returned to America in June 1798 as heroes for refusing to give in to the French corruption.

Upon Marshall's return from France, President Adams offered him an appointment to the U.S. Supreme Court, but again he declined. Encouraged by former President Washington to run for Congress, in 1798 Marshall was elected to the U.S. House of Representatives. There, he became a leading Federalist and supporter of Adams. After again declining an appointment as secretary of war, Marshall finally accepted the appointment by Adams as secretary of state in May 1800. In this position, Marshall became a strong supporter and chief personal advisor to Adams during the final year of his administration. Later in 1800, when Adams took leave from Washington, D.C., to return to his Massachusetts home for several months, Marshall essentially ran the country.

When Supreme Court chief justice Oliver Ellsworth (1745–1807) resigned due to ill health in late 1800, Adams's first choice to succeed him was Federalist **John Jay** (1745–1829; see entry in volume 1), who had served as the first chief justice in the early 1790s. However, Jay declined, in part because the position lacked power and any real authority. Adams then turned to Marshall, who was confirmed by the U.S. Senate on January 27, 1801. Marshall also continued to serve as secretary of state until March 4 when the Adams administration came to an end.

Having lost the presidential election to Democratic-Republican Thomas Jefferson and with Congress also strongly favoring Democratic-Republican candidates, Adams hoped to keep the federal courts as a Federalist stronghold through last-minute maneuvers before leaving office. The Federalist-controlled Congress passed the 1801 Judiciary Act, which created new federal courts, and Adams, with Marshall as close advisor, proceeded to make many federal court appointments during his last days.

Chief justice

Marshall took his seat on the Court in March 1801 and served in that position through the remainder of his life, for some thirty-four years. He was exceptionally knowledgeable in law and government operations. He was also very bright and could quickly understand and analyze complex legal issues. Marshall, through his personal abilities of charm and intellect, brought the Court above politics and brought about a major transformation in the judiciary. Party affiliation of the justices became less of a factor, and for a time the Court was strongly unified.

As in England, the U.S. Supreme Court through the 1790s made rulings on cases with each justice delivering a separate opinion on the case. However, in a young nation with its legal system barely formed, this approach only added confusion to this early period. Marshall established a rule that the Court issue a single opinion in cases. The unified rulings offered considerable legal certainty to the nation and greatly increased the Court's influence. During this time, the justices were housed together while in Washington, D.C., for the annual Court session that lasted several weeks. As a result, they constantly interacted on the issues before them. In this atmosphere, Marshall, who was open to different views and willing to change his own opinion, was often able to reach consensus (full agreement) among the Court justices.

The first years of Marshall's time on the Court were turbulent as the Democratic-Republicans led by President Jefferson, now in power, challenged Federalist judges. In 1803, fellow Supreme Court justice Samuel Chase (1741–1811) was impeached (charged by Congress) for injecting his strong Federalist views in the courtroom. Vice President **Aaron Burr** (1756–1836; see entry in volume 1) presided over the trial in the Senate, and Chase was found not guilty. Before long, political battles decreased, and a greater calm surrounded the Court.

The trial of Aaron Burr

Burr, himself, became a defendant when he was charged with treason in the summer of 1807. After leaving office a couple of years earlier, Burr became involved in mysterious plots that possibly involved invading Mexico or transforming

Courtroom scene during the trial of Aaron Burr on charges of treason. John Marshall was the presiding judge. *(© Bettmann/Corbis.)*

the region of the United States west of the Appalachians into a separate nation. The trial was held in the U.S. Circuit Court in Richmond. Marshall was the presiding judge. During this time, the Supreme Court justices still sat on U.S. Circuit Courts around the country when the Supreme Court was not in session. The Supreme Court met in the winter, and the circuit courts met in spring and fall.

Burr was found not guilty. Many, including President Jefferson, who was pressing hard for a conviction, blamed the unsuccessful prosecution directly on Marshall, who gave the jury such a narrow definition of treason that a finding of guilty was almost impossible. The Democratic-Republican Jefferson felt the Federalist Marshall had taken the action to politically frustrate him.

Judicial power

In addition to reforming the Court's operating procedures, Marshall brought even more change through individual case rulings. After a delay while the new Congress repealed the recently passed Judiciary Act, Marshall convened court in February 1803. Changes came quickly. Most important was the case of *Marbury v. Madison* in 1803 (see box). In this ruling, Marshall established the principle of judicial review. This principle meant that the Court could exercise considerable legal power in deciding whether federal laws are constitutional or not.

In an 1810 decision, Marshall extended the power of judicial review to determine the constitutionality of state laws in *Fletcher v. Peck*. Later, in rulings made in 1816 and 1821, the Court further extended judicial review to the review of state court decisions where federal issues were involved.

Through these series of decisions defining judicial review, Marshall established that the Constitution was the highest law of the land and that the courts were responsible for enforcing it. The independence of the judiciary was established and could be preserved through judicial review. Judicial review would later be used to keep states from encroaching on federal responsibilities and for protecting individual rights of citizens from government actions.

Creating economic stability

Many of Marshall's court decisions also supported the growth of corporations, a major Federalist goal earlier under Secretary of the Treasury Hamilton. The 1810 *Peck* decision had

Marbury v. Madison

The U.S. Supreme Court's 1803 *Marbury v. Madison* case launched a new era for the judicial system in America. In November 1800, the Federalists had lost the presidential election and many congressional seats to their rival political party, the Democratic-Republicans, who believed in a weak central government. The Federalists took action in their remaining months of political control before the inauguration date of March 4, 1801. The Federalist-controlled Congress passed the 1801 Judiciary Act creating additional federal courts. Then-President Adams, with assistance from Secretary of State John Marshall, filled the new court positions. Many appointments were made in the last hours of Adams's presidency, and the judges came to be known as the "midnight judges."

Some of the newly appointed judges had not received their formal papers, called commissions. Adams and Marshall signed and sealed the commissions, but some remained undelivered as Adams's time ran out on inauguration day, March 4, 1801. Adams appointed William Marbury, one of several new justices of the peace for the District of Columbia in the capital city. He was one of the justices who did not receive commissions. Upon taking office, President Thomas Jefferson ordered his new secretary of state, James Madison, not to deliver some of the remaining undelivered commissions to the newly appointed federal judges.

Marbury first unsuccessfully appealed to the State Department for his papers. Next, he filed a lawsuit with the U.S. Supreme Court against Madison. Upon hearing the arguments in the case, Marshall and the Court unanimously found that Marbury deserved his papers. However, Marbury needed to file his lawsuit with a lower federal court. The Court ruled it did not have constitutional authority to accept such cases.

other major implications besides expanding judicial review. It was the first ruling to establish the strong legal standing of business contracts. This created a strong national economic stability.

In *McCulloch v. Maryland* in 1819, the Court upheld the constitutional power of Congress to charter corporations, in this case the Second National Bank of the United States. The decision determined that Congress needed to stabilize currency and the national financial system. Creating a national bank, the Court determined, was a suitable way to achieve those goals. The decision most importantly supported a flexible, or "loose," interpretation of the Constitution by supporting the implied powers in the Necessary and Proper Clause of

William Marbury, plaintiff in the *Marbury v. Madison* trial. *(The Granger Collection, New York.)*

authorized the Court to issue writs of mandamus (court orders) to government officials forcing them to take some action. The Court claimed such authority was not granted by the Constitution.

Marbury did not receive his judgeship and Marshall gave up some small amount of Court authority. However, on the other hand, he claimed enormous power for the Court in its judicial review role. It was the first occasion for the Supreme Court to rule a federal law unconstitutional. The Court soon showed in another case that judicial review could support a federal government action, such as chartering a national bank. Thus, the *Marbury* decision defined and expanded the area of responsibility of the judicial system, a major step in shaping the national government.

It ruled that Section 13 of the 1789 Judiciary Act was unconstitutional by granting such a power to the Court. The section had the Constitution. Government had certain unwritten powers it could exercise to help it accomplish its explicit, enumerated, responsibilities granted in the Constitution.

Other decisions promoted economic growth. *Gibbons v. Ogden* (1824) involved a New York law restricting steamboat navigation in the state. Marshall again supported a broad interpretation of congressional powers over interstate commerce, striking down the state law as unconstitutional. The Court's decision essentially created a national free trade zone within the nation that greatly facilitated interstate commerce.

Through these decisions, the power of the national government was becoming well established, and the Supreme Court had become the final source for interpreting those powers. Many were upset with these newly defined powers of the Court. Despite efforts through Congress to limit the powers that Marshall had established, particularly over state laws and state court decisions, nothing resulted. The will of the public seemed to support Marshall.

New directions

The election of **Andrew Jackson** (1767–1845; served 1829–37; see entry in volume 1) as president in 1828 was a major blow to Marshall as was the death of his wife. Jackson supported strong state powers in conflict with Marshall's philosophy. When Jackson was in office, Marshall issued two historic Court decisions, *Cherokee Nation v. Georgia* (1832) and *Worcester v. Georgia* (1833). Marshall defined the legal relationship between the federal government and Native American tribes that persisted into the twenty-first century. He labeled tribes as "domestic dependent nations" having a distinction from state governments and established that only the U.S. Congress has the power to regulate tribal activities. However, the idea that states could nullify (ignore) federal laws was gaining strength by the early 1830s, and even Jackson as U.S. president refused to enforce the *Worcester* decision. It was a dark moment in the history of the Supreme Court.

The Court unity that Marshall had nurtured also began to decrease by the 1830s in his last years as chief justice. More decisions began including separate concurring statements, often supporting the Court's decision but perhaps for different reasons and representing dissenting opinions.

Away from the courtroom

For much of the year, the courts were not in session. During his time away from the bench, Marshall enjoyed novels and poetry and relaxing on his farm near Richmond. Between 1804 and 1807, he also wrote a five-volume biography of George Washington and, at the age of seventy-four, served in a Virginia constitutional convention in 1829. He also enjoyed entertaining, often hosting dinners for lawyers at his home. He lived the life of a Virginia gentleman, but he typically wore plain clothing and could be seen doing his own shopping at Richmond markets. He was very personable, charming, and informal.

By 1830, when Marshall was seventy-five, his own health began declining, but he remained mentally sharp. In 1831, he had surgery to remove kidney stones, but he recovered sufficiently to continue serving in the Court until his death on July 6, 1835.

For More Information

Books

Beveridge, Albert J. *The Life of John Marshall*. Boston, New York: Houghton Mifflin, 1916–19. Reprint, Holmes Beach, FL: Gaunt, 1997.

Hobson, Charles F. *The Great Chief Justice: John Marshall and the Rule of Law*. Lawrence: University Press of Kansas, 1996.

Newmyer, R. Kent. *John Marshall and the Heroic Age of the Supreme Court*. Baton Rouge: Louisiana State University Press, 2001.

Smith, Jean Edward. *John Marshall: Definer of a Nation*. New York: Henry Holt, 1996.

Stites, Francis N. *John Marshall: Defender of the Constitution*. Boston: Little, Brown, 1981.

Web Sites

Supreme Court of the United States. http://www.supremecourtus.gov/ (accessed on August 17, 2005).

Alexander McGillivray

Born 1759 (Present-day Alabama)
Died February 17, 1793 (Pensacola, Florida)

Creek Indian leader

"For the good of my Country I have sacrificed my all and it is a duty incumbent on me in this critical situation. . . . The protection of a great Monarch is to be preferred to that of a distracted Republic."

Alexander McGillivray was an important Native American political leader during the early years of the United States. He came to power in the Creek Confederacy at a time when white settlements were expanding farther into traditional Native American homelands and threatening Native American society. McGillivray used his influence to introduce reforms and protect Creek interests. As the son of a European father and a Native American mother, McGillivray made a unique contribution to the history of the newly formed United States.

McGillivray's domestic policy urged the centralization of power among the Native Americans; the concept of centralization was characteristic of European-style governments but had never been tried in the Creek nation. His foreign policy in the mid-1780s resulted in an alliance with Spain, the country that controlled the Gulf Coast region and the area that makes up present-day Florida. The alliance guaranteed the Creek their political and territorial rights within Florida. After **George Washington** (1732–1799; served 1789–97; see entry in volume 2) was inaugurated as the first president of the United States in

1789, McGillivray met with him to sign the Treaty of New York. The treaty established a formal relationship between the United States and the Creek nation and provided a federal guarantee of Creek territorial rights.

A native Creek

Alexander McGillivray was born around 1759 at his father's Little Tallassee plantation, near present-day Montgomery, Alabama. Little Tallassee was located close to the ruins of the old French fort Toulouse outside the Creek Indian town of Otcipofa, on the Coosa River. Alexander's mother was Sehoy Marchand, a Creek Indian of the influential Wind Clan. She was a member of the Koasati tribe of the Muskogee or Creek confederacy. The Koasati were a matriarchal tribe, which means they traced their descent and inheritance through female family members. Alexander developed close ties with his mother's family and culture as he was growing up. Because the Creek viewed heritage through the mother's side of the family, they considered McGillivray fully as a Native American despite his European name and schooling. As a child, he participated in Native American rituals, including annual public ceremonies celebrating the New Year and the change of seasons. He learned the unwritten Creek rules and expectations of the Creek people, and this knowledge equipped him in a unique way to serve them once he grew to be a man.

Alexander's father was Lachlan McGillivray, a wealthy trader from Scotland who established a trading post among the Creek Indian nation (see box). The Native Americans resisted white men who came to farm their land but welcomed those who brought the benefits of trade. Young Alexander was comfortable in the colonial environment of his father and learned the English language and culture from an early age. When he was about fourteen years old after growing up in Creek society, Alexander was sent to Charleston, South Carolina, where his cousin, the Reverend Farquhar McGillivray, became his tutor. Alexander studied Greek, Latin, English history, and literature. He was also sent briefly to Savannah, Georgia, where he studied business before returning to Charleston. However, the outbreak of the American Revolution (1775–83) cut short Alexander's formal education. In 1777, he returned from Charleston to his mother's people on the Little Tallassee.

The Creek Confederacy

The Creek confederacy was a loose alliance of various Native American groups. The members of the alliance occupied a large and fertile area in the Gulf Coast region of North America. Their land covered a major portion of the present-day states of Alabama and Georgia. Most of their white neighbors were situated to the east along the Atlantic seaboard. Neighboring Native American nations included the Seminoles to the southeast, the Choctaw and Chickasaw to the west, and the Cherokee to the north. Of these nations, the Creek were by far the largest, in land, population, and power; they added to their strength by adopting or absorbing other tribes into their confederacy. Throughout the Creek world, each tribe spoke its native language as well as a common language called the "trade language."

The Creek people were sometimes known as Muskogee, the name of their dominant tribe, but the English called them the Creek. The origin of the name is uncertain, but it may have come from the fact that they built their clustered towns on the many streams that watered their country. The Creek often gave their towns names that described the town location or a natural feature: Tallasi meant old or abandoned town, Wewoka meant barking or roaring water, and Concharty meant red earth. Sometimes a town was named for a historic event; for

A portrait of a member of the Creek nation.
(Painting by Frederic Remington. Library of Congress.)

example, Nuyaka was named to commemorate the signing of the Treaty of New York.

Although Creek women had little influence in religious or governmental ceremonies, eligibility for political office was determined through the female line. Creek headmen (chiefs) were chosen from particular clans in the mother's line, just as Alexander McGillivray was brought to power in the prominent Wind Clan. The clan system was of utmost importance to the Creek people. Clan members had strong obligations to one another, even if one did not know a fellow member personally.

Changing alliances

White traders who lived and worked among the Creek Nation for decades had close ties to Britain and placed their loyalties with the British. At the start of the American Revolution, many of these traders had their properties taken away by the American rebels. They either fled to Europe or in some cases were hanged. Lachlan McGillivray's estate in South Carolina was seized by the revolutionaries, and he immediately returned to Scotland. Alexander corresponded with his father on occasion throughout the following years but never saw him again. Back home on the Little Tallassee in 1777, his mother's position in the Wind Clan made him eligible for appointment as a lesser chief. With his linguistic ability and his understanding of both Creek and colonial societies, Alexander soon took a prominent place in Creek political life. He discovered that his father's departure had left the Native Americans without European trading goods that had become essential to them. McGillivray took action himself and arranged for renewed trade between the Creek and their French, British, and Spanish neighbors.

The British commissioned McGillivray as a colonel in the British army, and he went to work for the British superintendent of Indian Affairs. His job was to maintain the loyalty of the Creek to the British Crown (royalty) during the war. Although he was unable to move the Creek confederacy into an open alliance with Britain, he organized raiding parties that inflicted heavy damages throughout the Georgia frontier on American settlements and became known as a Creek war chief, even though he rarely participated in battle. When General **Anthony Wayne** (1745–1796; see entry in volume 2) killed the Creek chief Emistesigo in Savannah, Georgia, near the end of the war, McGillivray became leader of the Creek nation.

By this time, he had secured his place as a trustworthy interpreter and representative of his people to the outside world. It would be McGillivray's role to direct tribal affairs in the critical decade following the American Revolution. The Creek nation itself had been divided along pro-British and pro-American lines throughout the conflict. Still angry with the Americans for seizing his father's estate, McGillivray continued to support the British.

Shift away from the British

The Treaty of Paris in 1783 formally ended the American Revolution. Great Britain ceded (gave up) all its claims to lands east of the Mississippi River to the Americans and ordered all British troops to withdraw from the United States. The treaty betrayed Britain's Native American allies, because it made no mention of Native American claims of independence and separate political status within the new United States. At the end of the war, McGillivray found himself at the head of a Creek confederacy that was still only a loose alliance of independent tribes. The confederacy had originally banded together because of a mutual interest in defending tribal lands, but because of their independence the Creek bands were unable to make and carry out policies like the American colonists did.

McGillivray attempted to establish some unity among the separate Creek townships through a National Council. The Council met once a year in late spring and brought together all of the Upper and Lower Creek towns. The National Council was usually held at Tuckabatchee, capital of the Upper Creek, or Coweta, capital of the Lower Creek. Both towns had facilities for large gatherings. The Council was the place where the Creek addressed international affairs, which included issues involving the United States, European nations, and other Native American tribes. McGillivray used the Council to unite Creek tribes and increase their power. He proposed to further their cause in 1784 by signing a treaty with the Spaniards in Florida.

Tribal treaties

Because of the ongoing conflicts with the Americans over land, only the Spanish could offer the Creek confederacy the protection it needed and the trade that it desired in postwar times. Americans were interested in taking more and more land, not establishing trade relations. McGillivray secured a Spanish alliance for the confederacy when he signed the Treaty of Pensacola on June 1, 1784. The treaty was beneficial to both sides: The Spanish gained the pledge of continued Creek support, and the Native Americans maintained secure trade routes and an ally against the land-hungry Americans pushing against Creek boundaries. McGillivray arranged a Spanish-Creek trade arrangement for a British trading firm, a deal that worked to his advantage because he was a partner in the business. Although the Creek nation had many chiefs, McGillivray became known as the Great Beloved Man, or chief counselor, because he carried on all the tribe's correspondence, arranged their trade agreements, and acted as spokesman at the signing of treaties.

The state of Georgia soon challenged Creek independence by arranging treaties with McGillivray's political rivals within the Creek confederacy. Settlers began moving onto large sections of Creek lands, claiming them as their own. McGillivray denied the legality of these treaties and sent warriors to block the settlements. Between 1785 and 1787, he sent out numerous war parties, some as far north as the Cumberland River in present-day Tennessee. McGillivray became famous in the United States for his success in driving off would-be settlers from the contested areas.

President George Washington invited McGillivray to come to New York to discuss peace and a U.S. plan to promote "civilization" among the Creek. The civilization program consisted largely of encouraging the tribes to take up farming. In the summer of 1790, McGillivray led a delegation of twenty-six Creek chiefs to the U.S. capital in order to negotiate a settlement. McGillivray agreed to negotiate but refused any settlement that recognized the Georgia treaties, which he considered illegal.

On August 7, 1790, the U.S. government and the Creek nation signed the Treaty of New York, establishing a direct relationship between the two for the first time. The arrangements surrounding the treaty set a precedent: U.S. leaders asked the Native American chiefs to meet with them at the U.S. government seat rather than elsewhere. This allowed the U.S. leaders to impress upon the Native American chiefs the size, wealth, population, and power of the United States. In the Treaty of New York, Creek leaders relinquished millions of acres of Creek land and agreed to the U.S. demand that they turn over runaway slaves to the federal authorities. In return, the United States promised to defend Creek territorial rights and gave the confederacy the right to punish any American who invaded Creek lands.

The Treaty of New York was a personal victory for Alexander McGillivray. It affirmed his position as a legitimate Creek national leader. The treaty also strengthened his control over Creek trade by granting him permission to import goods through the Spanish port of Pensacola without paying American duties (taxes). These gains served McGillivray in his efforts to centralize power and protect the sovereignty (political independence) of the Creek nation. In addition, the treaty included some secret articles, which were not made public until the treaty was published in full, several months after the signing. McGillivray had sworn allegiance to the United States and received a commission in the U.S. military along with a salary of twelve hundred dollars a year for life. He had become a master at playing the British, Spanish, and Americans against each other and in receiving personal gains from his dealings; this resulted in many Creek viewing him with suspicion if not disrespect.

An untimely end

McGillivray did not live long enough to enjoy the provisions of the treaty or to see his dream of Creek national unity within a fully functioning confederacy. His health had been poor for some time as he suffered from the effects of several diseases throughout his adult life. His letters hold references to gout and rheumatism, splitting headaches, fevers, and long periods of bed rest. The rheumatism and pain would sometimes keep him from the administration of tribal business. Many times, he was so weakened that he could not mount a horse. Although McGillivray maintained active control over Creek affairs, continued internal rivalry in the Creek confederacy wore him down.

Eventually he was forced to turn away from the Treaty of New York because he could not get the various Creek groups to honor the treaty's conditions, including the boundaries it established between Creek and American land. In the summer of 1792, he renewed the alliance with Spain. The position of the southeastern Native Americans was further threatened in 1793 with the invention of the cotton gin, a device that made it easier to remove seeds from harvested cotton. Cotton quickly replaced deerskins as the most valuable commodity in the South, and white farmers wanted more land to grow more cotton. The Creek still possessed much of the land in the area; however, the rise of cotton as a cash crop brought increased pressure from American settlers.

McGillivray's personal life is not well documented, but it is known that he had at least two wives, which was customary for a Creek chief. He owned several plantations that resembled those of prosperous American planters. McGillivray kept about sixty slaves, all of whom lived in slave quarters; they were supervised by a white overseer. McGillivray had a plantation near Tensaw on the Little River, just above Mobile, Alabama, and another at Little Tallassee on the Coosa River. He built a log house with dormer windows (vertical windows set in a sloping roof) and a stone chimney and kept several small apple and peach orchards on his property. He owned a large stock of horses, hogs, and cattle, and he hired a crew to maintain them.

On February 17, 1793, Alexander McGillivray died at the Pensacola, Florida, home of his British business partner, William Panton. McGillivray was only thirty-four years old at the time of his death. He was buried in Panton's garden, far from his home in Little Tallassee. McGillivray left his estate to his three surviving children. This was contrary to Creek custom, which would have dictated that he leave all his property to his sisters.

McGillivray's death left the Spaniards and the United States without someone to represent their interests to the Creek confederacy. The increasingly vulnerable Creek nation was left to search for another leader with McGillivray's diplomatic gifts and influence. Future U.S. president Theodore Roosevelt (1858–1919) later observed that McGillivray's diplomacy allowed the Creeks to maintain their lands and customs for a generation longer than other tribes in the face of U.S. expansion during the late eighteenth century.

For More Information

Books

Caughey, John Walton. *McGillivray of the Creeks*. Norman: University of Oklahoma Press, 1938.

Debo, Angie. *The Road to Disappearance*. Norman: University of Oklahoma Press, 1941.

Ethridge, Robbie. *Creek Country: The Creek Indians and Their World*. Chapel Hill: University of North Carolina Press, 2003.

Web Sites

"Alexander McGillivray (ca. 1750–1793)." *The New Georgia Encyclopedia.* http://www.georgiaencyclopedia.org/nge/Article.jsp?id=h-690 (accessed on August 17, 2005).

"Pensacola, 300 Years, 1698–1998." *Pensacola Historical Society.* http://www.geocities.com/Heartland/Prairie/3226/Pensacola/index.html (accessed on August 17, 2005).

James McGready

Born 1760 (Pennsylvania)
Died February 1817 (Henderson County, Kentucky)

Presbyterian preacher

James McGready is known as the father of revivalism in the American West, which in the eighteenth and early nineteenth centuries was the region between the Appalachian Mountains and the Mississippi River. McGready's use of camp meetings brought religion to the masses on the western frontier of the United States. As a result, America experienced a "Second Great Awakening," a period of widespread revival in religious activity. (A first "Great Awakening" had occurred in the early eighteenth century.) Through McGready and others, Protestantism (Christian beliefs held by congregations that are independent of the Catholic pope and other central authority) continued to serve as an important force in the nation's history.

McGready was a powerful preacher who drew thousands to hear his message of faith at the beginning of the nineteenth century. His services provided a spiritual and emotional experience for all who attended, and his preaching often provoked a physical response among his audience. McGready based his camp meetings on the model provided by the early Scottish Presbyterians, who combined a continuous outdoor service

"No person seemed to wish to go home. . . . Little children, young men and women, and old gray headed people, persons of every description, white and black, were to be found in every part of the multitude."

with camping out. The term "camp meeting" was first used in 1802, and it soon became a familiar part of the American vocabulary.

The revivalist

James McGready Jr. was born around 1760 in the farm country of western Pennsylvania. James McGready Sr. and his wife, Jean, were poor farmers who had recently immigrated to America from Ireland and Scotland. In 1778, the McGreadys moved their growing family to Guilford County, North Carolina. They settled near the Presbyterian congregations of David Caldwell, a highly respected minister with churches in the towns of Buffalo and Alamance, North Carolina, just outside Greensboro. Caldwell combined teaching with his pastoral ministry and ran an academy that taught the classics in his home. The McGready children received their elementary education from Caldwell, the only teacher at the academy. James worked long hours in the fields with his brothers on the family farm, but he was serious about his religious duties and his education. A visiting uncle noticed his religious inclinations and persuaded the McGreadys to allow James to return to Pennsylvania for theological training.

In 1784, James McGready returned to his home state and settled in a town called Canonsburg, near Pittsburgh. He boarded with John McMillan, a Presbyterian minister who was a graduate of the College of New Jersey (later Princeton University). McMillan is believed to be the first Presbyterian minister to have a regular congregation west of the Allegheny Mountains. McGready helped with farm chores in exchange for his room, board, and private tutoring while living in the McMillan home. In 1785, a Presbyterian minister named Joseph Smith opened an academy nearby in order to prepare young men for the ministry. Smith was also a graduate of the College of New Jersey. McGready immediately enrolled in his school. He was not at Smith's academy very long before McMillan opened his own theological academy in Canonsburg.

McGready transferred to the new academy so he could study once again under his original mentor. Lectures were arranged in the form of questions and answers. Students were expected to take notes and memorize the information. This system of learning taught McGready to present his thoughts in a clear and logical form. McMillan continued his work as a Presbyterian minister, and his sermons often drew large crowds from a great distance; sometimes his revival meetings lasted all night. McMillan taught his students his own "New Side," or revivalist, beliefs, which encouraged a passionate conversion (rebirth) experience rather than a mere declaration of faith. McGready sought the emotional conversion that McMillan described. One Sunday morning in 1786, McGready experienced his own personal spiritual rebirth at a "sacramental meeting" by the Monongahela River. Church gatherings among evangelical (crusading) denominations were called sacramental meetings because the communion (bread and wine representing Christ's body shared among the meeting participants) received at the gatherings had become their greatest sacrament. McGready completed his formal education, and on August 13, 1788, he was licensed to preach in Pennsylvania. However, that fall McGready left Pennsylvania to return to his parents' home in Guilford County, North Carolina.

A son of thunder

In the early eighteenth century, a religious revival in England led by John Wesley (1703–1791) brought about a spiritual awakening in America, too. This is known as the Great Awakening. However, the years after the American Revolution (1775–83) marked a lifeless time for many churches in America. There was a desperate need for ministers. An urgent plea went out among pastors of all Christian denominations to their congregations asking them to pray for the new nation. Soon, a network of prayer meetings rose up among Baptists, Methodists, and Presbyterians. Gathering on the first Monday of each month, congregations began to pray for a religious revival in America. They did not have long to wait. By the end of the century, a "Second Great Awakening" would sweep the nation.

On his way home to North Carolina in late 1788, McGready stopped in Farmville, Virginia, to observe the interdenominational revival that was taking place there. He stayed at Hampden-Sydney College, where the Presbyterian part of the Virginia revivalist movement had begun in 1787.

Barton W. Stone

Barton Warren Stone was at David Caldwell's Guilford Academy in North Carolina when James McGready came to speak in 1790. McGready's powerful preaching led Stone to pursue ordination as a Presbyterian minister. In 1796, Stone was licensed to preach by the Orange Presbytery in North Carolina. Two years later, Stone became pastor of the united congregations of Cane Ridge and Concord in Bourbon County, Kentucky. Hearing of McGready's camp meetings, Stone traveled south in the spring of 1801 to witness the revival for himself. Impressed by the meetings at Red River, Stone organized similar services in his area at Cane Ridge, northeast of Lexington. Invitations went out for an August sacramental meeting. It was to become the standard by which all future revivals would be measured in America.

People began arriving early at the Cane Ridge site, and the roads were soon jammed with horses and wagons. The congregation had hosted such meetings in earlier years, but it soon became apparent that this would not be an ordinary summer sacramental meeting. By Saturday, over twelve thousand people had gathered. (At that time, the largest town in Kentucky had a population of less than two thousand citizens.) Some people had traveled hundreds of miles from neighboring Ohio and Tennessee.

The traditional central camp tent was set up at Cane Ridge, and neighboring farm families supplied such hospitality as they could. However, most people came prepared to camp. Farmers opened their fields and gathered extra feed for the visitors' horses. The crowd could be heard from a great distance; the noise was likened to the roar of Niagara Falls. As the host minister, Stone opened the meeting, but preachers from all

By the time McGready left Virginia, he was well trained in the techniques and powers of revivalism.

When McGready reached North Carolina, he was distressed by the poor religious condition of the state. The war had left congregations scattered, and people had become more concerned with materialism, an interest in acquiring property and wealth, and less concerned about spiritual matters. Furthermore, McGready was appalled to find people guzzling whiskey at funerals where he presided. McGready's reputation as a preacher grew quickly in Orange County; by 1790, he was known as a "son of thunder" for his fiery messages. McGready's preaching was particularly successful among his own congregations of Haw River and Stoney Creek. Also in 1790, McGready married

Religious reformation pioneer Barton W. Stone.
(Library of Congress.)

denominations formed teams to continue the preaching both day and night. A festive communion service was the high point of the final day, ending a full week of activities. Then everyone returned home.

Revival meetings were controversial, with the apparent seizures people were experiencing at the revivals. Stone was one of five revivalist preachers who withdrew from the Presbyterian Church in protest after being suspended in 1803. The following year, Stone founded the Christian church that came to be called the Church of Christ. In 1832, he negotiated an informal union with Alexander Campbell's Disciples of Christ church. Campbell's Christian church, which had been founded in 1808, was centered more in the East. The resulting Stone-Campbell movement, like other religious groups on the frontier, provided church-affiliated colleges that trained both pastors and other professionals who were needed for church ministry.

Nancy Thompson. They had six daughters, two of whom died in infancy.

McGready was 6 feet tall, plainly dressed, and rather solemn in appearance. He inspired people with his prayers and sermons and at the same time unsettled them with his message. McGready's preaching style was to begin calmly and progress in tempo and volume until he reached an impassioned end. He became a frequent guest speaker at David Caldwell's Guilford Academy, where he had once been a student. McGready's zeal inspired many young students to become Presbyterian revivalist preachers. One of those students was Barton W. Stone (1772–1844; see box).

McGready's work produced a strong renewal of interest in religion across north-central North Carolina. In the process of reviving religion in the state, McGready created some enemies. His pointed attacks on immorality and materialism greatly offended several of the wealthy families at his Stoney Creek congregation. After several sharp exchanges, McGready received a letter written in blood, threatening his life if he did not leave. He arranged a hasty reassignment with the head of the church and moved to Kentucky in August 1796. McGready preached for several months in Knoxville, Tennessee, on his way to Logan County, Kentucky, the heart of the untamed Cumberland region.

Kentucky ablaze

In January 1797, McGready began working with three small churches in Logan County, just across the state line from Tennessee. McGready's congregations were located in the southwest part of the state and named after local rivers, the Muddy, the Red, and the Gasper. Several of his friends and former congregation members from North Carolina had already settled in Logan County, which made the move more comfortable. Four other pioneer ministers had also settled in the Kentucky-Tennessee border area. McGready and the others were called the five "wild men" of the Cumberland. They were among the Presbyterian ministers who were willing to venture westward and follow the frontier rather than wait for a more developed civilization. The majority of people in Logan County were refugees from other states in the union. Those who fled from justice or punishment included murderers, thieves, and counterfeiters. Their presence earned the county the nickname "Rogues Harbour."

Of the five "wild men," McGready proved to be the agent of change and revival in the American West. He promoted prayer meetings on the first Monday of every month, fulfilling the wishes of Christian leaders in the East. In addition, McGready urged his followers to pray for him at sunset on Saturday evening and at sunrise on Sunday morning. He also recommended a day of prayer and fasting each month. A large man with a powerful voice, McGready delivered his carefully prepared sermons with great energy, challenging his audience to live a holy life. Signs of a revival appeared as early as 1797, but the leaders of the "Old Side," or antirevivalist Presbyterians, worked to stamp out any emerging enthusiasm. They believed it was not in keeping with appropriate reserved religious behavior and distracted from the work of ministers trained in traditional theological schools. McGready's churches experienced moderate growth through 1798, but the state of Kentucky was rapidly changing and presented a challenge to McGready. The population of Kentucky was estimated at over 70,000 citizens in 1790 and exploded to over 220,000 by 1800.

McGready had honed his skills as a revivalist back in North Carolina and began preparing his congregations for a revival. He modeled his sacramental meetings on the lengthy Communion services (consuming bread and wine as symbols of a union with Christ) of the Presbyterians in Scotland and set up a camp meeting for the summer of 1800. McGready's preaching had attracted a great deal of attention, so hundreds of people traveled up to 100 miles to hear him that summer. The visitors camped in fields surrounding the Red River church on Friday and began the weekend of social activities and spiritual experiences. Ministers from all denominations established makeshift pulpits wherever they could. They preached to the crowds from wagons, tables, or tree stumps throughout the woods.

The weekend meeting was marked with a religious intensity that expressed itself in emotional and physical outbursts. The physical phenomenon of "falling" was first observed at Red River. Large numbers of people fell down all at once, as if struck dead while McGready and other ministers at the camp preached. They would emerge out of their trance-like state with shouts of joy and thanksgiving. Observers wrote about what they had seen and tried to explain, or explain away, what had occurred.

McGready's camp meetings were a model of democracy. In keeping with the Christian scriptures, all members had the opportunity to share their testimony regardless of race, gender, or age. McGready's gathering in the summer of 1800 became the pattern for all camp meetings in America. For the next few years, revival meetings were a regular part of the frontier culture. These revivals provided the fire that

An example of a camp revival. *(Library of Congress.)*

ignited the "Second Great Awakening" Protestant leaders had so earnestly prayed for after the Revolution.

Presbyterian unity

The Second Great Awakening brought spiritual renewal to the churches and significant increases in their membership. The movement provided a unity among the Christian denominations it affected and did much to develop the regions west of the Appalachians. The Transylvania Presbytery consisted of all the congregations in Kentucky, southern Ohio, and the Cumberland area across the mountains in Tennessee. The Cumberland district experienced such success that the synod (national or regional church leadership) separated it from the overgrown Transylvania Presbytery and formed the Cumberland Presbytery in 1802.

Despite the success of the "New Side," or revivalist Presbyterians, resentment continued among the "Old Side," or antirevivalist Presbyterians. McGready's methods and beliefs angered the more conservative group of the Cumberland Presbytery. One particularly divisive issue was his use of unordained preachers. McGready was also accused of preaching and encouraging doctrines contrary to the Presbyterian Confession of Faith. In 1805, the synod suspended McGready and several other ministers in the Cumberland Presbytery. In protest, some of the ministers formed the Cumberland Presbyterian Church. The synod reacted by abolishing the Cumberland Presbytery in 1806 and moving administration of the congregations including the Cumberland Presbyterian Church back to the Transylvania Presbytery.

McGready was distressed by the split and decided not to participate in the new Cumberland church, for fear the issue would hinder the revival movement still continuing in the region. He remained loyal to his Presbyterian heritage and successfully sought reinstatement to the Transylvania Presbytery. In 1806, McGready began work at a congregation on the Ohio River in Henderson County, Kentucky, and moved there the following year. He spent his final years establishing churches in southern Indiana. James McGready enjoyed a quiet and peaceful ministry in his last years. He died in 1817 at his home in Henderson County.

For More Information

Books

Boles, John B. *The Great Revival 1787–1805.* Lexington: University Press of Kentucky, 1972. Reprint, 1996.

Cleveland, Catharine C. *The Great Revival in the West, 1797–1805.* Chicago: University of Chicago Press, 1916. Reprint, Gloucester, MA: Peter Smith, 1959.

Conkin, Paul K. *Cane Ridge: America's Pentecost.* Madison: University of Wisconsin Press, 1990.

Foster, Douglas A., Paul M. Blowers, Anthony L. Dunnavant, and D. Newell Williams, eds. *The Encyclopedia of the Stone-Campbell Movement.* Grand Rapids, MI: W. B. Eerdmans, 2004.

Web Sites

"James McGready: Presbyterian Minister 1763–1817." *Historical Foundation of the Cumberland Presbyterian Church and the Cumberland Presbyterian Church of America.* http://www.cumberland.org/hfcpc/McGready.htm (accessed on August 17, 2005).

"Nineteenth Century Revivals." *Christian Word Ministries.* http://www.christianword.org/revival/2-1800.html (accessed on August 17, 2005).

James Monroe

Born April 28, 1758 (Westmoreland County, Virginia)
Died July 4, 1831 (New York, New York)

Diplomat, governor, U.S. president

James Monroe was the first of the early prominent U.S. leaders to deliberately choose public service as his career. Spanning forty-three years, Monroe's career included the roles of state legislator, governor, foreign diplomat, U.S. secretary of state, U.S. secretary of war, and U.S. president.

Young James

James Monroe was born on April 28, 1758, the first of four children born to Colonel Spence Monroe and Elizabeth Jones Monroe. James was tutored at home before entering a private school at twelve years of age. He entered the College of William and Mary at the age of sixteen. After two years, his studies were interrupted when he decided to join the Continental Army, to fight for American independence. The American Revolution (1775–83) had begun, and James wanted to help his country break free from British rule.

Monroe saw action in New York at Harlem and White Plains. He was wounded at the Battle of Trenton in New Jersey, and after recovering he went on to battle in Pennsylvania at

"The American continents, by the free and independent condition which they have assumed and maintain, are henceforth not to be considered as subjects for future colonization by any European powers."

From the Monroe Doctrine

James Monroe. *(© Bettmann/Corbis.)*

Brandywine (September 1777), Germantown (October 1777), and Monmouth (June 1778).

Monroe left the Continental Army in 1780 with a high commendation from the commander in chief, General **George Washington** (1732–1799; see entry in volume 2). Washington would go on to become the first president of the United States. That same year Monroe began law studies under Virginia governor **Thomas Jefferson** (1743–1826; see entry in volume 1), whom he met in 1778 while serving in the army.

Continental Congress, 1783–86

Monroe's public service career began in 1782 when he won a seat in the Virginia legislative assembly, the House of Delegates. The next year, the assembly named him a delegate to the Continental Congress, America's national legislative body. He served in this position from December 1783 to November 1786. As a Virginia delegate to Congress, Monroe took a strong interest in three major issues confronting the new nation: regulation of trade, the Old Northwest, and navigation of the Mississippi River.

Under the Articles of Confederation, the nation's first constitution, the national government had no power to regulate trade among the states or with other countries. To remain competitive in trade, states imposed taxes on each other: import taxes on goods coming into the state and export taxes on goods being shipped out of the state. The states also made individual trade agreements with foreign countries. The situation caused confusion and bickering among the states. Monroe advocated giving control of trade to a central authority, the national government. He proposed that the national government collect import and export taxes and then pay out this money to the states. This was one of the few times when Monroe supported a strong centralized government. However, no immediate action was taken on this matter.

As a Virginian, Monroe took a strong interest in the future of the Old Northwest. In 1784, Virginia had ceded (given up) its claims on land in the Old Northwest to Congress, with the understanding that Congress would manage the land for the good of all the states. **James Madison** (1751–1836; see entry in volume 2) had written the cession plan. Monroe was concerned about how these western lands would be dealt with. The Old Northwest included land north of the Ohio River to Canada and west of the Appalachian Mountains to the Mississippi River.

During the 1784 summer recess of Congress, Monroe made an extended tour of the Old Northwest. He wanted to learn about the British forts in the area; relations between the Native Americans and the whites who had settled there; and the general lay of the land, soil, and water. Monroe encouraged Congress to set up committees to consider dividing the region into several territories and plan for a temporary form of government for them.

Navigation of the Mississippi River was Monroe's third main interest while he was serving in the Continental Congress. Spain held claim to the Mississippi and to the port at New Orleans. Monroe joined with other Virginia delegates to demand free navigation of the Mississippi for American frontier farmers.

Brief return to private life

While serving in the Continental Congress, twenty-seven-year-old Monroe courted seventeen-year-old Elizabeth Kortright (1768–1830), daughter of a wealthy New York merchant. They married in New York on February 16, 1786. When Monroe's term in Congress ended, in November 1786, he and Elizabeth moved back to Virginia. Their first child, Eliza, was born in December. The family lived in Fredericksburg, in Spotsylvania County, from late 1786 until 1789. The Monroes had two more children. Their son, James Spence, was born in May 1799; he died while still a toddler on September 28, 1800. A second daughter, Maria Hester, was born in 1803.

In Fredericksburg, Monroe began a private law practice and was again elected to serve in the Virginia Assembly. However, in 1787, much to his dismay, he was not elected to the Constitutional Convention in Philadelphia that began in late May. The purpose of the convention was to revise the Articles of Confederation, the nation's first constitution, but the delegates instead wrote an entirely new constitution. Monroe's friend, James Madison, one of the delegates from Virginia, was the chief author of the new constitution, which significantly strengthened the federal government.

Virginia ratifying convention of 1788

In 1788, Monroe represented Spotsylvania County at the Virginia convention to consider ratification of the new constitution. Madison knew Monroe was not in favor of a strong central government but thought Monroe would vote to ratify the Constitution. However, Monroe joined with fellow Virginia statesmen Patrick Henry (1736–1799) and George Mason (1725–1792) in opposing ratification. Monroe's specific complaints about the Constitution were as follows: (1) It provided no adequate check on exercise of power by the executive (president); (2) it would lead to serious power struggles between national and state governments; and (3) it put no limit on the president's term. Another objection many delegates expressed was that the new constitution did not contain a bill of rights (basic liberties considered fundamental to citizens).

Upset that the majority of Virginia delegates voted in favor of ratifying the Constitution, Henry tried to prevent Madison from winning a seat in the U.S. House of Representatives of the newly established U.S. Congress. He convinced Monroe to run against Madison in the district that included Spotsylvania County. However, much to Henry's dismay, Madison was victorious. Monroe and Madison, having avoided personal attacks during the campaign, remained friends.

U.S. senator

Although Monroe lost his bid for the House, he found himself in the U.S. Senate in 1790. The Virginia legislature appointed Richard Henry Lee (1732–1794) and William Grayson (1736–1790) as the state's first two U.S. senators, but Grayson died soon after his appointment. The legislature selected Monroe to fill the vacant Senate slot. He took his seat in the Senate on December 6, 1790, and held the position until May 1794.

During this period, Monroe was one of the fiercest opponents of the policies of President Washington's administration. Washington and his top advisors favored strengthening the federal government over the state governments. Monroe especially opposed the financial measures introduced by Secretary of the Treasury **Alexander Hamilton** (1755–1804; see entry in volume 1).

Federalists and Republicans

Gradually, America's early leaders split into two political camps. Those favoring a strong central or federal government were known as Federalists. Federalists tended to believe that highly educated Americans would run the government best; this generally meant people who were wealthy enough to afford the privilege of education. Federalists did not believe that the common people could make good decisions on government matters. Washington, Hamilton, and **John Adams**

Friendship of Three Virginians

James Monroe and Thomas Jefferson admired each other's intellect and commitment to American independence. They began a friendship in 1778 that would last until Jefferson's death in 1826. Jefferson, the older statesman, supported and counseled Monroe on many occasions during Monroe's long career of public service. He was the key influence in Monroe's political career.

James Madison, a close friend of Jefferson and later the fourth U.S. president, also became a friend of Monroe's after Jefferson introduced the two in 1784. Although Madison left the Continental Congress in 1783, just when Monroe was arriving, they frequently sought advice from each other on matters related to the new nation. Many years later, Monroe would serve in President Madison's administration. Except for brief interruptions over political matters, Monroe and Madison remained lifelong friends.

Statues of three prominent Virginians—James Madison, Thomas Jefferson, and James Monroe—decorate the front of the Charlottesville, Virginia, City Hall.
(© *Mark E. Gibson/Corbis.*)

(1735–1826; see entry in volume 1), Washington's vice president, were considered Federalists.

Americans aligning with Monroe, Madison, and then secretary of state Thomas Jefferson were known as Republicans (later called Democratic-Republicans). Although Madison had been the primary author of the Constitution, which strengthened the federal government, he did not believe the Constitution gave Congress authority to establish a national bank, one of the financial measures recommended by Hamilton. Republicans of the 1790s believed that the executive branch was quickly becoming too powerful. The term "Republican" comes from the word "republic"; a republic is a government run for and by consent of the people. Republicans trusted the common people, ordinary citizens, to make decisions on how the government should be run.

Minister in France

In his Neutrality Proclamation of 1793, President Washington declared the United States a neutral country. This meant that the United States would not favor either France or Britain in the battles these two enemies continued to fight. Washington knew America could not afford to fight another war. However, America's neutrality was not respected. Both the British and the French seized U.S. commercial ships, and the British "impressed" American seamen. Impressment meant capturing seamen and forcing them to work on British vessels. The U.S. public was outraged.

Given his forthright opposition to many of President Washington's ideas, Monroe was surprised when Washington selected him as minister to France. Monroe, a Republican, was commissioned for the job on May 28, 1794. American states-man **John Jay** (1745–1829; see entry in volume 1), a Federalist, was the minister to Britain. Republicans such as Monroe favored good relations with France, a country that had helped the United States defeat Britain in the American Revolution. Republicans still considered Britain the enemy and were strongly pro-French. Federalists desired improved trade relations with Britain; they were pro-British and anti-French. Because of Monroe's pro-French feelings, Washington hoped Monroe could have success in negotiating with the French.

The biggest barrier to improved U.S.-French relations was the Jay Treaty, an agreement between America and Britain that Jay negotiated in late 1794. The treaty improved U.S. trade with Britain, but it did not require the British to stop their practice of impressment, Americans' biggest concern. Nevertheless, a Federalist-dominated Congress approved the Jay Treaty in June 1795. Republicans were outraged and so was France. The French believed the United States should honor its Treaty of Alliance of 1778 and support France against Britain. The French had not expected the United States to improve its relations with Britain, but that is exactly what the Jay Treaty did. France was exceedingly upset with the United States from the moment the treaty was signed, and Monroe openly said he regretted that Congress had approved the treaty. The Washington administration was angry with Monroe for not downplaying the importance of the Jay Treaty; President Washington had expected him to soothe French misgivings. Believing Monroe mishandled the entire situation, Washington removed him from the minister post on August 22, 1796.

Return to Virginia

Monroe traveled across the Atlantic in the spring of 1797 and spent the rest of the year writing *A View of the Conduct of the Executive,* which strongly criticized Washington and Jay. It was published in December 1797. Although Monroe's opinion of Washington and Jay softened over time, Washington never forgave his fellow Virginian for the words contained in the publication.

Within two years, Monroe reentered public office. He was elected governor of Virginia in 1799. The governor's term of office was only one year, but Monroe was elected for three straight years. In November 1799, Monroe moved his main home from Fredericksburg to Albemarle County, Virginia, to property called Highland, later Ash Lawn-Highland. This home was near the homes of his friends Jefferson and Madison.

Louisiana Purchase diplomatic victory

Thomas Jefferson became the third U.S. president in 1801. Jefferson learned that same year that Spain had ceded its rights to a huge expanse of land then known as Louisiana. By the Treaty of San Ildefonso, Spain had handed over this land to France. Louisiana encompassed approximately 800,000 square miles, stretching from the mouth of the Mississippi River at New Orleans northwest all the way to Canada and west to the Rocky Mountains. For the United States, having powerful France as a next-door neighbor on the western frontier was a threatening prospect. Having France in control of New Orleans and navigation on the Mississippi River was intolerable.

Determined to settle the situation peacefully, President Jefferson sent Monroe back to France with instructions to aid the American minister already in France, Robert R. Livingston (1746–1813). Jefferson wanted them to try to purchase the port of New Orleans from the French. Congress had allotted

$2 million for the purchase of New Orleans. On April 12, 1803, Monroe joined Livingston in Paris; Livingston was already in negotiation with the French. To the amazement of the two Americans, France offered to sell the United States all of Louisiana. After negotiations over price, Monroe, Livingston, and the French settled on $15 million. They signed a treaty of agreement on May 2, 1803, and hoped Congress would approve the additional $13 million. Congress readily approved the purchase on October 20, and the United States took over the region—which came to be called the Louisiana Purchase—on December 20, 1803. This purchase was the largest land deal the world had ever known; it doubled the size of the United States. President Jefferson, Monroe, and Livingston were astonished and ecstatic.

Difficult missions to Britain and Spain, 1804–7

By early 1804, the British were still seizing U.S. ships and impressing American seamen. President Jefferson, pleased with Monroe's success in France, dispatched him to Britain in April. Britain was not receptive to negotiators, so Jefferson sent Monroe to Spain in the fall to help Charles Pinckney (1757–1824) with negotiations to acquire the Floridas. Monroe and Pinckney were in constant communication with Spanish minister Don Pedro Cevallos from January to May 1805. Again negotiations led nowhere, so Monroe returned to his residence in London and resumed talks with Britain. At last, in the fall of 1806, serious negotiations with Britain began. The United States signed a treaty in December 1806 for improved relations with Britain. Because of the long time required for communication across the Atlantic, President Jefferson received the treaty on March 15, 1807. The treaty had two fundamental flaws: It made no provision against the impressment of American seamen, and it secured no promise of payment for losses Americans had incurred in the seizure of their goods and vessels. Dismayed with Monroe's treaty, Jefferson never presented it to the Senate for ratification; he simply terminated negotiations without any agreement. He then replaced Monroe and Monroe returned to the United States.

Monroe's failed missions to Spain and Britain were not due to any lack of intelligence or expertise on his part. These missions were doomed from the start, because Spain was not ready to give up the Floridas and Britain had no intention of giving up the practice of seizing U.S. vessels and seamen. Within a few years, the United States would be at war with Britain. However, Monroe was embarrassed and angry that Jefferson and Madison had refused to take his negotiated treaty to the Senate. He felt slighted by his two old friends.

Ill-fated run at the presidency

In 1808, a few old Virginia Democratic-Republicans talked Monroe into opposing Madison in his run for the presidential nomination. Monroe's candidacy went nowhere. Madison went on to become the Democratic-Republican presidential nominee and the fourth president of the United States. Monroe's family life served to cheer him. On October 17, 1808, his oldest daughter, Eliza, married Judge George Hay (1765–1830). Hay, twenty years older than Eliza, was a well-known lawyer and a political activist in Virginia. Hay and Monroe would become close friends. As Monroe regrouped from his diplomatic difficulties and renewed his political career, Hay became a close adviser.

In the spring of 1810, Monroe was elected for the third time to the Virginia House of Delegates. By the end of 1810, he was again elected as governor of Virginia. Monroe served only part of his term as governor, from January until November 1811. President Madison, fully aware of Monroe's political and diplomatic talents and holding no ill feelings toward him, asked him to join his administration as secretary of state. Monroe relished the opportunity and gladly accepted the assignment. He would hold the position until 1817.

Secretary of state, secretary of war

On June 18, 1812, the United States declared war on Britain. The start of the war went so badly for the United States that the secretary of war, Dr. William Eustis (1753–1825), left his Cabinet position. President Madison asked Monroe to temporarily serve as both the secretary of state and secretary of war. Soon, General John Armstrong (1758–1842) took over the war secretary's position. In August 1814, the battle reached Washington, D.C. Convinced the British would never march on the nation's capital city, Armstrong had not dispatched troops to defend it. On August 22, Monroe informed President

Madison that he believed the capital was in direct danger. On August 24, the British marched into Washington and burned the public buildings, including the Capitol and the president's mansion.

Dismissing Armstrong immediately, President Madison asked Monroe to again take charge of the War Department. Monroe at once infused vigor into the military operations. His hopes were bolstered when Fort McHenry at Baltimore held firm against a British advance. Monroe was enthusiastic, determined, and confident of public support. By the end of 1814, peace was at hand.

President

In 1816, Monroe was elected the fifth president of the United States. He received 183 electoral votes, defeating Federalist candidate Rufus King (1755–1827) of New York, who received only 34. Monroe was inaugurated on March 4, 1817. That same year, he participated in laying the cornerstone for the University of Virginia. Former president Jefferson founded the university, but both Monroe and Madison aided in the plans. In 1820, Monroe was reelected to a second term. By then, the Federalist Party no longer existed. Monroe received every electoral vote except one cast by a New Hampshire elector for Monroe's secretary of state, John Quincy Adams (1767–1848). The Monroe presidential years are known as the Era of Good Feelings. The eight years proved very positive for the young nation.

The first major event of the eight-year Monroe administration was the Seminole War of 1817–18. Members of the Seminole living in Spanish-held Florida made frequent raids into southern Georgia, stealing property and terrorizing Americans. General **Andrew Jackson** (1767–1845; see entry in volume 1) and his troops crossed into Florida, subdued the Native Americans, and seized territory. By 1819, the Spanish realized they could not hold Florida and ceded it to the United States.

In 1818, Missouri applied for admission to the union as a slave state (a state that allows slavery in contrast to free states that make slavery illegal), setting off a bitter controversy over the expansion of slavery in America. In 1820, Congress agreed

President James Monroe (standing) with his Cabinet: (left to right) John Quincy Adams, William H. Crawford, William Wirt, John C. Calhoun, Samuel Southard, and John McLean. *(Library of Congress.)*

on the Missouri Compromise, which remained in effect for thirty years. Missouri was admitted as a slave state, but slavery was prohibited in the region of the Louisiana Purchase north of the southern boundary of Missouri, except in the state of Missouri itself which could allow slavery.

On December 2, 1823, Monroe delivered a message to Congress that became a lasting legacy of his administration. The three main points of the message, later known as the Monroe Doctrine, set directions for U.S. foreign policy throughout the nineteenth and twentieth centuries. Monroe stated that there was to be no further European colonization in the Western Hemisphere, chiefly meaning Mexico, Central America, and South America; that the United States would stay out of the political affairs of European nations; and that

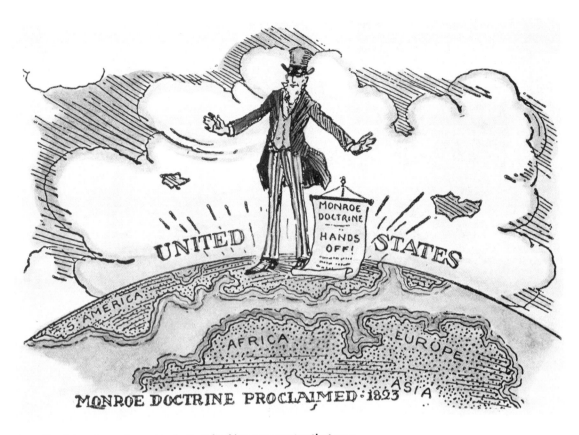

An editorial cartoon shows Uncle Sam looking at a poster that says, "Monroe Doctrine: Hands Off!" The reference is to two of the key points of the Monroe Doctrine: the United States would stay out of European nations' political affairs, and Europe would not interfere with Western Hemisphere governments. *(The Granger Collection, New York.)*

he expected European governments not to meddle in the affairs of governments in the Western Hemisphere.

Last years

Monroe retired from the presidency in 1825 and moved to his estate, "Oak Hill," near Leesburg, Virginia. His last act of public service came in 1829, when he served as president of the Virginia convention to revise the state constitution. Madison joined him as a member of the convention. Monroe's wife died in 1830, and he moved to his daughter Maria's residence in New York City. Monroe died at Maria's home on July 4, 1831.

For More Information

Books

Ammon, Harry. *James Monroe: The Quest for National Identity*. New York: McGraw-Hill, 1971. Reprint, Charlottesville: University Press of Virginia, 1990.

Dangerfield, George. *The Era of Good Feelings*. New York: Harcourt, Brace, 1952.

Gilman, Daniel C. *James Monroe: In His Relations to the Public Service during Half a Century, 1776 to 1826*. Boston: Houghton, Mifflin and Company, 1883.

Kelley, Brent. *James Monroe: American Statesman*. Philadelphia: Chelsea House, 2001.

Levy, Debbie. *James Monroe*. Minneapolis: Lerner Publications, 2005.

Web Sites

"James Monroe (1817–1825)." *American Presidents.* http://www.american president.org/history/jamesmonroe/ (accessed on June 14, 2005).

James Monroe Foundation. http://www.monroefoundation.org/ (accessed on August 17, 2005).

James Monroe's Ash Lawn–Highland. http://www.ashlawnhighland.org/ (accessed on August 17, 2005).

Judith Sargent Murray

Born May 1, 1751 (Gloucester, Massachusetts)
Died July 6, 1820 (Natchez, Mississippi)

Author, social activist

Judith Sargent Murray was a well-known author in the United States during the late eighteenth century. Although she used fictitious names—and sometimes a male identity—when writing, Murray's identity was not a secret, and she established a distinguished literary reputation. She is believed to be the first woman to regularly publish essays with her series titled *The Gleaner*. Considered a minor classic in America, the work has been favorably compared to that of her contemporaries, **Philip Freneau** (1752–1832; see entry in volume 1) and Noah Webster (1758–1843). Murray entered the national debate on the role of women in the emerging United States, which made her works important to late-twentieth-century historians.

Murray's lengthy writing career covered a number of topics and took on a variety of forms, including prose (ordinary language) and poetry. She was a pioneer in the field of playwriting and was the first American-born writer whose work was performed on the Boston stage. Murray is also thought to be the first American woman to have her plays performed professionally. As a leading member of the first Universalist church in America, Murray used her position to help spread Universalist religious and social ideas in the United States.

"The idea of the incapability of women is, we conceive, in this enlightened age, totally inadmissible. . . . To argue against facts, is indeed contending with both wind and tide."

Judith Sargent Murray. *(© Terra Foundation for American Art, Chicago/Art Resource, NY.)*

Universalism in Gloucester

Judith Sargent was born on May 1, 1751, in the coastal town of Gloucester, Massachusetts. She was the first of eight children born to Judith Saunders and Winthrop Sargent. Judith's father was primarily interested in the sea and became a wealthy shipowner and merchant like his father before him. Four of the Sargents' children died in infancy, but three of the remaining four went on to achieve distinction as adults. As a youth, Judith received the same basic, elementary training in reading and writing as all New England girls. However, Judith was very intelligent, and she wanted more. She was not permitted to enter college, but her brother, Winthrop Jr., was studying for admission to Harvard. Judith was allowed to share his lessons with a local tutor. During vacations from Harvard, Winthrop also aided her in continuing her studies.

Judith was eighteen years old when she married a young sea captain and trader named John Stevens, who was ten years older than her. Stevens came from a prominent Gloucester family, but financial problems had left the family without real wealth. Married on October 3, 1769, the Stevenses moved into a beautiful mansion overlooking the harbor and Eastern Point. Times were uncertain in the colonies during the early 1770s because of the threat of war with England. Judith began to write down her feelings in poetry and essays. John served as a member of the Committee of Safety at Gloucester in 1775, and he and Judith were both actively involved in Patriot politics when the American Revolution (1775–83) broke out. Patriots were American colonists who supported the rebel cause to gain independence from British rule.

The war brought financial disaster to the area. Coastal traffic was greatly hindered, and the fishing trade became dangerous due to the naval activity in the waters. Judith's focus in her writing turned more toward social questions and human rights during the war. She found herself questioning the status of women in the new social order of a democracy (a government ruled by the people through majority decisions), much like her contemporaries **Mercy Otis Warren** (1728–1814; see entry in volume 2) and **Abigail Adams** (1744–1818; see entry in volume 1) were doing. In 1779, Judith wrote an essay stating her belief that women and men had equal minds and deserved an equal opportunity for an education. When John's sister died in 1780, the Stevenses took her daughter Anna to raise as their own; they later took in Anna's sister Mary as well. They had no children of their own.

Early in the 1770s, John Murray (1741–1815; see box), an itinerant (traveling) preacher of the doctrine of universal salvation (all humans would be saved from their sins by God; known as Universalism), had visited Gloucester from England. When Murray first arrived from England in 1770, the Sargent family was among the first to welcome him. He was a frequent visitor at the Stevens home, and Judith became a champion of the

Reverend John Murray: "Father of Universalism"

Though Universalist religious beliefs had their roots in England, an organized movement of Universalism first began in the American colonies in the mid-1700s. Universalism was greatly influenced by the new ideas of the eighteenth century concerning the reasoning powers of humans and the growth of science. Universalist teachings emphasized that all humans would be saved from their sins by God—the doctrine of universal salvation. Hallmarks of Universalism were the freedom of individual interpretation or reason, a tolerance of human diversity, and a belief in the natural dignity of humans. The Universalist doctrine was a reaction to the sterner aspects of other religions at the time, many of which taught that God's salvation would be granted to only a few chosen individuals.

The first person to preach Universalist ideals in America was George De Benneville (1703–1793), who emigrated from Europe to Pennsylvania in 1741. However, it was John Murray, an immigrant to America in 1770, who spread Universalist beliefs with such success that he inspired the birth of an organized movement and a Universalist denomination. Murray and his followers faced much opposition from various religious denominations whose leaders believed that the Universalists held too tolerant of an attitude toward humankind, which would lead to immorality.

Murray traveled through the colonies preaching before settling in Gloucester,

Reverend John Murray. *(© Hulton Archive/Getty Images.)*

Massachusetts, in 1774. He became chaplain for the Continental Army in Rhode Island in 1775 as the American Revolution broke out, but he soon suffered a severe illness. Returning to Gloucester, he served as pastor of the newly created Independent Church of Christ beginning in 1779.

In 1785, Murray participated in the Universalist convention at Oxford, Massachusetts, that formed the Independent Christian Universalists. Murray was head of the Universalist Society of Boston from 1793 until his death in 1815. The organization later became the Universalist Church of America. It merged with the American Unitarian Association in 1960 to form the Unitarian Universalist Association.

liberal (open to new ideas) religious doctrines of Universalism. Murray received such enthusiastic support that he decided to make Gloucester his home base. He developed quite a following over the years as he preached that God and Jesus Christ were the same and that the sacrifice of Christ would save all. This interpretation caused a split from the First Parish Church in town, a Congregationalist church whose members did not believe that all would be saved but only those who had personally sought forgiveness and salvation in their lives. In 1780, Winthrop Sargent Sr. donated land to build a meetinghouse in Gloucester, and Murray dedicated the building, which became the first Universalist church in America. In 1782, Judith anonymously published the Universalist catechism, a personal declaration of her faith that was to be used for the instruction of children.

Equal minds

The Treaty of Paris was signed in 1783, officially ending the American Revolution. However, the financial distress experienced in many places, including Gloucester, continued. Those forced into bankruptcy faced debtors' prison. Judith had continued writing throughout the war and had a desire to use her work to contribute to discussions surrounding current events. Judith knew that if she wrote under an assumed name, she could voice her opinions publicly, and she hoped her writing could also bring in some money to help out the family finances. Using the name "Constantia," she published "Desultory Thoughts Upon the Utility of Encouraging a Degree of Complacency in the Female Bosom." The essay argued for more-advanced education for girls. She linked the self-respect that a woman receives from education with achievements and economic independence that frequently follow. "Desultory Thoughts" was published in the *Gentleman and Lady's Town and Country Magazine* in October 1784. "Constantia" was the name Judith's closest friends called her. She would continue to use the name regularly for both published and personal writing.

John Stevens was unable to recover from his financial problems after the war, and his creditors threatened him with imprisonment. In the winter of 1786, Stevens left Gloucester aboard a vessel belonging to Winthrop Sargent Sr. and set sail for Saint Eustatius in the West Indies. His plan was to earn enough money elsewhere so that he could repay his debts and return to America. Stevens had not been on the island long when he died of an unknown illness in March 1787.

Judith Sargent Stevens married her pastor, John Murray, in October 1788. Shortly after their wedding, John took Judith to meet Abigail and **John Adams** (1735–1826; see entry in volume 1) at their home in Braintree, Massachusetts. John Murray had first met the Adamses on their return voyage from England in September 1788. They had shared passage across the ocean and formed a lifelong friendship.

The Murrays traveled extensively while John preached throughout New York, New Jersey, and Pennsylvania. On these tours, Judith became acquainted with a number of the nation's leading citizens, including President **George Washington** (1732–1799; served 1789–97; see entry in volume 2) and his wife, **Martha Washington** (1732–1802; see entry in volume 2), and the family of scientist and diplomat **Benjamin Franklin** (1706–1790; see entry in volume 1). In a letter to her parents, dated August 14, 1790, Judith told of having tea that day with President and Mrs. Washington and then passing the rest of the day at the home of Vice President and Mrs. Adams. She described the scenery and the other guests she encountered throughout the day. Judith was especially impressed by the presence of Southern businesswoman **Catharine Littlefield Greene** (1755–1814; see entry in volume 1).

In August 1789, the Murrays' first child, a son, died soon after his birth, and Judith turned to poetry to deal with her grief. She renewed her writing efforts and began contributing poetry to the new *Massachusetts Magazine*. Her topics were varied and included political, cultural, and religious issues. The following year, Judith published an essay titled "On the Equality of the Sexes" in which she argued for educational and employment opportunities for women. On August 22, 1791, the Murrays' second child was born, and they named her Julia Maria Murray.

"The Gleaner"

Judith Sargent Murray became a regular contributor to the *Massachusetts Magazine* beginning in February 1792 with a series of essays titled "The Gleaner." The monthly essays were written from the point of view of an imaginary man named Mr. Vigillius. Murray used her male character to promote her own position on education and economic self-sufficiency for women. The series was a favorite with the magazine's readers and continued until August 1794. Murray wrote a second popular series of essays for the magazine during the same time period. The series was called the "Repository."

In 1793, the Murrays moved to Boston. There, Judith was able to pursue her interest in the development of American drama. In April of that year, an old ban on theatrical entertainment in Boston had been lifted, and Murray wanted to try her hand as a playwright. By 1795, her first play was presented at the Federal Street Theater, making Murray the first American-born writer to have her work appear on the Boston stage. However, her play, *The Medium, or Virtue Triumphant,* was not well received, and it had a short theater run. The following year at the Federal Street Theater, her production of *The Traveler Returned* was equally short-lived after it drew a blast of criticism from reviewers.

Financial difficulties once again began to affect Judith and her family. John suggested she publish her essays. Judith gathered together one hundred of her essays in a three-volume set she titled *The Gleaner.* The volumes contained most of her essays and poetry as well as her two plays. The entire collection was dedicated to President John Adams. *The Gleaner* was released in 1798 but had only modest success.

Virtue triumphant

Murray made one more attempt as a playwright with *The African,* which was performed at the Federal Street Theater in 1808. *The Gleaner* volumes had not produced the desired response, and Murray failed to arrange a second edition. She continued to publish a few of her poems in Boston periodicals under the pen names "Honora-Martesia" and "Honora." However, family concerns increasingly took most of her attention. John suffered a stroke in 1809 and was bedridden because of the resulting paralysis. He was working on his autobiography when he died in 1815. Murray completed the work herself and published it the following year.

In 1816, Murray moved to Natchez, Mississippi, to live with her daughter and be close to her young granddaughter. She died in 1820 at the age of sixty-nine. Murray was buried in the Bingamon cemetery on Saint Catherine's Creek, overlooking the Mississippi River. Nearly two centuries after her death, historians recognized Murray for her contributions to American literary history. As relayed in Sharon M. Harris's 1995 book *Selected Writings of Judith Sargent Murray,* Murray in her introductory comments to *The Gleaner* wrote, "My desires are . . . I would be distinguished and respected by my contemporaries; I would be continued on grateful remembrance when I make my exit; and I would descend with celebrity to posterity."

For More Information

Books

Field, Vena Bernadette. *Constantia: A Study of the Life and Works of Judith Sargent Murray 1751–1820.* Orono, ME: The University Press, 1931.

Harris, Sharon M., ed. *Selected Writings of Judith Sargent Murray.* New York: Oxford University Press, 1995.

Skemp, Sheila L. *Judith Sargent Murray: A Brief Biography with Documents.* Boston: Bedford Books, 1998.

Smith, Bonnie Hurd. *From Gloucester to Philadelphia in 1790: Observations, Anecdotes, and Thoughts from the Eighteenth-Century Letters of Judith Sargent Murray.* Cambridge, MA: Judith Sargent Murray Society, 1998.

Web Sites

"Abigail Adams." *Dictionary of Unitarian and Universalist Biography.* http://www.uua.org/uuhs/duub/articles/abigailadams.html (accessed on August 17, 2005).

Judith Sargent Murray Society. http://www.hurdsmith.com/judith/ (accessed on August 17, 2005).

"Perspectives in American Literature: Judith Sargent Murray (1751–1820)." *Department of English, California State University, Stanislaus.* http://www.csustan.edu/english/reuben/pal/chap2/murray.html (accessed on August 17, 2005).

Sarah Pierce

Born June 26, 1767 (Litchfield, Connecticut)
Died January 19, 1852 (Litchfield, Connecticut)

Educator

S arah Pierce was an educator who opened and operated the first school in the United States dedicated to the higher education of women. The Litchfield Female Academy was the leading institution for women during the first decades of the nineteenth century. It attracted students from fifteen states and territories, Canada, Ireland, and the West Indies. Pierce greatly influenced the history of education through the many young women she trained as teachers. While some of her students returned to teach at Litchfield Female Academy, others, inspired by Pierce, went on to establish their own schools. Many of the Female Academy's graduates devoted their energies to improving educational opportunities for other women.

> "A new tone to female education was given by the establishment of a Female Seminary, for the instruction of females in this village, by Miss Sarah Pierce, in 1792. This was an untried experiment."
>
> *Connecticut Superior Court chief justice Samuel Church*

An untried experiment

Sarah Pierce was born on June 26, 1767, the youngest of seven children of John Pierce, a potter, and his first wife, Mary Paterson. When Sarah's mother died, her father married Mary Goodman. Three more children were added to the large family living in Litchfield, Connecticut. Sarah

Sarah Pierce. *(Litchfield Historical Society.)*

received an excellent education as a child, far better than most New England girls at the time. When Sarah was fourteen years old, her father died. Responsibility for the family fell to her elder brother, Colonel John Pierce. John was paymaster general of the Continental Army and a friend of General **George Washington** (1732–1799; see entry in volume 2). John sent Sarah and her older sister, Nancy, to New York City to continue their education so that they could eventually support themselves by teaching. John died in 1788, and the girls returned to Litchfield while the family's estate was settled. In 1792, Sarah Pierce obtained local government approval (charter) to open a school for female students and began teaching several pupils in the dining room of her home.

The town of Litchfield was a cultural and commercial center at the close of the eighteenth century. The first medical society and the first temperance society (an organization opposed to the consumption of alcoholic beverages) in the United States were organized in the little country town. The Litchfield Law School had been established a decade before Pierce began her own school there. The law school held the distinction of being the first one formally operating in the United States. The law school's founder, Judge Tapping Reeve (1744–1823), was among the townsmen who supported advanced education for women and championed their right to hold property. Pierce was continually encouraged in her efforts to build a nationally respected women's academy in the progressive town of Litchfield. With the help of her sister, Nancy, Sarah began by teaching basic core classes, including reading, writing, arithmetic, history, and religion. The academic curriculum reflected Sarah's belief that women and men were intellectually equal. "Miss Pierce's Litchfield School" gained a reputation for excellence, and the number of pupils increased rapidly.

Growing institution

By 1798, Pierce's school had become an important element of the town of Litchfield. Financial backing was gathered to move the growing school out of Pierce's home. A building was erected on land she owned on North Street. The school became known as the Female Academy. It soon housed the young female relatives of the socially elite. Before long, young women were coming from as far away as Georgia to attend the Female Academy. Travel was not easy for these women. The railroad was not yet in existence, so many arrived on horseback; later, when stage lines were established, they traveled by stagecoach.

At the Litchfield school, the students did not live in dormitories but boarded with approved families in town. The rules of conduct and behavior in the houses where the women stayed were strict, in keeping with Pierce's ideals of Christianity, morality, education, and character. Pierce encouraged her students to volunteer their time to charitable organizations. However, she also allowed the Female Academy students time to mingle with the men of the law school. The prestige of the two schools gave Litchfield a reputation as a leading center of education in the United States.

Harriet Beecher Stowe

Sarah Pierce's Female Academy created an educated, elite group of women who often turned their energies to shaping the future of the young nation. Harriet Beecher Stowe (1811–1896) was one former graduate who used her education and writing talents to shape public opinion in the last half of the nineteenth century. One of her books heightened the publicity surrounding the fight against slavery in the United States.

Born in Litchfield, Connecticut, Harriet Beecher was only eight years old when she entered the Litchfield Female Academy in 1820. She was an eager student who loved to write and often took home awards for her compositions. In 1824, she moved to her sister Catharine's Hartford Female Seminary, where she took increasingly difficult subjects and aspired to become an artist like her mother. She soon discovered her true gift was in writing and dedicated herself to becoming a literary woman. Harriet Beecher married Calvin Ellis Stowe (1802–1886),

a professor, in 1836. He encouraged her to continue with her writing. He would remain her biggest supporter throughout their fifty-year marriage.

Harriet Beecher Stowe was one of many women who began writing sketches and stories for publication in magazines, even though it was not particularly respected or profitable at the time. Her stories began appearing in 1839 in the periodical *Godey's Lady's Book.* It was the first magazine in America to solicit and pay for original material, and it welcomed female as well as male contributors. Most of the literature was written for entertainment, amusement, or instruction and was meant to be read aloud. It was called "parlor literature" because it was read in the homes of polite society.

Stowe raised seven children and at the same time contributed to the family's finances with her writing. In 1849, the Stowes lost their eighteen-month-old son, Samuel Charles, in a cholera epidemic that swept their hometown of Cincinnati, Ohio. Deep feelings on the subject of slavery were prominent in the United States at the time, and Harriet equated her loss of

The Female Academy remained a Pierce family project throughout its early years, with Sarah bringing in her own sisters and her brother-in-law as staff. Pierce would also hire women, frequently former students, to teach additional courses as needed. In 1814, Pierce brought her nephew, John Pierce Brace, onto the faculty to introduce more-advanced courses. Brace, a Williams College graduate, instituted classes in logic, philosophy, Latin, botany, mineralogy, and astronomy.

Writer Harriet Beecher Stowe. *(© Bettmann/Corbis.)*

Uncle Tom's Cabin is a story of a faithful slave named Tom who is sold away from his family. Tom is ultimately beaten to death on a Louisiana plantation by the cruel Simon Legree. The story appeared in regular installments in the *National Era* magazine from June 5, 1851, through April 1, 1852, and a huge number of readers followed the story and waited eagerly for the next installment. When *Uncle Tom's Cabin* was published in book form in 1852, more than three hundred thousand copies were sold. The story was cast as fiction, but it touched the conscience of a nation already on edge due to the passing of the Fugitive Slave Law.

Stowe published *A Key to Uncle Tom's Cabin* in 1853 to counter the critics who complained that her novel had exaggerated the brutality of slavery. Stowe's book generated new discussions about slavery and morality, and historians agree that it played a role in sparking the American Civil War (1861–65). When Stowe visited the White House in 1862, President Abraham Lincoln (1809–1865; served 1861–65) reportedly greeted her with the words, "So you're the little woman who wrote the book that started this great war."

a son with what a slave mother would feel when torn away from her child. She felt the North encouraged such tragedies by passing the Fugitive Slave Law of 1850. Stowe responded by writing what would be her most famous book, *Uncle Tom's Cabin: Or, Life among the Lowly.*

Pierce continued teaching history and the arts. She showed great care and concern for her pupils. When her students found their existing textbooks dull, she wrote and published her own four-volume Universal History texts. They were written in the form of questions and answers to stimulate the students' interest. Pierce experimented with innovative ways to reinforce geography and history lessons, encouraging students to draw and paint maps and charts of historical events. Botany lessons were often illustrated with watercolor drawings. Although she was primarily interested in a strong academic curriculum, Pierce saw to it that her students also received adequate physical exercise. She was often seen leading the entire student body on brisk morning and evening walks through Litchfield. Until poor health prevented it, Pierce would take her customary walk through the hills even during the roughest of Connecticut winters.

Enrollment peaked in 1816, when 150 students attended the Female Academy. Students ranged in age from seven years to early twenties. A small number of local boys were later included at the school. The Reverend Lyman Beecher (1775–1863), a prominent clergyman in town, provided religious instruction. In return for teaching, Reverend Beecher received free tuition at the school for three of his children, including his daughter Harriet Beecher Stowe (see box). The curriculum of the Female Academy was similar to that of men's colleges in New England. Requirements for graduation were very demanding. Because educational opportunities for women were so few, and the cost so high, a woman's advanced degree became a status symbol among the wealthy. Many affluent parents became willing to invest as much in their daughters' education as they did in the education of their sons.

Loss of prominence

John Pierce Brace took on additional responsibilities as associate principal of the school and in 1825 became principal. In 1827, the school once again expanded its property and was incorporated with a board of directors under a new name, the Litchfield Female Academy. The Litchfield Law School began to lose its prominent position in the late 1820s because competing law schools had opened at Harvard (in 1817) and Yale (in 1824). The town of Litchfield began to feel the loss of students and a resulting loss of influence as two other Connecticut towns, New Haven and Hartford, surpassed it in importance.

Sarah Pierce retired from teaching in 1833, and the Litchfield Female Academy officially closed its doors in 1856. In a way, Pierce's own influence became a factor in causing the decline of her academy: She so inspired her students that many of them opened competing schools of their own. Catharine Beecher, sister to Harriet Beecher

Stowe, was a former Female Academy student who opened the Hartford Female Seminary and drew away many students to her institution. John Pierce Brace left Litchfield in 1827 and moved to Hartford, where he accepted the post of principal at the rival Hartford Female Seminary.

In 1851, Connecticut Superior Court chief justice Samuel Church (1785–1854) declared that the Female Academy was historically and socially significant in the cause of advancing educational opportunities for women in the United States. Happily, Sarah Pierce lived long enough to hear these words of recognition. Former students described Pierce as a small woman with a slender build. She had bright blue eyes, a fair complexion, and an ability to faithfully follow all of the standards that she demanded of her students. Pierce never married or had any children of her own; instead she dedicated her life to running her school and teaching her students. Not long before her death, she lost her sight and much of her stamina because of an illness that caused a slight paralysis. Sarah Pierce died in Litchfield on January 19, 1852, at the age of eighty-four. She was buried in West Cemetery in Litchfield; her school closed shortly thereafter.

For More Information

Books

Hedrick, Joan D. *Harriet Beecher Stowe: A Life*. New York: Oxford University Press, 1994.

James, Edward T., ed. *Notable American Women 1607–1950: A Biographical Dictionary*. Cambridge, MA: Belknap Press of Harvard University, 1971.

Kirkham, E. Bruce. *The Building of Uncle Tom's Cabin*. Knoxville: University of Tennessee Press, 1977.

Vanderpoel, Emily Noyes. *More Chronicles of a Pioneer School: From 1792 to 1833*. New York: Cadmus Book Shop, 1927.

Web Sites

"A History of the Litchfield Female Academy." *Litchfield Historical Society.* http://www.litchfieldhistoricalsociety.org/history/histfemacademy.html (accessed on August 17, 2005).

Eliza Lucas Pinckney

Born December 28, 1723 (Antigua, West Indies)
Died May 26, 1793 (Philadelphia, Pennsylvania)

Agricultural innovator

"I wrote my father . . . on the pains I had taken to bring the Indigo, Ginger, Cotton, Lucern [alfalfa], and Cassada [cassava] to perfection, and had greater hopes from the Indigo . . . than any of ye rest of ye things I had tryd."

Eliza Lucas Pinckney was a teenager when she was assigned to manage three large plantations for her family. She was still a young woman when her horticultural (plant-growing) experiments succeeded in the cultivation of the first indigo plants in British North America. Lucas shared her discovery with her South Carolina neighbors, creating an industry that would sustain the Carolina economy for three decades. The so-called Indigo Bonanza saw indigo planters double their money every three to four years from 1745 until 1775, when the American Revolution (1775–83) brought an end to trade with Britain. By 1775, South Carolina was exporting over 1 million pounds of indigo annually, with a present-day value of over $30 million. Thanks to Pinckney's efforts, the Southern economy had grown strong by the time the United States won its independence in 1783.

Pinckney supported the American Revolution and saw her plantations destroyed by British raiders during the war. Her eldest son, Charles Cotesworth Pinckney (1746–1825), fought in the Continental Army and later became one of the signers of the U.S. Constitution. Her youngest son, Thomas Pinckney (1750–1828), also fought in the war and later served as governor of South Carolina. President **George Washington** (1732–1799; served 1789–97; see entry in volume 2) paid tribute to Eliza Pinckney's contribution to the newly independent United States by requesting to serve as a pallbearer at her funeral in 1793. Although there are numerous portraits of her famous family, no painting or other likeness of Eliza Lucas Pinckney has ever been found. However, her surviving journal and letters create their own portrait and represent one of the most complete accounts of plantation life in early America. Eliza was one of the major matriarchs who helped shape America.

The planter

Elizabeth Lucas was born on December 28, 1723, on a sugar plantation overlooking Willoughby Bay in Antigua, West Indies. She was the eldest of four children born to Anne and George Lucas. From her earliest days, Elizabeth was called Eliza. Her father was a lieutenant colonel in the British army, and he became lieutenant governor of the island colony of Antigua. Eliza, intelligent and ambitious, was sent to London, England, to complete her education. She studied philosophy, French, and music, always setting high standards for herself and others.

In 1738, George Lucas moved his family to South Carolina, hoping the climate change might benefit his wife's poor health. Fifteen-year-old Eliza and her sister Polly joined their parents on a plantation George had inherited from his father, John Lucas of Antigua. The 600-acre plantation along Wappoo Creek was just 17 miles by land from Charles Town, later renamed Charleston, South Carolina.

The War of Jenkins' Ear, a maritime conflict between Britain and Spain, forced George Lucas to return to his post in Antigua in 1739. At sixteen years of age, Eliza was left in charge of Wappoo and two other large plantations owned by her father. In a large blank parchment-bound book, she began recording personal and plantation affairs, including details on her horticultural experiments. In addition to running the three family plantations, Eliza tutored her sister Polly. She also taught reading to two black women whom she intended to employ as schoolmistresses for the rest of the black children on her plantations.

George challenged Eliza to find a crop that would grow successfully on the high land which was drier with less fertile lands. South Carolina desperately needed a new export to invigorate its economy. The outbreak of war in Europe between France and Britain interrupted the market for Carolina rice, South Carolina's one staple (a crop produced regularly in large amounts). Eliza's father sent her seeds from the West Indies and encouraged her to plant them and experiment with the various crops. She tried many different kinds of seeds, including ginger, cotton, and alfalfa, but it was the indigo seeds that finally offered the greatest potential for success. If an American farmer could prepare a fine grade of blue dye-cakes from indigo for cloth manufacturers, English merchants would buy the American product rather than the one produced in the French West Indies.

Indigo lady

Eliza shared her father's sense of enterprise and his love of horticulture, and she recorded their correspondence. Beginning in 1740, she experimented with the best soil and the proper season for sowing indigo. Frost damaged Eliza's first crop before the seeds had sufficient time to dry in their small pods. This left her without enough seed for the next spring planting. Eliza had to write to her father and ask him to send more seeds from the West Indies. Worms ate the second crop, but Eliza's efforts to adapt the tropical indigo to the Carolina temperatures showed promise.

By September 1742, Eliza was able to report to her father that she had saved enough seed for the next annual planting. The manufacture of quality dye was a complex process; it took a skilled hand to produce good dye from fresh plants. Recognizing the success of Eliza's efforts, George Lucas sent a dye maker from the island of Montserrat to construct a small factory at Wappoo. Nicholas Cromwell built the vats, but he intentionally spoiled the dye because he feared that Carolina dye manufacturing might soon compete with dye production in his own country and ruin the island's economy. Eliza's experiments continued annually, and in 1744 Eliza finally grew a successful indigo crop, the first in North America. Her father sent Patrick Cromwell, a professional dye maker and a brother of Nicholas, to direct the manufacturing of the indigo dye-cakes (see box).

The 1744 crop of plants produced 17 pounds of dye for the Lucas family. Of this amount, 6 pounds were sent to England

The Manufacture of Indigo

Originally indigo was geographically restricted to areas of the world that had hospitable climates for the plant's growth. India supplied indigo dye to the ancient Middle East and the Greco-Roman world. During the expansion of European power into the Far East, many companies traded in indigo. The species found in Asia was always considered the most valuable indigo to trade, but lesser species were common in parts of Africa and the Americas. By the end of the seventeenth century, Britain was importing indigo for civilian use and for military and naval uniforms. Americans also made use of the dye: Almost half of the flags of the original thirteen states featured blue backgrounds. During the American Revolution, the colonists used indigo to dye the blue coats that became the uniform of the Continental Army.

The manufacture of dye-cakes required a factory consisting of a series of vats or tubs for steeping, beating, mixing, and draining the indigo before it was put into sheds for drying and packing. Slaves would clear and plow the fields and then sow the indigo seeds. Weeding typically began when the plants were 2 to 3 inches tall. When the plants were about a foot tall, the rows between them were plowed to add oxygen to the soil. If a drought lasted for more than six weeks at this point, the plants would start to blacken and die. The indigo was harvested when it was almost ready to flower, at about 2 to 5 feet tall. Slaves would then cut the stalks and bundle the plants together by tens before hauling them to the factory, where they would be processed the same day.

About one hundred bundles at a time were placed in the "steeper," a vat filled with water. The plants were weighed down with logs or stones. After twelve to twenty-four hours, the indigo began to ferment, making the water bubble and turn amber green as it drew the pigment grain from the leaves. The fermented mixture was drawn down into the "beater" vat, where unwanted particles were picked out of the liquid. It was then stirred with paddles for about two hours to add oxygen until the mixture turned a violet blue. The stirring caused the indigo to condense into specks, flake off, and sink like mud to the bottom of the vat. The water was then drawn off into a third container, leaving the indigo at the bottom of the second vat. From there it was scooped up and put into cloth bags to drain overnight.

The indigo now resembled blue mud. It was packed into square, brick-size containers with drainage holes. After additional pressing and drying, it was removed from the molds and cut into pieces about an inch and a half square. When completely dry, the pieces of "pigeon neck" indigo were very hard, lightweight, and gleaming blue. When it was needed for dying, the dried indigo dye-cake was dissolved in stale urine, tannic acid, or wood ash. The mixture was then put into water, where it produced a yellow-green solution. Cloth dipped into the dye turned yellow green until it was removed and exposed to oxygen. The cloth would then turn blue after drying.

and were enthusiastically received by the merchants of London. The rich blue dye was rated equal to that of the French indigo. European consumers were demanding more and more indigo products. They wanted indigo-dyed fabrics, paints, and laundry bluing, which made white fabrics appear whiter. The blue dye was used for adornment and religious ritual and as a symbol of political and social status. To encourage a commercial supply of indigo from Carolina, Eliza distributed the seed from her 1744 crop to a large number of planters in hopes of increasing trade with England. By 1747, Carolina plantations had produced enough indigo to export over 100,000 pounds of the blue dye-cakes. The British parliament supported a bounty (payments to farmers to help with their farming expenses) on indigo from South Carolina and allowed the colony to establish impressive credits in London banking houses. South Carolina's success in growing indigo in the dry, high ground balanced nicely with its established rice plantations in the marshes and lowlands. The two lucrative crops made South Carolina one of the wealthiest of the thirteen colonies.

The Belmont Plantation

Most of Eliza's energies were given to her plantation duties, but she did enjoy brief visits to Charleston, a town that offered its residents and visitors music, theater, balls, and a weekly newspaper. After 1748, the town also offered a library society, but Eliza had her own well-furnished library made up of the books her father had left when he returned to Antigua. The year 1744 marked not only the success of her indigo experiments but her marriage to Charles Pinckney (1699–1758). Charles was a childless widower more than twenty years older than Eliza. He had studied law in England and was the first native South Carolina attorney. Soon after the wedding, Eliza's mother returned to Antigua, and Charles Pinckney began building a mansion in Charleston for his young bride. The Pinckneys lived in Charleston for almost a decade and had four children. Charles, Harriott, and Thomas all lived to see old age, but George died in 1747, only months after his birth.

Eliza continued her pursuits of horticulture and agriculture on her husband's Belmont Plantation on the Cooper River. She directed experiments with flax, hemp, and the culture of silkworms; her silkworm production aroused great hopes in

Carolina but was only briefly profitable. Eliza continued to supervise the indigo experiments on her father's plantations and managed the marketing and sale of her crops.

In 1753, the Pinckney family moved to London, where Charles Pinckney served as a commissioner from the colony to the Board of Trade and Plantations. Eliza enjoyed her return to English society as the wife of a South Carolina representative, and the Pinckney children were enrolled in English schools. In May 1758, after nearly five years in Britain, Eliza and Charles took nine-year-old Harriott home to South Carolina. Charles and Thomas remained in England to complete their education. When Charles, Eliza, and Harriott arrived in America, Charles devoted himself to his neglected plantation, but he was soon stricken with malaria. He died on July 12, 1758, after a three-week illness. Heartbroken by her husband's death, Eliza returned to plantation business, directing her husband's seven separate landholdings in the low country.

Charles Cotesworth Pinckney, eldest son of Eliza Pinckney.

The Pinckneys of South Carolina

Plantations were largely self-sufficient operations in the eighteenth century. In addition to a cash crop, plantations produced most of the goods the Pinckneys used on a daily basis. They also made their own cloth and leather, constructed their own barrels, and raised their own food. In running multiple plantations, Eliza oversaw a varied workforce consisting of planters, carpenters, and artisans. She also exerted a strong influence upon the lives and careers of her children, who were to play major roles in shaping America.

Eliza's sons were devoted to the American cause in spite of their long years in England. They returned to Charleston before the outbreak of the American Revolution, and both served in the Continental Army during the war. Charles served as General Washington's aide in 1777. After the war, he represented South Carolina at the Constitutional Convention in Philadelphia, Pennsylvania, in the summer of 1787. Thomas attained the rank of general, and in 1787 he became governor of South Carolina. Both of Eliza's sons were Federalist Party candidates in the nation's early presidential elections. Eliza's daughter, Harriott, married Daniel Horry in 1767 and moved to Hampton Plantation on the Santee River. After the American Revolution, Eliza spent most of her time at Hampton, surrounded by her grown children and grandchildren.

In May 1791, President Washington stopped by Hampton to visit Eliza during his Southern tour to rally support for the new national government. The following year, Eliza was diagnosed with cancer. By the spring of 1793, her condition had grown so painful that she decided to travel to Philadelphia, to seek the cures of a highly recommended physician. Eliza Lucas Pinckney died on May 26, shortly after her arrival in Philadelphia. President Washington served as one of her pallbearers when she was buried in the city's St. Peter's Churchyard.

For More Information

Books

Barker-Benfield, G. J., and Catherine Clinton, eds. *Portraits of American Women: From Settlement to the Present.* 2nd ed. New York: Oxford University Press, 1998.

Pinckney, Elise, ed. *The Letterbook of Eliza Lucas Pinckney 1739–1762.* Chapel Hill: University of North Carolina Press, 1972. Reprint, Columbia: University of South Carolina Press, 1997.

Ravenel, Harriott Horry. *Eliza Pinckney.* New York: C. Scribner's Sons, 1896. Reprint, Spartanburg, SC: Reprint Co., 1967.

Roberts, Cokie. *Founding Mothers: The Women Who Raised Our Nation.* New York: William Morrow, 2004.

Web Sites

West, Jean M. "The Devil's Blue Dye: Indigo and Slavery." *Slavery in America.* http://www.slaveryinamerica.org/history/hs_es_indigo.htm (accessed on August 17, 2005).

Edmund Randolph

Born August 10, 1753 (Williamsburg, Virginia)
Died September 12, 1813 (Clark County, Virginia)

Attorney general, secretary of state, governor

Edmund Randolph was highly influential in the political shaping of America, particularly between 1776 and 1800, when he served as Virginia's first attorney general, Virginia state governor, the first U.S. attorney general, and the nation's second secretary of state. Coming from a family with a colonial legal background, Randolph was very intelligent and highly respected for his legal knowledge. Randolph played a key role at the 1787 Constitutional Convention, serving on a committee that developed an early draft of the U.S. Constitution.

"I am certain that a national government must be established, and this is the only moment when it can be done."

Family of lawyers

Edmund Randolph was born in August 1753 to John Randolph and Ariana Jenings at Williamsburg, Virginia. Their home was called Tazewell Hall. The family was well established in colonial politics and legal matters, having moved to America from England in the mid-1600s. His father, uncle, and grandfather all served as attorneys for the British Crown in the Virginia colony. Ariana's father was also a king's attorney in the colony of Maryland.

Edmund Randolph. *(Library of Congress.)*

Many colonial leaders visited the home of the prominent Randolph family on a regular basis. Young Edmund grew up hearing discussions at the dinner table and in the parlor on a wide range of important topics of the day. As a young man, he attended the College of William and Mary in Williamsburg and then studied law under his father. Like other young men seeking a law career in those days, he performed clerical tasks around the law office while studying law books in his free time. He successfully received a license and began his law practice at the age of twenty-one.

A Patriot

When the American Revolution (1775–83) erupted in April 1775, Randolph's family, including his parents and sisters, hurriedly left the colonies, as did many other Loyalists (those who supported continued British rule). However, Randolph was very much a Patriot (supporter of independence from British rule). In August, he gathered letters of recommendation from various prominent Virginians and presented them to General **George Washington** (1732–1799; see entry in volume 2) in Boston, hoping to become an army camp aide. He was successful in gaining the appointment. However, Randolph found that military life did not appeal to him. Upon the sudden death of his uncle, Peyton Randolph (c. 1721–1775), who was in Philadelphia serving as president of the First Continental Congress, Edmund took leave from his brief military assignment. He accompanied his uncle's body back to Virginia for burial and remained there to manage his uncle's estate.

Back in Williamsburg, Randolph turned to politics. In 1776, at twenty-three years of age, he became the youngest member of the Virginia constitutional convention. He helped draft and adopt the Virginia Declaration of Rights as well as a new state constitution in 1776. With a new state government formed, Randolph was appointed its first attorney general. He would serve for ten years, during which time he was also elected mayor of Williamsburg, an even more demanding position. Also in 1776, Randolph married Elizabeth Nicholas, daughter of Virginia's new state treasurer. They had four children. Like many elected officials at the time, Randolph continued his private interests—running his estate and his law practice—while he was in office.

Delegate to the Continental Congress

The Virginia Assembly elected Randolph as a delegate to the Continental Congress in 1779 and again in 1781 and 1782. He focused on his role as state attorney general through the mid-1780s. Change came for Randolph in 1786. In November, he was elected governor of Virginia and also sent as a Virginia delegate to a meeting among states in Annapolis, Maryland, in September. The purpose of the meeting was to discuss common problems under the Articles of Confederation, the nation's first constitution, which had become effective in 1781. However, only five states sent delegates. The delegates at the Annapolis meeting sent a proposal to the Continental Congress to bring together delegates from the thirteen states the following May in Philadelphia to improve the Articles.

Constitutional Convention of 1787

Not surprisingly, Virginia chose to send Randolph to the convention in Philadelphia in May 1787. Though no one knew it at the time, this meeting would become what is now called the Constitutional Convention; the delegates who attended the meeting voted to abandon the Articles of Confederation and create a new U.S. constitution. Randolph was in very select company. Other Virginia delegates were George Washington, **James Madison** (1751–1836; see entry in volume 2), **John Marshall** (1755–1835; see entry in volume 2), and George Mason (1725–1792). Randolph had the privilege of presenting the opening address to the convention, a lengthy speech calling for a much stronger central government.

A major debate developed at the convention; it concerned how the states should be represented in a newly proposed two-house Congress. The large states naturally wanted representation to be based on the size of a state's population or on its wealth. The smaller states wanted each state to have equal representation in Congress. Virginia delegate Madison drew up a proposal known as the Virginia Plan. However, Madison was quite short and not gifted in public speaking. Randolph was tall and had a commanding voice. So Madison asked Randolph to present the proposal to the convention delegates. Because Madison was from one of the states with a large population, his proposal favored representation based on population in both houses of Congress. In the end, the delegates reached a compromise: Senate representation would be equal for all states; the number of representatives in the House would be based on the population of each state.

At the Constitutional Convention, Randolph served on the committee to develop a draft, called the Committee of Detail. Madison was the lead author. However, when the Constitution was adopted in final form, Randolph and fellow Virginia delegate George Mason refused to sign it. They believed the

Constitution did not provide sufficient protection of individual rights. They also thought the newly created position of president was too much like a monarch, holding excessive power. Randolph tried to promote the idea of a three-person executive committee rather than a single president; he also argued that the proposed single president should not be allowed to run for reelection. Randolph was so concerned over the new Constitution that he published a letter opposing it when he returned to Virginia from the Philadelphia convention. He also recommended that the delegates hold a second convention but to no avail.

The following year, in 1788, Randolph attended the Virginia convention for ratifying the Constitution. However, now Randolph chose to support its approval, joining fellow Virginia delegates Madison and Marshall. Eight other states had already ratified the Constitution at the time of the Virginia gathering. Randolph had concluded that its acceptance was inevitable and that Virginia should throw in its support. Randolph played a key role in the close vote favoring ratification. A number of Virginians were angered by Randolph's change in position concerning the Constitution.

The first U.S. attorney general

Following the ratification convention, Randolph resigned his post as governor in November 1788 and returned to the Virginia general assembly. However, as the new national government under the Constitution took shape, President George Washington selected Randolph as the nation's first attorney general. Like future attorney generals, he maintained a private law practice while serving as advisor to the president. He also performed personal legal work for the president and became one of Washington's most trusted advisors. He wrote speeches and official papers for Washington on many occasions.

Randolph spent many of the next several years trying to ease the growing split between Secretary of the Treasury **Alexander Hamilton** (1755–1804; see entry in volume 1) and Secretary of State **Thomas Jefferson** (1743–1826; see entry in volume 1). Hamilton and Jefferson represented different political factions that disagreed over economic and foreign policies. The political division widened after

Edmond Charles Genet. *(Library of Congress.)*

France declared war on Britain in early 1793. Some American political leaders wanted to support France; others preferred Britain. With Randolph's support, President Washington chose a position of neutrality (not favoring either warring party) in the spring of 1793.

Almost immediately thereafter, France's new minister to the United States, Edmond Charles Genet (1763–1834), appeared on the scene. Genet ignored basic international diplomatic procedures by going straight to the American people and asking them for military support for France. Even Jefferson, an ardent supporter of France, was taken aback. Randolph was given the task of demanding that France recall Genet. The newly established French leadership distrusted him and responded by issuing a warrant for Genet's arrest. Randolph protected Genet and allowed him to stay in the country as France sent a new minister.

Secretary of state

Jefferson resigned as secretary of state in December 1793, and Washington selected Randolph to replace him. He served in the position until August 1795. The position was a challenge, in part because of Hamilton's continued involvement in foreign issues, which were normally the responsibility of the secretary of state.

Major foreign issues lingered since the end of the American Revolution (1775–83), the nation's battle to win independence from Britain. The British were ignoring the terms of the 1783 Treaty of Paris, the peace agreement that ended the war. They were keeping troops on American soil at trading posts on the frontier west of the Appalachian Mountains. They also had not returned slaves taken during the war.

President Washington sent Supreme Court chief justice **John Jay** (1745–1829; see entry in volume 1) to Britain in the summer of 1794 to negotiate a new treaty. Randolph had objected to this course of action. He believed a Court justice should not be involved in executive office business, and he urged keeping a sharp separation between the branches of government. Randolph thought Jay should at least resign from the Court, but Jay did not. Nonetheless, with assistance from Hamilton, Randolph drew up instructions for Jay to follow in negotiating with Britain and asked him specifically to negotiate a new trade agreement. However, because of Hamilton's continued meddling and the length of time needed for communication across the Atlantic Ocean, Jay did not follow Randolph's guidance very closely. Disappointed with the results of Jay's negotiations, Randolph advised President Washington not to sign the treaty. His advice attracted strong criticism from Hamilton and others who supported adoption of the new treaty by Jay. The Senate ratified the Jay Treaty in June 1795.

When the French learned of the treaty, they strongly protested. French political leaders claimed that by signing the treaty the United States had violated its 1778 alliance agreement with France. Randolph denied this was the case. The new treaty did set the stage for negotiations for a new treaty with Spain to secure navigation rights for Americans on the Mississippi River. These negotiations proved very successful and resulted in the signing of the Treaty of San Lorenzo in October 1795.

In an effort to embarrass Randolph, the British intercepted a message from Jean Antoine Joseph Fauchet, France's minister to the United States, to Randolph that gave the appearance that Randolph was secretly dealing with Fauchet. The British then accused Randolph of influencing policy favorable to France in exchange for personal financial payments. President Washington summoned Randolph to his office to answer the charges. Humiliated, Randolph angrily resigned in August 1795. Fauchet denied any such dealings, and Randolph immediately wrote and published a long defense of his actions and revealed the British plot to embarrass him. No wrongdoing on Randolph's part was ever uncovered. Fauchet may have bragged to his superiors in France that he was winning favors, when in fact Randolph had not cooperated with him.

Randolph returned to a very successful private law practice in Richmond, Virginia. In 1807, he successfully represented former vice president **Aaron Burr** (1756–1836; see entry in volume 1). Burr was being tried for treason before Supreme Court chief justice John Marshall in the U.S. Circuit Court in Richmond. Burr was found not guilty.

Though a successful lawyer, Randolph did not manage his personal finances well and fought debt problems through his last years. Randolph's wife died in 1810, and he suffered ill health for some time. He lived his final years with his daughter in Charles Town in present-day West Virginia. Randolph died in September 1813. He was buried in Millwood, Virginia, where over a century later, in 1940, a monument was erected in his honor.

For More Information

Books

Randolph, Edmund. *History of Virginia.* Charlottesville: University Press of Virginia, 1970.

Reardon, John J. *Edmund Randolph.* New York: Macmillan, 1975.

Betsy Ross

Born January 1, 1752 (Philadelphia, Pennsylvania)
Died January 30, 1836 (Philadelphia, Pennsylvania)

Businesswoman, seamstress

B etsy Ross, the legendary maker of the first American flag known as the "Stars and Stripes," was a successful businesswoman during the early years of the nation. Ross did not just supplement the family income as many women did in the early years of the nation; she actually supported her family with her business skills. She trained as a seamstress and apprenticed as an upholsterer before becoming an official flag-maker for the Pennsylvania State Navy Board. She resided in Philadelphia her entire life and experienced firsthand the effects of the American Revolution (1775–83). Ross lost two husbands to the war, and at one point her home was taken over by the British to lodge soldiers.

Disowned by the Quaker Society as a young woman, Ross became a faithful member of the new Society of Free Quakers. The group was commonly called the "Fighting Quakers" because they participated in civil affairs and the military defense of the country. This group contrasted with the regular, pacifist Quakers. Ross operated a successful upholstery and flag-making business for over fifty years, but a lifetime of sewing cost Ross her eyesight. She spent her final years with her children and grandchildren, telling them the story of how she made the first "Stars and Stripes."

> "I remember having heard my mother . . . say frequently that she, with her own hands . . . made the first Star-spangled Banner that ever was made."
>
> *Rachel Fletcher, daughter of Betsy Ross*

Betsy Ross. *(© Bettmann/Corbis.)*

Learning a trade

Betsy Ross was born Elizabeth Griscom on the first day of January in 1752. Rebecca James and Samuel Griscom were Quakers, a religious group that strongly opposed violence and war. Elizabeth, called Betsy, was the eighth of their seventeen children. The family lived in Philadelphia, where Samuel worked in the building trades. It is believed that he assisted in the construction of the Pennsylvania State House, now known as Independence Hall, the building in which the 1787 Constitutional Convention took place. The children attended the

Friends' School on South Fourth Street. Rebecca also taught Betsy to do needlework. Betsy went on to work as an apprentice to an upholsterer. She learned to make and repair a variety of items, including rugs, umbrellas, and venetian blinds.

While learning her new trade, Betsy fell in love with fellow apprentice John Ross. John was of the Anglican faith; his father was the rector at Emmanuel Church in New Castle, Delaware. Betsy's family did not approve of her plans to marry John. The couple crossed over the Delaware River to New Jersey, where they wed on November 4, 1773. Because she married a non-Quaker, Betsy was disowned by her family and the Quaker Society. The Rosses attended Christ Church, an Anglican church in Philadelphia, where their family pew was just across the aisle from the pew of General **George Washington** (1732–1799; see entry in volume 2). Washington was an acquaintance of the family, and Betsy sewed and embroidered the general's shirts on occasion. John's uncle, Colonel George Ross (1730–1779), was a prominent Philadelphian and a friend of Washington. The two would sometimes drop by the Rosses' home for a friendly visit.

John and Betsy Ross opened an upholstery shop on Chestnut Street and later moved their business to Arch Street. When the American Revolution broke out, John joined the local militia and was assigned to guard munitions near the Delaware River. He was killed in an explosion of gunpowder in January 1776, leaving twenty-four-year-old Betsy a widow. She continued running the upholstery business and supplemented her income with military orders. Records show that the Continental Army placed orders for a variety of supplies including tents and blankets. In May 1777, Ross received payment for an order of flags for the State of Pennsylvania. Her business prospered, and Ross was able to acquire properties in Philadelphia and Cumberland Counties.

A symbol of liberty

In June 1776, Ross received a secret visit from a three-member committee of the Continental Congress. The group's leader was George Washington; the other two men were George Ross, uncle of Betsy's late husband, and Pennsylvania delegate Robert Morris (1734–1806). Congress had authorized them to design a flag for the emerging

Mary Young Pickersgill

Mary Young Pickersgill (1776–1857) was a young widow living in Baltimore, Maryland, at the beginning of the nineteenth century. She established a profitable flag-making business in order to support her daughter, Caroline, and her widowed mother, Rebecca Young. Pickersgill had learned the trade from her mother, who made flags for ships, forts, and organizations in Philadelphia during the American Revolution.

Pickersgill's business in Baltimore was equally as successful as her mother's had been. She made a good living designing and sewing flags for the U.S. Army and U.S. Navy. She also supplied banners and pennants to the many privateer ships operating out of Baltimore. Privateers were privately owned ships commissioned to fight or harass the enemy. They looted British merchant ships, seized the cargo, and transported it to foreign ports. During the War of 1812 (1812–15), business slowed considerably as the British blockaded Chesapeake Bay and made plans to attack Baltimore in response to the privateer attacks.

In the summer of 1813, Pickersgill received an order for two flags from Major George Armistead (1780–1818), the commander of Fort McHenry, an army post near Baltimore. The smaller flag was designed to fly in bad weather. The larger flag measured 30 feet by 42 feet and was designed to be visible from a great distance. It had fifteen stars and fifteen stripes representing the thirteen original American states plus Vermont and Kentucky. Pickersgill received a payment of $500 for both flags. She employed her daughter and several other women in order to finish the flags before hostilities erupted. They laid the immense flag out on the spacious floor of nearby Claggett's Brewery and worked night and day in order to complete the project in only six weeks.

They presented the flags to Armistead that summer, but as it turned out, more than a year would pass before the British attacked Baltimore. Pickersgill's large flag flew over Fort McHenry on the morning of August 14, 1814, inspiring Francis Scott Key (1779–1843) to write a poem that was later set to music and renamed "The Star-Spangled Banner." That flag was preserved and placed on permanent public display at the Smithsonian Institution in Washington, D.C.

Pickersgill was not only a successful early American businesswoman like Betsy Ross; she was also a philanthropist (one who gives to charities). She addressed social issues such as housing, job placement assistance, and financial aid for disadvantaged women. Pickersgill served as president of the Impartial Female Humane Society from 1828 until 1851. The society helped poor families with government funding support for children and employment opportunities for women. In 1850, the society established a home for aged women, and by 1863 a men's home was added. As testimony to her humanitarian efforts, the society became known as the Pickersgill Retirement Community.

nation. The committee presented Ross with a sketch of the proposed flag and commissioned her to make it. She changed the design slightly by substituting five-pointed stars for the six-pointed ones in the sketch, and she arranged the stars neatly in a circle instead of scattered over the field. The proposed flag was square, but Ross recommended changing it to a rectangle that was one-third longer than its width.

Ross quickly made the flag, and Congress unanimously approved it. The "Stars and Stripes" created by Ross became a symbol for the new nation. In June 1777, the Continental Congress passed the Flag Act, making the "Stars and Stripes" the official flag of the United States. The act stated that the American flag must have thirteen alternating red and white stripes as well as thirteen white stars on a blue background. The stars represented the thirteen colonies and were meant to symbolize the nation as a new constellation, unwavering in the night sky. History shows that flag-making was rather informal at that time and there were still many interpretations on the basic design. The arrangement of the stars in a circle became known as the Betsy Ross flag. For her efforts, Ross was given a contract to manufacture flags for the government for decades to come.

An early American businesswoman

In the summer of 1777, Ross married Joseph Ashburn. Serving as first mate on an American ship named the *Patty,* he was often away from home. Ross remained in Philadelphia, where their daughter, Zilla, was born in 1779. After Zilla's birth, Ashburn returned to the sea. Later, the British captured his ship and imprisoned him at Old Mill Prison in Plymouth, England. Ashburn was unaware of the death of his nine-month-old daughter, Zilla, and he would not live to see his daughter Eliza, born in 1781. Ashburn died in prison of an unknown illness in March 1782. Ross was once again a widow. She continued to support herself and her daughter with her upholstery and flag-making business.

John Claypoole, a family friend, had been a fellow prisoner of Joseph Ashburn in England. When the British released American prisoners in 1782, Claypoole made his way back to Philadelphia and contacted Ross. He told her of Ashburn's death and brought farewell messages from him to her. On May 8, 1783, Betsy married Claypoole. The couple had five children, but the youngest one died in infancy. Claypoole worked for the U.S. Custom House before his death in August 1817. His war injuries had left him disabled for nearly twenty of their thirty-four years together, so Ross supported the family with her business ventures.

Shortly after Ross married Claypoole, she sought to renew her association with the religion of her childhood. A new religious society calling themselves the Free Quakers had formed in Philadelphia in 1781 to meet the needs of those who had been disowned by the Society of Friends, or Quakers. The new society also welcomed those who were attracted by the Quaker ideas but who had no previous association. They initially met in homes but then accepted an offer from the trustees of the University of Pennsylvania to meet on the university campus. A flyer titled *An Address to Those of the People called Quakers* was distributed in several states, inviting others to join the Free Quakers. The *Address* explained that the society was based on the fundamental principles and beliefs of the Friends. Their intended purpose was to allow the disowned to worship freely. The outstanding difference between the two societies was that the Free Quakers encouraged civil participation in the defense of the country as well as military action. Ross and her husband joined the Free Quakers in 1784. She remained a faithful member throughout the remainder of her life.

Ross continued her upholstery and flag-making business until her eyesight began to fail. After fifty years in her chosen profession, she retired at the age of seventy-six. Ross moved to a daughter's farm in the remote suburb of Abington, where her children and grandchildren visited her often. Ross frequently told her family the story of the fateful day when George Washington and his committee visited her home to ask that she make a flag for the new nation. Before she became completely blind, Ross took a carriage ride into the city once a week to attend church meetings. In 1833, Ross returned to Philadelphia, where she lived with her daughter's family on Cherry Street until her death at the age of eight-four. Ross was buried in the Free Quaker Burying Ground until 1857, when her remains were moved to Mount Moriah Cemetery, Philadelphia.

Betsy Ross (center) presents the first American flag to President George Washington (second from right). (© *Bettmann/Corbis.*)

History of a legend

For many years through the early American period, Ross's story of sewing America's first flag was known only by her family. In March 1870, her grandson, William J. Canby, delivered a paper to the Historical Society of Pennsylvania, describing Ross's role in the creation of the first "Stars and Stripes." His paper was based on his own conversations with his grandmother over twenty years earlier when he was still a child. Canby presented his research along with affidavits from several of his aunts to verify the story. He noted that his search for supporting documents outside the family had been unsuccessful. Canby called for research by others to confirm the matter.

Canby's story appeared in *Harper's Monthly* in July 1873. It was soon immortalized in print and illustrations. The centennial of the Flag Act in 1877 brought renewed interest in the flag and the symbolism that accompanied it. By the middle of the 1880s, the tale of Ross and her flag appeared in school textbooks and was one of the most familiar stories about the American Revolution.

In 1893, at the World's Columbian Exposition in Chicago, Charles H. Weisberger's painting *Birth of Our Nation's Flag* was put on display. The painting depicts Betsy Ross presenting her finished "Stars and Stripes" to George Washington, Robert Morris, and George Ross. A reproduction of the painting was printed on certificates sold in 1898 for a contribution of ten cents to the Betsy Ross Memorial Association. Over two million of the certificates were sold, and the proceeds funded restoration of the Betsy Ross House, where the flag was likely made.

For More Information

Books

Armentrout, David, and Patricia Armentrout. *Betsy Ross*. Vero Beach, FL: Rourke Publishing, 2004.

Duden, Jane. *Betsy Ross*. Mankato, MN: Bridgestone Books, 2002.

Guenter, Scot M. *The American Flag, 1777–1924: Cultural Shifts from Creation to Codification*. Rutherford, NJ: Fairleigh Dickinson University Press, 1990.

Miller, Susan Martins. *Betsy Ross: American Patriot*. Philadelphia: Chelsea House, 2000.

Randolph, Ryan P. *Betsy Ross: The American Flag, and Life in a Young America*. New York: PowerPlus Books, 2002.

St. George, Judith. *Betsy Ross: Patriot of Philadelphia*. New York: Henry Holt, 1997.

Web Sites

"The Betsy Ross Homepage." *Independence Hall Association*. http://www.ushistory.org/betsy/ (accessed on August 17, 2005).

"Mary Young Pickersgill." *The National Flag Day Foundation, Inc.* http://www.flagday.org/Pages/Lessons_bios/Pickersgill_bio.html (accessed on August 17, 2005).

Sacagawea

Born 1786 (Present-day Idaho)
Died December 20, 1812 (Present-day South Dakota)

Shoshone interpreter

S acagawea is an extraordinary figure in the history of the American West. She was the only woman to participate in the Lewis and Clark expedition (1804–6), an exploration of the West arranged by President **Thomas Jefferson** (1743–1826; served 1801–9; see entry in volume 1). Sacagawea's indispensable role in the expedition made her a legendary figure in her own right. Over time, Sacagawea's documented history became mixed with frontier myth (a traditional story) to create a woman shrouded in mystery. Sacagawea became a popular subject of books, movies, and tribal lore during the twentieth century. More monuments, memorials, rivers, lakes, and mountain ranges have been named for Sacagawea than for any other American woman. In the twenty-first century, Sacagawea remains one of the most familiar figures of the Lewis and Clark party.

> "The Indian woman . . . has been of great service to me as a pilot through this country."
>
> *Explorer William Clark*

Child of the Snake people

Sacagawea was born around 1786 as a member of the Shoshone nation. Her parents lived in the western Rocky Mountains of the United States. Her birthplace was most likely

Sacagawea. *(© Hulton Archive/Getty Images.)*

southeast of the town of Salmon, in the central Salmon River country of present-day Idaho. Sacagawea belonged to the Agaiduka, or Salmon Eater, band of the Shoshone nation. Other Native Americans called the Shoshone "Snakes," associating them with the Snake River of their homeland. The Shoshone believed wolves, not snakes, were their ancestors and claimed a close association with coyotes and dogs. The Shoshone tribes called themselves Nermenuh, or "People." In her native language, Sacagawea's name means "boat pusher" or "boat launcher." Not much is known of her personal life until she reached her early teens and became a popular figure in the history of the American West.

Around the year 1800, Sacagawea traveled eastward across the Rockies with her family and tribe to the Three Forks area of the Missouri River in Montana. Sacagawea's band was camped between the present-day town locations of Butte and Bozeman, Montana, when they encountered a group of Hidatsa warriors. The Shoshone were outnumbered, and Sacagawea was among those captured. She was taken to live with the Hidatsa in their Knife River village near what is now Bismarck, North Dakota. In the Hidatsa language, Sacagawea's name means "Bird Woman." Sacagawea's name has alternately been spelled Sakakawea and Sacajawea.

Toussaint Charbonneau (1758–1843) was a French Canadian fur trader who had been living with the Hidatsa in their earthen lodges along the Knife River for about eight years. Sacagawea lived as a captive of the Hidatsa until she was sold or gambled away to Charbonneau, along with another girl called Otter Woman. The girls became the property and wives of Charbonneau. Soon, sixteen-year-old Sacagawea found she was pregnant.

Exploration of the American West

In April 1803, the United States acquired the area then known as Louisiana from Napoléon Bonaparte (1769–1821) of France. The Louisiana Purchase (see box) included an area in the center of North America larger than Great Britain, France, Germany, Italy, Spain, and Portugal combined. President Thomas Jefferson put Meriwether Lewis (1774–1809) and William Clark (1770–1838) in charge of an expedition to explore this land and the area farther west, all the way to the Pacific coast. The Lewis and Clark party, named the Corps of Discovery, set out on their journey in May 1804.

In the winter of 1804, Sacagawea met Lewis and Clark when they arrived at the Hidatsa and Mandan villages located in North Dakota. The Corps hired several men, including Toussaint Charbonneau, as interpreters and advisors for the push westward. They also saw Charbonneau's young Native American wife as potentially helpful: She

The Louisiana Purchase

On April 30, 1803, American ambassadors Robert Livingston (1746–1813) and **James Monroe** (1758–1831; see entry in volume 2) signed the Louisiana Purchase Treaty in Paris, France, on behalf of the United States. The treaty added over 800,000 square miles of land west of the Mississippi River to the United States for the price of 60 million francs (French currency), equal to about 15 million American dollars. The new territory, rich in natural resources, cost the United States approximately three cents an acre. The Louisiana Purchase opened up the land west of the Mississippi to settlement and ended the threat of war with France at the same time. The land was eventually divided into all or part of thirteen states, including Louisiana, Arkansas, Missouri, Iowa, North and South Dakota, Nebraska, Kansas, Wyoming, Minnesota, Oklahoma, Colorado, and Montana.

President Thomas Jefferson was a strict interpreter of the U.S. Constitution, but he also dreamed of an empire that covered the continent. Although the Constitution did not provide authority for the president to purchase territory, Jefferson stretched the limits of his office and submitted the Louisiana Purchase Treaty to Congress. Congress approved the treaty, and as a result, the United States, barely a generation old, doubled in size, becoming one of the largest nations in the world. The purchase was announced on July 4, 1803, and the United States formally took possession of the region in December of that year.

Jefferson had anticipated that the United States might expand westward, so he had already assigned Meriwether Lewis as commander of an exploratory expedition in the spring of 1803. Lewis wrote to William Clark and asked him to share command in the venture, during which

would be an ideal interpreter for the expedition when it reached the Shoshone lands at the headwaters of the Missouri River. For Sacagawea, it was an opportunity to escape the Hidatsa and return to the place of her birth and her native tribe.

In North Dakota, the Lewis and Clark expedition built Fort Mandan across the river from the Native Americans' main village and made it their winter quarters. On December 17, the Corps recorded a temperature of 45 degrees below zero Fahrenheit, colder than they had ever experienced in the existing United States. Fort Mandan was finished on December 24, 1804. The Corps moved into the fort and waited for the spring thaw and the continuation of their journey.

Sacagawea points out something to explorers Meriwether Lewis and William Clark. (© Bettmann/ Corbis.)

they would attempt to map the territory across the western part of the continent to the Pacific Ocean. On March 10, 1804, Lewis and Clark traveled to St. Louis, Missouri, to attend ceremonies celebrating the transfer of the Louisiana Purchase to the United States. The Corps of Discovery officially began their expedition on May 14, 1804. As they traveled, Lewis and Clark sent shipments of artifacts and plant specimens back to President Jefferson. They took notes on previously unknown animals and sent samples that included everything from prairie dogs to grizzly bears.

The expedition returned to St. Louis on September 23, 1806. The two men were treated as national heroes when they arrived in Washington, D.C. They received double their usual military pay and gifts of land as rewards for completing the journey. Lewis was named governor of the Louisiana Territory, and Clark was made brigadier general of the territory's militia and Native American agent for the West.

Sacagawea gave birth to her son, Jean Baptiste Charbonneau (1805–1866), at the fort on February 11, 1805. Lewis assisted in the birth, and Clark, who took an immediate liking to the boy, nicknamed him "Pomp" or "Pompey." Clark's journals reveal that he developed a special relationship with Sacagawea, too. Although both Lewis and Clark referred to her as "the Indian woman," or as "Charbonneau's wife," Clark used the nickname "Janey" for Sacagawea in one journal entry. Because her name was difficult to say and even more difficult to write, Sacagawea's personal contributions were often recorded in an impersonal way in the journals of Lewis and Clark. From the time she first appeared in their records until the summer of 1806, when her part in the journey ended, Sacagawea's name was used only seventeen times. However, Sacagawea played an important role in the Corps: She served as a peace symbol when the party encountered Native Americans. The presence of a woman with an infant signaled to the Native Americans that Lewis and Clark and their Corps of Discovery were not a war party.

Sacagawea's baby was the youngest of the thirty-three permanent members of the expedition when the Corps left Fort Mandan and headed west on April 7, 1805. Jean Baptiste rode on his mother's back in a papoose cradleboard of the kind traditionally used by the Shoshones. Even though she had an infant to care for, Sacagawea joined other Corps members each day in digging for roots, picking berries, and collecting edible plants that were used as food and sometimes as medicine. The party included Lewis's Newfoundland dog, Seaman, whose bark kept grizzly bears from getting close to camp and whose hunting skills brought wild ducks to his master's table.

On May 16, the expedition was traveling on the Missouri River when their boats were nearly overturned during a storm. Lewis and Clark credited Sacagawea for remaining calm and being the one who saved valuable instruments and records from being lost to the waters in the chaos that followed. Although Sacagawea did not know the country well enough to direct the expedition to its final goal of the Pacific Ocean, she was familiar with the geography near her homeland in the Three Forks area of the upper Missouri River.

The transferring of loyalties

As part of their official duties, the Corps developed a ritual that they used when encountering Native American tribes for the first time. Lewis and Clark would explain to the tribal leaders in a formal meeting that their land now belonged to the United States. They told them that a man far in the east named President Thomas Jefferson was their new "great father" and presented them with a peace medal that showed Jefferson's image on one side and an image of two hands clasping on the other. The Corps also presented trade goods along with American flags that had fifteen stars to represent the existing states of the union. Corps members would follow the ceremony with a parade in which they marched in uniform and fired their guns.

When the expedition reached the Great Falls of the Missouri in June 1805, they discovered five massive waterfalls that forced them to portage, or carry, all of their gear over the next 18 miles. The portage upstream past the waterfalls took them over a month to accomplish. In late July, the Corps reached the Three Forks of the Missouri, which they named the Jefferson, the Gallatin, and the Madison in honor of President Jefferson, Secretary of the Treasury **Albert Gallatin** (1761–1849; see entry in volume 1), and Secretary of State **James Madison** (1751–1836; see entry in volume 2). Continuing up the Jefferson fork of the river, Sacagawea realized they were coming close to Shoshone lands in Idaho.

Sacagawea recognized the landmark Beaverhead Rock that prompted Lewis to go out ahead and scout the area. He reached the headwaters of the Missouri River, crossed the Continental Divide, and climbed a final ridge expecting to see plains and a river flowing to the Pacific. Instead, he found even more mountains and deduced that a northwest passage to the ocean did not exist. Lewis pressed on to the nearest Shoshone camp, where he tried to negotiate for horses. Clark and the rest of the Corps soon followed, and when they arrived, Sacagawea found herself unexpectedly reunited with her brother, Cameahwait. Lewis and Clark discovered they were now in a favorable situation with the Native Americans because of Sacagawea's family connection. The pair named the site "Camp Fortunate" in their journal entries.

Sacagawea's long-lost brother had become chief of the band of Shoshone during her many years of absence. Cameahwait sketched a map and offered the Corps of Discovery guidance across the Bitterroot Mountains. He agreed to sell the party the horses they needed and to guide them through the Salmon River country. That would put them onto the navigable waters of the Clearwater and Columbia Rivers, where they could resume traveling by boat toward the Pacific Ocean. The negotiations were not simple. Sacagawea would talk with her people and then translate into Hidatsa for Charbonneau. He would then translate into French for Corps member François Labiche. Labiche made the final translation into English so that Lewis and Clark could understand what was going on.

Trail's end

Cameahwait said goodbye to Sacagawea and sent a Shoshone guide called Old Toby, along with twenty-nine horses and a mule, to see her party safely across the Bitterroot Range of the Rocky Mountains. With young Jean Baptiste riding on her back in his cradleboard, Sacagawea reluctantly left her brother and her people. The Corps began the steep ascent into the mountains on horseback on September 11, 1805, and emerged on the other side eleven days later, half-starved, at the villages of the Nez Perce; near present-day Weippe, Idaho. The Nez Perce taught the expedition party a new way to make dugout canoes. With the new canoes, they set off down the Clearwater River on October 7. The expedition reached the Columbia River, the last waterway to the Pacific Ocean, on October 16, 1805. Clark recorded seeing Mount Hood (near present-day Portland, Oregon) in the distance. It had been named by a British sea captain in 1792. Spotting it proved by their maps that they were near the ocean.

The Corps was still 20 miles away from the ocean when they were met by terrible winter storms that halted their progress for nearly three weeks. On November 24, 1805, they finally reached the place where the Columbia River empties into the Pacific Ocean. The entire expedition, including Sacagawea, voted on where to build their winter quarters. They chose the Clatsop tribe side of the Columbia River by majority vote. Crossing to the south side of the Columbia, near present-day Astoria, Oregon, the Corps built Fort Clatsop, which they inhabited during the winter of 1805–6. Having not yet seen the ocean, Sacagawea insisted she be included in a group that made the final trip to the Pacific shore, where she would witness the novelty of a whale that had beached on the sand.

After a winter of only twelve days without rain, the Corps of Discovery presented their fort to the Clatsop tribe, for whom it was named, and set out for home in March 1806. On the return journey, Sacagawea proved to be a valuable guide to Clark, who praised her in his journal as his "pilot" through Bozeman Pass in Montana. The Corps returned to the Hidatsa-Mandan villages on August 14, 1806, where Sacagawea, Charbonneau, and their son, Jean Baptiste, parted from the expedition. Charbonneau was paid for his contribution, but Sacagawea, never an official member of the expedition, received no monetary compensation for her part in the venture.

Legend of the Bird Woman

There are two contradictory accounts of Sacagawea's life following her return to South Dakota. Little was officially documented after her years with the expedition. The account favored by many historians records her death from fever in late 1812. The written account of Sacagawea's final years is sketchy but includes documentation by Clark himself that she died at Fort Manuel in South Dakota. It is believed that Sacagawea gave birth to a daughter named Lisette before her death, but it is not known whether the child survived past infancy. It is known that William Clark legally adopted young Jean Baptiste Charbonneau and assumed responsibility for his education.

The oral account of Sacagawea's life after the expedition is favored by most Native Americans and maintains that she lived to be an old woman. These oral traditions say Sacagawea left Charbonneau and wandered from tribe to tribe. She became known as Porivo (Chief Woman), Wadze Wipe (Lost Woman), and Bo-i-naiv (Grass Woman). It is said that she remarried and had other children before being reunited with Jean Baptiste and an adopted nephew whom she named Bazil. These tribal traditions trace Sacagawea's death to a Wyoming tribe reservation in 1884 after nearly a century of life.

National interest in Sacagawea gained momentum in the early twentieth century with the centennial observances of the Louisiana Purchase and the Lewis and Clark expedition. A women's association raised funds for a statue of Sacagawea that was unveiled at the Lewis and Clark Exposition of 1905 in Portland, Oregon. Social activist Susan B. Anthony (1820–1906) was one of several prominent people who made speeches at this event. Anthony and Sacagawea share the honor of having their likenesses stamped on a U.S. dollar coin.

For More Information

Books

Clark, Ella E., and Margot Edmonds. *Sacagawea of the Lewis and Clark Expedition*. Berkeley: University of California Press, 1979.

Hebard, Grace R. *Sacajawea*. Glendale, CA: Arthur H. Clark Co., 1933.

Howard, Harold P. *Sacajawea.* Norman: University of Oklahoma Press, 1971. Reprint, 2002.

Kessler, Donna J. *The Making of Sacagawea: A Euro-American Legend.* Tuscaloosa: University of Alabama Press, 1996.

Nelson, W. Dale. *Interpreters with Lewis and Clark: The Story of Sacagawea and Toussaint Charbonneau.* Denton: University of North Texas Press, 2003.

Slaughter, Thomas P. *Exploring Lewis and Clark: Reflections on Men and Wilderness.* New York: Alfred A. Knopf, 2003.

Web Sites

"Jefferson's West: The Louisiana Purchase." *Monticello: The Home of Thomas Jefferson.* http://www.monticello.org/jefferson/lewisandclark/louisiana.html (accessed on August 17, 2005).

Public Broadcasting Service. "Sacagawea." *Lewis & Clark: The Journey of the Corps of Discovery.* http://www.pbs.org/lewisandclark/inside/saca.html (accessed on August 17, 2005).

Elizabeth Ann Seton

Born August 28, 1774 (New York, New York)
Died January 4, 1821 (Emmitsburg, Maryland)

Educator, religious leader

Elizabeth Ann Seton was a convert to Roman Catholicism who formed a religious community and opened a school for poor children in Maryland. In 1809, she founded the Sisters of Charity of St. Joseph's, the first religious order of women in the United States. In 1813, Seton was elected mother superior, or head, of the Sisters of Charity—the same year the organization set up a national Catholic school system. By 1814, Mother Seton and her Sisters of Charity were also managing the first Catholic orphanage in the United States.

In 1828, shortly after Seton's death, the Sisters of Charity of St. Joseph's began the first Catholic hospital in the United States, located in St. Louis, Missouri. Seton left a large body of writing in the form of journals and correspondence that helped document the historical development of American Catholicism in the nation's early years. In 1975, she became the first person born in the United States to be named a saint when she was canonized by Pope Paul VI (1897–1978).

"Faith lifts the staggering soul on one side, hope supports it on the other. Experience says it must be, and love says—let it be."

Elizabeth Ann Seton. *(© Hulton Archive/Getty Images.)*

New York charity

Elizabeth Ann Bayley Seton was the daughter of Catherine Charlton and Dr. Richard Bayley. The couple had three daughters, Elizabeth arriving second in 1774. Her family called her by a number of nicknames including Betty, Betsy, Bette, and Eliza. Elizabeth's place of birth was most likely New York City, where her father was a prominent surgeon. Dr. Bayley's position gave his family access to the rich social and cultural life of New York society. The Bayley and Charlton families were among the earliest colonial settlers of the New York area. Catherine's father had come from Ireland and was pastor at St. Andrew's Episcopal Church on Staten Island. When Elizabeth was born, her grandfather had been a rector at St. Andrew's for nearly thirty years.

Elizabeth was a little over a year old when the American Revolution (1775–83) began. However, the biggest event in her early life was not the war, but the loss of her mother, who died in 1777. Catherine died after giving birth to her third daughter and namesake, Catherine Bayley. Richard Bayley remarried in 1778, and with his new wife, Charlotte Amelia Barclay, he had seven more children. Elizabeth's father was largely absent because of his career, and her young stepmother was busy raising her own children. Elizabeth's baby sister died in 1778, leaving her and her elder sister, Mary Magdalen, to be passed among relatives around New York. Elizabeth and Mary attended a school called "Mama Pompelion's," where they learned to speak French and studied music and dance. Elizabeth took comfort in her religious faith and immersed herself in her education as well as the social life of the city. She was fourteen years old in April 1789 when **George Washington** (1732–1799; served 1789–97; see entry in volume 2) was sworn in as the first president of the United States in downtown New York.

On January 25, 1794, at the home of her sister, Elizabeth was married to William Magee Seton by the Episcopal bishop of New York. William was a merchant from a wealthy trading family. Elizabeth gave birth to their first child, Anna Maria, in 1795. While her husband's business prospered during this period, Elizabeth united with several close friends to pursue charitable work. In 1797, they organized the Society for the Relief of Poor Widows with Small Children in order to provide for the needy women and children in their community. Elizabeth served as the society's treasurer until 1804. She also continued in her own studies to deepen her spiritual life at Trinity Episcopal Church of New York. By 1802, the Setons had added two sons and two more daughters to the family.

Family tragedies lead to change

William Seton was the eldest of thirteen children, and when his father died in 1798, he inherited Seton, Maitland and Company, the family's importing business; he also inherited responsibility for the ongoing care of his siblings. Elizabeth, six months pregnant with her third child, managed the welfare of both families by day and balanced the firm's account books at night. Financial troubles began plaguing the business, and the company was finally forced to file a petition of bankruptcy.

During this time, William was diagnosed with tuberculosis (a lung disease), and his health was deemed critical. In a final attempt to save him, the Setons placed their hopes in the warm climate of Italy. They booked passage aboard the *Shepherdess,* bound for Livorno, Italy, and set sail from New York on October 1, 1803. Anna Maria accompanied her parents, while the younger children were left in America in the care of relatives. Yellow fever was prevalent in New York when the *Shepherdess* left port, so Italian authorities at the port of Livorno imposed a quarantine when the ship docked. The Setons were confined to a cold, damp public hospital outside Livorno for thirty days, which left William completely disabled. Upon their release, the Setons traveled to Pisa, Italy, where William died on December 27. He was buried in the little English cemetery in Livorno, leaving Elizabeth a widow at age twenty-nine.

With no husband and with five small children to raise, the impoverished (poor) Elizabeth Seton found herself in the same position as the women she had served through her charity work in New York. However, she found friendship with the Filicchi family while awaiting passage back to the United States. The Filicchis were business partners in her husband's firm. They introduced her to the culture of Leghorn and Florence in Italy. During her three-month stay, Seton toured museums and churches and was introduced to the teachings and devotions of the Roman Catholic Church. The Filicchis provided gracious hospitality along with financial, emotional, and spiritual support, helping the young widow and her daughter through their grief.

Antonio Filicchi accompanied Seton and her daughter, Anna Maria, now called Annina, as they boarded a ship christened the *Flamingo* for the return trip to New York. After nearly two months at sea, the ship arrived at port on June 8, 1804. Seton's exposure to the Roman Catholic Church in Italy, along with the Filicchis' influence, left her determined to join the Church upon her return to the United States. It was not an easy decision for Seton, because there was considerable anti-Catholic sentiment in New York City at the time. Many Americans still viewed Catholicism as associated with the strong central governments of Europe and worshiping the pope rather than God. The United States had only recently gained its independence from these heavy-handed authorities and gained their individual freedoms. Despite the objections of her friends and relatives, Seton left the Episcopal Church to become a Catholic on March 14, 1805. She was received into the Catholic faith at St. Peter's Church on Barclay Street in lower Manhattan in New York City. At this time, she added the name of Mary to her own names and often signed herself "MEAS," an abbreviation for Mary Elizabeth Ann Seton.

Moving on to Maryland

Elizabeth Seton spent the next three years in New York City trying to support her family as a teacher. She was in a difficult financial situation with five young children but she considered them her primary responsibility over every other commitment. In order to place her own sons in the Catholic academy in Georgetown, Maryland, Seton found it necessary to accept financial aid from family and friends. When the opportunity presented itself, she accepted a one-year assignment to open a Catholic school in Maryland.

In June 1808, Seton left New York to move to Baltimore, Maryland, where she established a small boarding school for girls. Classes began that September in a small house located next to St. Mary's College and Seminary on Paca Street. By December, several other women arrived to assist her at the school. The following spring, two of her late husband's sisters, Cecilia and Harriet Seton, who had also converted to Catholicism, joined Elizabeth.

On March 25, 1809, Elizabeth Ann Seton took vows of poverty, chastity, and obedience in the presence of Archbishop **John Carroll** (1735–1815; see entry in volume 1). These vows, required annually, commit the person to an economic condition similar to those they will serve so they can relate to them more easily. The vows also include a full commitment to the religious mission without distractions of other commitments such as marriage. Carroll, from a prominent Maryland family, was elected bishop of Baltimore in May 1789. He was the first American bishop in the Catholic Church. His older brother, Daniel Carroll (1730–1796), was a member of the Continental Congress and one of only two Catholics to sign the U.S. Constitution in 1789. Archbishop Carroll's cousin Charles was the only Catholic to sign the Declaration of Independence. Carroll worked to form a national church that was independent from government, which differed from the European experience where church and state were tied to one another. His primary concern was to provide educational opportunities for lay (nonclergy) leaders and to develop native clergy for the Catholic Church in America.

The archbishop gave Seton the title of "Mother Seton" when she took her vows. Seton's goal of beginning a new religious community became a reality on June 1 with the organization of the Sisters of Charity of St. Joseph's (see box). It was the first religious order of women in the United States. Shortly after the organization formed, its members appeared in public dressed alike for the first time. Their religious garb consisted of a black dress with a shoulder cape and a white cap tied beneath the chin. The outfit was essentially the same as that worn by widows in Italy. It was not a major change for Elizabeth; she had been wearing similar clothing since her husband's death in Leghorn.

Sisters of Charity

On June 21, 1809, Mother Seton moved with her sisters-in-law and other women who had joined her sisterhood community to a larger property purchased for them near Emmitsburg, in Frederick County, Maryland. The purpose of their move was to establish an institution for the education of young women, an urgent need in America. Initially, the Sisters of Charity experienced a good deal of hardship as they prepared the primitive facilities and tried to attract pupils to the new school in Emmitsburg. However, Elizabeth's friend, Archbishop Carroll, introduced her to the leading Catholic families of Maryland, and their daughters soon became Elizabeth's students.

By February 1810, the Sisters of Charity had experienced enough financial success to allow Mother Seton to open a separate school for the needy of Emmitsburg. St. Joseph's

The Sisters of Charity of St. Joseph's

Eighty-six members joined the Sisters of Charity of St. Joseph's during Elizabeth Seton's lifetime. Other communities who claimed Mother Seton as their founder in the nineteenth century include: The Sisters of Charity at Mount St. Vincent-on-the-Hudson (New York, 1846); The Sisters of Charity of Mount St. Joseph (Cincinnati, Ohio, 1852); The Sisters of Charity of St. Vincent de Paul (Halifax, Nova Scotia, Canada, 1856); The Sisters of Charity of St. Elizabeth (Convent Station, New Jersey, 1859); and The Sisters of Charity of Seton Hill (Greensburg, Pennsylvania, 1870).

In 1947, all the existing communities of the Sisters of Charity in North America formed the conference of Mother Seton's Daughters. This conference developed into the Sisters of Charity Federation in the Vincentian-Setonian Tradition in 1996 with member congregations in the United States and Canada. By the beginning of the twenty-first century, thirteen religious congregations represented more than five thousand members located in seven states and two provinces. The Sisters of Charity is a voluntary membership association of Roman Catholic women who do not live in religious residences, or cloisters. Their mission in the Church calls them to a state of charity through ministry among the sick and the poor.

Academy and Day School was the first free Catholic school for girls staffed by the Sisters in the United States. Classes included reading, writing, arithmetic, music, needlework, and languages. Mother Seton excelled in her role as organizer, encourager, and spiritual director, and the school ran smoothly right from the start. She remained a devoted mother to her own children, but she also watched over the physical and spiritual welfare of each pupil entrusted to her.

The Rule of the Sisters of Charity of St. Joseph's was formally adopted in 1812. The French Common Rules of the Daughters of Charity, written by Vincent de Paul (1581–1660) in Paris in 1634 and adopted in final form thirty-eight years after his death, were adapted to fit the needs of the Catholic Church in America. The Rules establish the way in which the poor and needy would be administered, including how the sisters would lead their own lives in humility (having a modest self-awareness) and simplicity. Members of her community elected Elizabeth Seton to be the first mother superior, or head, of the Sisters of Charity. She held this position for the remainder of her life. By 1814, the sisterhood and its two schools in Emmitsburg were thriving, and

NEW YORK, SEPTEMBER 20, 1879.

A member of the Sisters of Charity administers aid to the sick and dying victims of yellow fever in Memphis, Tennessee, in 1879. *(© Bettmann/Corbis.)*

although education remained the Sisters' main mission, they took on the added responsibility of managing St. Joseph's Asylum in Philadelphia, Pennsylvania. It was the first Catholic orphanage in the United States. Three years later, the Sisters began the New York City Orphan Asylum, later named St. Patrick's Orphan Asylum.

By 1818, Mother Seton had lost three children to illness, and her own health was on the decline. Elizabeth died of tuberculosis in 1821 at the age of forty-six and was buried at St. Joseph's in Emmitsburg. Pope Paul VI canonized her St. Elizabeth Ann Seton on September 14, 1975.

For More Information

Books

Dirvin, Joseph I. *Mrs. Seton: Foundress of the American Sisters of Charity.* New ed. New York: Farrar, Straus and Giraux, 1975.

Gillis, Chester. *Roman Catholicism in America.* New York: Columbia University Press, 1999.

James, Edward T., ed. *Notable American Women 1607–1950: A Biographical Dictionary.* Cambridge, MA: Belknap Press of Harvard University Press, 1971.

Melville, Annabelle M. *Elizabeth Bayley Seton, 1774–1821.* New York: Scribner, 1951. Reprint, New York: Paulist Press, 1993.

Stone, Elaine Murray. *Elizabeth Bayley Seton: An American Saint.* New York: Paulist Press, 1993.

Web Sites

"History." *The Sisters of Charity Federation in the Vincentian-Setonian Tradition.* http://www.sisters-of-charity.org/history.htm/ (accessed on August 17, 2005).

McNeil, Betty Ann. "St. Elizabeth Ann Seton." *National Shrine of Saint Elizabeth Ann Seton.* http://www.emmitsburg.net/setonshrine/bio.htm (accessed on August 17, 2005).

"St. Elizabeth Ann Seton." *Catholic Online.* http://www.catholic.org/saints/saint.php?saint_id=180 (accessed on August 17, 2005).

John Sevier

Born September 23, 1745 (Rockingham County, Virginia)
Died September 24, 1815 (Fort Decatur, Alabama)

First governor of Tennessee

"In the state of Tennessee . . . be assured the Government will have my hearty support in opposing the aggressions of any invader whatever."

John Sevier served as the first, and only, governor of the state of Franklin from 1784 until its collapse in 1788. He went on to serve six terms as governor of the state of Tennessee after participating in the organization of the state in 1796. When his term as governor ended in 1809, Sevier was elected as a state senator representing Knox County, Tennessee. Sevier began his career as a pioneer and a soldier, but his leadership abilities soon carried him into public service. He exercised a lifelong commitment to western and southern expansion of American settlement during the early formative years of the United States. Sevier ended his political career as a member of the U.S. House of Representatives and advisor to U.S. president **James Madison** (1751–1836; served 1809–17; see entry in volume 2).

A soldier of fortune

John Sevier was born in September 1745 in the Shenandoah Valley of Virginia. His birthplace was on the frontier near present-day New Market, Virginia, a town Sevier himself founded as a young man. John was the eldest of seven children born to Joanna

John Sevier. *(Library of Congress.)*

Goade and Valentine Sevier. The Seviers were farmers, but Valentine also worked as a merchant, trader, and land speculator (one who buys unsettled land at inexpensive prices and resells it to settlers at higher prices for a profit). During a time of increased Native American attacks on the frontier, the family moved briefly to Fredericksburg, Virginia, where the children attended school. When the Seviers returned to the valley, John spent the next several years attending school in nearby Staunton. Sevier would never be sympathetic to Native Americans in the future as the nation expanded rapidly into Native American lands. By the time he was a teenager, John left the school and began to work at his father's store, becoming a partner around 1763.

At the age of sixteen, John Sevier married fifteen-year-old Sarah Hawkins. The couple spent the next decade moving around the Shenandoah Valley, farming and speculating in land. Wherever they settled, Sevier would also open a trading store and tavern to supplement the family's income. At one point, Sevier purchased a tract of land near his birthplace and laid out the town in lots. He sold the lots, erected a tavern and a store, and continued with the business of farming. Sevier named the town New Market and gave 3 acres of land to the Baptists to build a church for the growing community.

In 1773, the couple moved with Sevier's parents and several brothers to the southwest and settled on the Holston River in North Carolina (now Tennessee). Like many other speculators, the family was searching for larger tracts of land that were fertile and inexpensive but would soon become valuable as the population pushed westward. For the next few years, Sevier served as a militia captain under General **George Washington** (1732–1799; see entry in volume 2) while fighting Native Americans in what was called Lord Dunmore's War.

In 1776, the Seviers packed up and moved once again. They immigrated to the Watauga River region, along what is now northeast Tennessee, which had previously been home to the Cherokee nation of Native Americans. Sevier had visited the area over the past several years prior to the move and was already a commissioner for the Watauga Association, an organization formed to bring orderly settlement to the area. He was a member of the first court the association established to maintain order in the new settlement, serving as both a clerk and a judge. In 1776, Sevier was chosen to represent North Carolina as a delegate to the provincial congress, marking his entry into state politics. John and Sarah Sevier had ten children together before she died in 1780. A short time later, John married Catherine Sherrill, with whom he had eight more children.

The state of Franklin

When the provincial congress met in Halifax, North Carolina, Sevier was promoted to lieutenant colonel in the state militia. This post placed him in charge of the troops in Washington

District. The district was sparsely settled but covered the entire area of the future state of Tennessee. In the fall of 1780, as the American Revolution (1775–83) came to the frontier regions, Sevier led his troops to join gathering forces at the Battle of King's Mountain, just south of the North Carolina line. The resulting British surrender was a significant victory for the colonists. Sevier continued to lead his troops in surprise attacks against the British and their Native American allies throughout the war. He received high commendations from the North Carolina legislature for his efforts. His military success against British forces enhanced Sevier's reputation as a frontier leader and made him one of the most popular citizens in the West.

Shortly after the war ended in 1783, the Continental Congress passed a resolution declaring that Virginia, North Carolina, and Georgia must cede (give up) portions of their territory to provide for the formation of new western states. The resolution caused a division in the government of North Carolina: Some government officials agreed with the resolution; others did not want to surrender the western lands to the union. North Carolina's representative in Congress, William Blount (1749–1800; see box), supported the resolution and wanted to see the unimproved western lands developed. Some settlers in Greene, Sullivan, and Hawkins Counties began a movement to separate from the state of North Carolina. Leaders in the movement proposed the formation of the "State of Franklin," named after American statesman **Benjamin Franklin** (1706–1790; see entry in volume 1), within the disputed territory west of the Allegheny Mountains.

John Sevier was elected governor of the newly independent state of Franklin in March 1784. However, he faced strong opposition from those who remained loyal to North Carolina. Sevier served as governor of the proclaimed State of Franklin for three years. During that time, he was in communication with Spanish government officials about the possibility of forming an alliance with Spain. Sevier hoped to gain access to Spanish-controlled trading ports including New Orleans and spur Franklin's economic growth. In 1788, North Carolina declared the State of Franklin to be in revolt, and on October 10 Sevier was arrested. Sevier was accused of treason, but because of his popularity with the western pioneers, he was never tried. In fact, that same year

William Blount

William Blount was born and raised on a plantation in North Carolina. The Blounts were wealthy land speculators who dealt in large tracts of land on the American frontier. The family business prospered during the American Revolution, while Blount was serving in the state legislature. North Carolina had developed a plan to pay its soldiers with frontier land in the wilderness areas of present-day Tennessee. Blount and his business partners gained financially because of his position in the legislature dealing with soldiers' claims and land titles.

In 1784, Blount was elected Speaker of the House of Commons and then served two terms in the state senate. In the critical years after the war, Blount became interested in national politics and the creation of new states in the area west of the Appalachians. He expanded his influence when he was elected to serve in the Continental Congress of 1782–83 and reelected for 1786–87. Blount introduced policies that strengthened national control over Native American tribes in order to protect his company's extensive western land investments.

In 1790, President George Washington appointed Blount as governor of the new Southwest Territory and also superintendent

William Blount. *(© Bettmann/Corbis.)*

of Indian affairs in the region. In 1796, Blount presided over the state's constitutional convention that paved the way for organizing the state of Tennessee. He was then elected to serve as a U.S. senator for the new state. Personal financial problems led Blount to enter into a conspiracy with England to join the western Mississippi area with Britain. Blount resigned from the Senate in order to avoid impeachment for treason when his participation in the conspiracy was discovered.

he became a candidate for the North Carolina senate and was elected as the representative for Greene County. Before the end of the year, Sevier had received a full pardon on the treason charges and was commissioned brigadier general in the militia.

First governor of Tennessee

Sevier voted in favor of ratification of the U.S. Constitution at the North Carolina ratification convention in November 1789. In March 1790, he was again elected to the state legislature, where issues regarding the financial policy of the new government were addressed. With his term ending in 1791, Sevier was nominated to serve on a legislative council with Blount. In June 1790, President George Washington appointed Blount governor of the new "Territory South of the River Ohio." This territory consisted of land ceded to the United States by North Carolina in 1789. President Washington confirmed Sevier's nomination to serve on the legislative council of the new territory. The first session met in the summer of 1794. One of the council's responsibilities was to ensure that the territory met the federal government's conditions to organize a new state government. These conditions included appointing top officials of the territory including secretary and three judges, electing a legislature and sending nonvoting delegates to Congress when the population reached five thousand male residents, and developing a state constitution and applying to Congress for statehood when the population reached sixty thousand free inhabitants.

The Tennessee River provided the name for the proposed new state. The government of Tennessee began to function when the legislature organized in March 1796. Sevier was elected as the state's first governor and inaugurated on March 30. Blount and William Cocke (1748–1828) were selected to serve as U.S. senators. They left immediately to take their new posts in Philadelphia, Pennsylvania, where the national government was located at that time. Complications in Congress delayed Tennessee's admission into the union until June 1, 1796. Sevier completed the organization of the state and began to confront the problems of establishing a government on the frontier. The state underwent tremendous growth from 1796 until the beginning of the nineteenth century, going from less than 90,000 to more than 250,000 residents in a dozen years.

Sevier dealt with everything from land disputes and civic improvements to strained Native American relations and competition for militia commands. Military appointments were in great demand because officers wielded an even greater influence than civil officials in the state. Early in 1798, Sevier himself received an appointment as one of the brigadier generals of the provisional army. War between the United States and France was threatening to break out that spring. Sevier wrote to Washington expressing his willingness to raise an army and serve as its commander if the war became a reality.

Sevier served three consecutive, two-year terms as governor of Tennessee, the constitutional maximum. He then waited out the governorship of Archibald Roane (1760–1819) and returned in 1803 to serve another three terms, ending his run in 1809. Sevier had a long-standing feud with future U.S. president **Andrew Jackson** (1767–1845; see entry in volume 1), who was a judge on the state's superior court at the time. Sevier's vast holdings from land speculation produced accusations of land fraud by Jackson and others. Hostilities continued to grow, and eventually Jackson and Sevier agreed to settle the matter in a duel. However, the highly publicized confrontation never took place. No one was ever able to prove Sevier guilty of fraud, and people generally decided that Jackson's charges against Sevier must be false. Most people agreed that Sevier's ambition for achievement and wealth was tempered by an honorable character and a generous spirit.

Congressman Sevier

Several months after completing his final term as governor, Sevier was elected to the state senate. He entered the senate on September 20, 1809, representing Knox County. Initially, Sevier held positions on the land committee and the committee on militia law. His interest in the development of the western country earned him an appointment to a joint committee studying the navigation of different streams in the territory. The state assembly received, and adopted, the committee's report. The report recommended eliminating the Native American title to lands between the Tennessee River and the rivers flowing into Mobile Bay in order to secure free navigation. Throughout his life, Sevier had little sympathy for Native Americans, and he continually favored a policy of expansion into their territories. He had no intention of giving up any of the lands claimed by the Native Americans, and he took every opportunity to add to the land already possessed by the whites.

In 1811, Sevier left state politics and moved on to the national level. He was elected to represent his district in the U.S. House of Representatives of the Twelfth Congress on

March 4, 1811. Sevier used his influence to promote further western and southern expansion and eagerly supported war with England in 1812. Sevier was reelected in 1813 to serve in the Thirteenth Congress of the United States. He enjoyed his time in the capital and was an active part of the social life of the city. Sevier was a frequent guest at the home of President James Madison and other leading government officials. Sevier was never considered well-read, but he always made an effort to keep himself well-informed in his political dealings.

In March 1815, the same month Sevier began serving in the Fourteenth Congress, Madison appointed him to a commission to settle a boundary dispute resulting from a treaty signed with the Creek nation of Native Americans. The commission was charged with surveying and determining a boundary between Georgia and the land of the Creeks in Alabama. Sevier left Philadelphia in early June to begin his assignment. He worked through the summer and into the early fall on the border commission while stationed on the east bank of the Tallapoosa River near Fort Decatur in Alabama. Sevier died suddenly while reclining in his tent on the riverbank just one day after his seventieth birthday. He was buried at Fort Decatur, but his remains were removed in 1889. More than seventy years after his death, Sevier was laid to rest in a grave on the courthouse lawn in Knoxville, Tennessee, beneath a monument erected in his honor.

For More Information

Books

Driver, Carl S. *John Sevier: Pioneer of the Old Southwest*. Chapel Hill: University of North Carolina Press, 1932.

Gilmore, James R. *John Sevier as a Commonwealth-Builder*. New York: D. Appleton and Company, 1887. Reprint, Spartanburg, SC: Reprint Co., 1974.

Masterson, William H. *William Blount*. Baton Rouge: Louisiana State University Press, 1954. Reprint, New York: Greenwood Press, 1969.

Wilkie, Katharine E. *John Sevier: Son of Tennessee*. New York: J. Messner, 1958.

Web Sites

"John Sevier." *The Architect of the Capital*. http://www.aoc.gov/cc/art/nsh/sevier.cfm (accessed on August 22, 2005).

The Life and Times of General John Sevier. http://www.johnsevier.com/ (accessed on August 22, 2005).

"William Blount - North Carolina." *U.S. Army Center of Military History.* http://www.army.mil/CMH-pg/books/RevWar/ss/blount.htm (accessed on August 22, 2005).

Tecumseh

Born 1768 (Old Piqua, Ohio)
Died October 5, 1813 (Chatham, Ontario, Canada)

Shawnee tribal leader

T ecumseh was one of the greatest and most trusted leaders of the Shawnee nation. He aggressively resisted American settlement and influence in his native land and worked to build a united Native American front against the Americans. He spent much of his time traveling through the Ohio River valley and in the South, rallying other Native American groups to defend their lands. Tecumseh was a member of the Algonquian tribe, a widespread group that shared a common language. The Algonquians include the Shawnee, Delaware, Miami, and Ottawa, among others. Algonquian was one of the largest language groups in native America.

Tecumseh was an eloquent speaker and often served as the spokesman for the Shawnee at councils between white officials and the tribes of the Ohio River valley. His dignity of character brought him to the forefront in dealing with the leaders of the United States and Britain during a time of significant change throughout the world. Tecumseh's international importance earned him a place in history as one of the most influential Native Americans who ever lived.

"But have we not courage enough to defend our country and maintain our ancient independence. . . . The annihilation of our race is at hand unless we unite in one common cause against the common foe."

Tecumseh. *(© Bettmann/Corbis.)*

A shooting star

Tecumseh, also known as Tecumtha, was born along the Scioto River near Old Piqua in the Ohio Country during the winter of 1768. Ohio Country was the name given to the territory west of the Appalachian Mountains and north of the Ohio River in the early eighteenth century. Its borders roughly surrounded present-day Ohio, eastern Indiana, western Pennsylvania, and northwestern West Virginia. Tecumseh's mother was Methoataaskee, and his father was Pukeshinwa, a respected statesman and warrior of the Shawnee tribe. Tecumseh's name is often translated as Shooting Star or Blazing Comet. Although Shawnee names were highly symbolic, some people believe the name may have also been inspired by an actual astronomical event. Legend has it that Methoataaskee saw a meteor in the sky on the evening of Tecumseh's birth.

Methoataaskee and Pukeshinwa had four sons and a daughter before the remarkable birth of triplets in 1774. One of the three boys born that day died at birth. The remaining two would never know their father, because Pukeshinwa died in battle several months before they were born. Tecumseh was six years old when the triplets arrived.

When Tecumseh was born, the family was living in Old Piqua, the tribal capital since 1760. This village held the majority of warriors then living in the Ohio Country. Tecumseh's birth added to the numbers of Shawnee resettling in the Ohio River valley, which had been the Shawnee homeland prior to the French and Indian War (1754–63), a battle between Britain and France for control over North America that ended in 1763 with a British victory (see box). The increasing size of their population during this time helped ensure the survival of the Shawnee during a time when white settlement in the region was also increasing. Over the next several decades, the increased Shawnee population intimidated many non–Native Americans who opted against settling in the region. As a result, the Shawnee were able to gather sufficiently large forces to defend their lands.

A vanishing culture

The British fought in the French and Indian War, in the hopes of forcing France out of North America and gaining control over the North American frontier. However, after winning the war, British leaders were immediately faced with a Native American uprising. The Shawnee joined the revolt in June 1763 because they distrusted the British and were determined to defend against continued threats to their land. The Native Americans launched attacks on white homesteads and settlements until a tentative peace was reached in 1764. Pukeshinwa eventually moved his family out of Chillicothe and helped found Kispoko Town. There, he rose to the rank of chief. The Shawnee had a council of civil chiefs, both male and female, who led the tribe during times of peace. During

The French and Indian War

Tecumseh was born into a society that had experienced war between distant European powers over claims to the very land the Shawnee still occupied. Much resentment among Native Americans resulted from these foreign incursions. In addition, European interest in the Ohio Country increased around the same time that Native American tribes from the Atlantic Coast were being pushed westward by expanding colonial settlement along the Atlantic seaboard. The arrival of these Native Americans from east of the Appalachian Mountains placed more pressure on the homelands of peoples who had traditionally lived there for centuries.

Both the French and the British had claimed ownership of the Ohio Country since the early eighteenth century. French explorers first went to the region in search of animal furs in the 1660s. They built trading posts there to exchange European goods for furs trapped by local Native Americans. When Native American tribes exhausted the fur supply in their own area, they often moved and took control of land occupied by weaker tribes in order to continue supplying the Europeans.

Living with the Europeans had advantages and disadvantages for the Native Americans. European tools, materials, and weapons brought the Native Americans more efficient means of gathering food and fighting tribal enemies. However, the trade also made them dependent upon the whites. Many tribes feared the loss of their lands and culture. European settlers built fences, burned vast prairies, dammed free-running streams, and cut down woodlands. Even tribes who wanted peaceful relations with the new settlers were subject to extinction by new diseases the whites brought with them.

Both French and British merchants engaged in the fur trade, but the British were more interested in eventually farming the fertile land in the Ohio Country. In the mid-1750s, the French began pushing further eastward toward the Appalachians, establishing military and trading posts. Alarmed by the French expansion onto lands Britain thought it controlled, Britain launched a defense of the lands. The use of force marked the start of the French and Indian War in North America. The French gained an early advantage because of their stronger alliance with Native Americans, who feared that the growing number of British colonists along the Atlantic coast would continue moving west and drive them from their land. The British were ultimately victorious in the war and acquired most French possessions in North America, including the Ohio Country. They owned most of present-day Canada and all land between the Atlantic seaboard and the Mississippi River, with the exception of Florida.

A treaty was signed in 1763, signaling the end to open hostilities. However, owning the land and controlling it were two different matters. Native Americans still stood ready to defend their territory. The British government issued the Proclamation of 1763, which made it illegal for British colonists to settle the Ohio Country. The purpose of the proclamation was to prevent bloodshed and reduce military expenses in the American colonies. However, the colonists believed the war had been fought to open access to the rich farmland. The proclamation fueled the fire of the American Revolution, because the colonists were determined to claim more land and they were willing to fight for that cause.

times of conflict, the war chief became the principal leader and held his own councils.

A peaceful decade followed the move to Kispoko, but then Virginians began to move westward to settle the area now known as Kentucky. The arriving frontiersmen and the high Shawnee birthrates fueled the need for more land. Before long, white settlers were soon spilling over the Appalachian Mountains in greater numbers onto Native American land. Conflicts over the land intensified with each passing year. The Shawnee banded together against the forces of the British colonial governor of Virginia, John Murray (1732–1809), Earl of Dunmore. They met at the Battle of Point Pleasant on the Ohio River on October 10, 1774, where the Shawnee were defeated. Pukeshinwa was killed, and the two sides reached a temporary agreement to end the hostilities. However, the arrangement was not satisfactory to all the Shawnee and drove a wedge between the various groups who belonged to the tribe. The division within the tribe would intensify with the onset of the American Revolution (1775–83).

During the American Revolution, both the British and the Americans recognized the military potential of the armed warriors living on the frontier, and they competed for Native American support. The Native Americans mostly wanted to protect their territory against the colonists' westward expansion. For that reason, they sided with the British, who had banned white settlement of the Ohio Country. The colonists were willing to go to war to gain control of the region but faced tremendous opposition from the British and their native allies.

The Panther and the Prophet

Beginning in 1777, the Shawnee assisted the British by attacking American settlers on the Kentucky and Virginia frontiers. Tecumseh was too young to participate in these raids. After the death of their father, Tecumseh's oldest brother, Cheeseekau, was left to raise him. Cheeseekau trained Tecumseh to hunt and had him spend time with tribal elders so he would learn the stories that made up the history of their proud people. Tecumseh was very athletic and led his companions in childhood sports. He excelled in the use of the bow and arrow and showed an early interest in war games. His brother trained him as a warrior and taught him courage in battle, but he also schooled Tecumseh in the virtues of justice, compassion, and a love of truth. Tecumseh carried these lessons with him and gained respect from both his allies and his enemies. Tecumseh was taller than most Shawnee and grew to be a very strikingly handsome man with a commanding presence. He developed into a brave warrior and eventually became a Shawnee leader.

The American Revolution ended in 1783 with the defeat of the British, but tensions remained high between the Americans and the Native Americans. Violence escalated as American settlers moved into the territory they had won from the British. The United States formed the Northwest Territory in 1787; this area included the land that would become the states of Ohio, Illinois, Indiana, Michigan, Wisconsin, and parts of Minnesota. The Native Americans of the Northwest Territory wanted to keep their lands and fought a series of successful battles to secure the areas they inhabited and their hunting grounds. Tecumseh's reputation grew during this series of victories. President **George Washington** (1732–1799; served 1789–97; see entry in volume 2) assigned General **Anthony Wayne** (1745–1796; see entry in volume 2) to challenge the Native Americans, and Wayne defeated them at the Battle of Fallen Timbers on August 20, 1794. The Native Americans surrendered and signed the Treaty of Greenville in 1795. The agreement released the Native Americans' claim on most of southern and eastern Ohio to the United States.

Not all Native Americans agreed to the surrender of lands. Tecumseh would not attend the signing of the treaty. He believed the best way to stop the advancing white population was to form a confederacy of Native American tribes. He reasoned that a Native American alliance stood a better chance against the increasing pressures from the settlers and from the American military. To increase support for his alliance, Tecumseh visited the Native American tribes located throughout the region west of the Appalachian Mountains. He traveled the length of the region, from Canada to the Gulf of Mexico, urging Native American peoples to band together. Tecumseh did not intend direct hostility against the United States, but he condemned white influence and land purchases and called for Native Americans to return to a traditional way of life, free from foreign influences.

Tecumseh's younger brother was named Lalawethik (also Laloeshiga; c. 1768–1834), which means Panther with a Handsome Tail. In 1805, this brother had a vision, and his name was changed to Elskwatawa (also Tenskwatawa), or the Prophet. Claiming to be a medium of the Supreme Spirit, he revealed his vision. It called for the Native Americans to return to their traditional ways and turn their backs on the contaminating influence of the whites. The two brothers established a village called Prophetstown in the Indiana Territory in 1808. It was located on the Wabash River, below the mouth of the Tippecanoe River. A large following of supporters joined the two brothers, and the population of Prophetstown grew. Tecumseh put a great deal of energy into his goal of intertribal unity. He continued meeting with British and American officials, and by 1810 he announced that his confederacy was nearing completion.

Tecumseh's brother Elskwatawa, also known as the Prophet. *(© Hulton Archive/Getty Images.)*

The War of 1812

William Henry Harrison (1773–1841), governor of the Indiana Territory, was becoming increasingly alarmed at the number of Native Americans gathering at Prophetstown. While Tecumseh was away recruiting in the South, Harrison led an army toward the village. On November 7, 1811, the American army defeated the Native Americans, who were led by Tecumseh's brother, the Prophet. The village and its provisions were destroyed at what became known as the Battle of Tippecanoe. Upon his return, Tecumseh tried to bring his followers back together, but his brother's reputation was tarnished because he had taken no active role in the fighting, and as a result, the confederacy weakened. However, the battle brought public attention to the Native American confederacy and inspired continued British support for the Native American cause.

In 1812, President **James Madison** (1751–1836; served 1809–17; see entry in volume 2) asked Congress to declare war on Britain. In addition to supporting Native American resistance to American settlement in the Northwest Territory,

The Battle of Tippecanoe. *(© Bettmann/Corbis.)*

Britain had been kidnapping sailors from American ships and hindering U.S. trade with France. Tecumseh and his remaining followers allied themselves with the British when war was declared. The Native Americans hoped that if the British won, they would return the Native Americans' homeland to them. In turn, the British needed their Native American allies in order to defend Canada from an invasion by the United States.

The British and Indian forces were able to work together because of the leadership skills of Tecumseh, who was able to keep a wide range of tribal leaders organized as an effective alliance. The U.S. assault on Canada was driven back, and Tecumseh led his warriors in a division of the British army that captured Detroit. However, the United States won a key naval battle against a British fleet on Lake Erie, breaking Detroit's supply line. The combined British and Native American force retreated from Detroit through Ontario, Canada. American forces pursued them and then defeated them at the Battle of the Thames on October 5, 1813. Tecumseh died in the battle. His united Native American resistance to American settlement died with him.

Two children are reported to have survived Tecumseh. He had a daughter with a Cherokee wife and a son, Paukeesaa, by a Shawnee wife named Mamate. The war reached a draw in late 1814, and resulting peace negotiations failed to adequately protect Native Americans. Between 1831 and 1833, the U.S. government relocated the Shawnee from their land in Ohio to reservations (areas of land set apart by the government on which the Native Americans would live) in Oklahoma and Kansas.

Several war veterans tried to gain political advantage in the form of election votes by claiming to have killed the great chief Tecumseh. Numerous accounts of his death were recorded and were subject to debate for years. Richard Mentor Johnson (1780–1850) was known as "Old Tecumseh" and "Tecumseh Johnson." He claimed to have personally killed the chief at the Battle of the Thames and rose to the position of vice president of the United States, serving from 1837 until 1841. William Henry Harrison was dubbed "Old Tippecanoe" and was elected to Congress in 1816. His association with Tecumseh proved useful in his presidential campaign, too. Helped by the slogan "Tippecanoe and Tyler, Too" (Tyler being U.S. senator John Tyler [1790–1862] of Virginia, Harrison's running mate), Harrison became the ninth president of the United States in 1841.

For More Information

Books

Clark, Jerry E. *The Shawnee.* Lexington: University Press of Kentucky, 1993.

Eckert, Allan W. *A Sorrow in Our Heart: The Life of Tecumseh.* New York: Bantam Books, 1992.

Klinck, Carl F., ed. *Tecumseh: Fact and Fiction in Early Records.* Englewood Cliffs, NJ: Prentice-Hall, 1961.

Sugden, John. *Tecumseh: A Life.* New York: Henry Holt and Company, 1998.

Turner, Wesley B. *The War of 1812: The War for Canada.* Toronto, Ontario: Grolier Limited, 1982.

Web Sites

"Tecumseh." *The Ohio Historical Society.* http://www.ohiohistorycentral.org/ohc/history/h_indian/people/tecumseh.shtml (accessed on August 22, 2005).

Mercy Otis Warren

Born September 25, 1728 (Barnstable, Massachusetts)
Died October 19, 1814 (Plymouth, Massachusetts)

Historian, poet

M ercy Otis Warren was an American poet and a historian of the nation's early years. She is often referred to as the first lady of the American Revolution (1775–83), because leading political figures from the colonies consulted with her about their plans for independence. She participated in the revolutionary cause through her publications, which promoted democracy (a government ruled through majority decisions made by the people) at a time when most Americans still thought of it as an impossible notion. Warren promoted political and legal rights for women along with American independence. As the colonists' rebellion against British rule increased, Warren became one of the most important women in early American history. Her books provide historians with details and commentary on the founding of the United States from a woman's perspective.

"History . . . the deposite [description] of crimes, and the record of everything disgraceful or honorary to mankind, requires a just knowledge of character, to investigate the sources of action."

The beginning of Mercy

Mercy Otis was born September 25, 1728, in Barnstable, Massachusetts, on Cape Cod. She was the first daughter and the third of thirteen children born to Mary Allyne and Colonel James Otis. Mercy was named for her father's mother. Her

Mercy Otis Warren. *(Library of Congress.)*

ancestors included Puritans (a Protestant group who advocated strict moral conduct and reform of the Church of England) who arrived at Plymouth, Massachusetts, on the *Mayflower* in 1620. The passengers on board this ship were among the hearty settlers who began the British colonization of North America. By the eighteenth century, the Otis family was well established in Barnstable.

James Otis was a farmer and militia officer whose income allowed the family to live comfortably. He later studied law and served as a judge in the county court. Mercy was especially close to her eldest brother, James, who was called Jemmy. The Otises ensured that their sons were prepared for college, but the Otis daughters received no formal education; this was the common practice at that time. However, Mercy was a highly intelligent girl, and she wanted to learn. She was allowed to sit in on her brothers' lessons in history and literature, but not their formal study of Latin and Greek. Their uncle, the Reverend Jonathan Russell, tutored the children. Mercy spent a great deal of time browsing through his library.

As the daughter of one of the county's leaders, Mercy frequently overheard political discussions. She found that she enjoyed politics and eagerly joined in the conversations with Jemmy and her father. When Jemmy graduated from Harvard College (now Harvard University) in 1743, Mercy took a rare trip away from Cape Cod to attend the commencement ceremony. She continued to sit in on Jemmy's lessons again when he returned home to prepare for his master of arts degree.

The rock at Plymouth

On November 14, 1754, at the age of twenty-six, Mercy married James Warren. Warren was a farmer, merchant, and, like Jemmy Otis, a Harvard graduate. The couple met through their families, who shared business and legal dealings. Mercy and James had very similar backgrounds and interests, including strong religious and political beliefs. They even shared the same great-great-grandfather, who was a passenger on the *Mayflower*. Their marriage was one of mutual love and respect and would last more than fifty years.

Mercy moved a few miles north of Barnstable to join James at the Warren family estate in Plymouth, Massachusetts. The main farm, located on the Eel River, was called Clifford Farm. Mercy cared for her ailing father-in-law while James began developing a career in the colonial legislature. In 1757, James inherited his father's estate, which included a house in Plymouth called Winslow House. The home stood at the intersection of North and Main Streets, the thoroughfare between Boston and Cape Cod. That summer, the Warrens moved to Plymouth to prepare for the birth of their first child, James Jr. Four more sons followed: Winslow arrived in 1759, followed by Charles, Henry, and finally George in 1766.

Mercy found herself at the center of a lively family of politicians, who were also Patriots (people who supported American independence): Her husband had been elected to the Massachusetts House of Representatives in 1765; her father was working as a justice of the peace; and her brother Jemmy Otis was a leading spokesman for the Whig Party (a British political party that opposed a strong monarchy). As conflicts between the American colonies and the British government increased, the family's political activities drew Mercy closer to public affairs. The Warren home became a common meeting place for leading opponents of British royal policy within Massachusetts. Among them were **George Washington** (1732–1799; see entry in volume 2), **John Adams** (1735–1826; see entry in volume 1), **Alexander Hamilton** (1755–1804; see entry in volume 1), and the radical Samuel Adams (1722–1803). When the meetings shifted to Boston, Mercy was able to closely follow the political events through her husband's involvement and through correspondence with her brother.

Revolutionary thoughts

Jemmy Otis, an attorney with many contacts, had resigned his royal appointment in 1760 to become a leading spokesman for independence. He was one of the first colonial leaders to challenge Britain's authority in the colonies. Otis wrote a paper protesting British taxes and defining a concept of government based on the natural rights of the people. On February 24, 1761, he gave a famous speech declaring that taxation without representation by elected legislators was tyranny. However, Otis assured Britain that rebellion would be a last resort because the British American colonists would never desert their mother country unless they were driven to it. In 1769, Otis's fierce temper landed him in a fight that left him permanently injured from a blow to the head. After his injury, Mercy began to play a bigger role in the Revolution. Women had limited opportunities in politics at that time, so she chose a different path: She began to use pen and paper to champion the cause of independence in America.

In October 1772, the Warrens hosted a meeting at their home. Samuel Adams and other revolutionaries attended. They came up with the idea to form "committees of correspondence." These groups were formed in many Massachusetts towns to share opinions about Britain's policies. As the colony's rebellion against British rule grew, Mercy began to write political plays that she intended to have read, but not necessarily performed, to support the Patriot cause. Like the men of her family, Mercy was among those ready to throw out the colonial governor. She believed that America would be better served by a republican government: elected representatives who would govern by the consent of the people for the benefit of the people.

Mercy's first published work appeared in 1772. It was a five-act play titled *The Adulateur: A Tragedy As It Is Now Acted in Upper Servia*. The satire (a literary work that uses humor to criticize) cast the royal governor of Massachusetts, Thomas Hutchinson (1711–1780), as the villain "Rapatio." As the ruler of the mythical country of Servia, Rapatio is eager to destroy the colony. On the other side is the patriotic Brutus. He delivers passionate speeches of warning and resistance

James (Jemmy) Otis's temper often got him in trouble. Here, he responds to someone pouring water on him by throwing a stone at a window. *(The Granger Collection, New York.)*

and is modeled after Mercy's brother, Jemmy. Selections of the play were published in the *Massachusetts Spy* in two installments between March 26 and April 23. The play was released anonymously (without the author's name) because being a playwright was not considered proper for a woman at the time. *The Adulateur* was printed as a political pamphlet the following year with additional material added by another author.

Continues writing

Although still busy raising her five young boys, Mercy was now making her own contribution to the revolutionary cause. She had been writing poems and patriotic correspondence since the mid-1700s, but she shared her work only with friends and family. Mercy's views now reached a wide, welcoming audience of both male and female readers. In 1773, her Rapatio character appeared again, this time in a drama called *The Defeat*. Selections were published anonymously in the *Boston Gazette* and later in the *Massachusetts Spy*. In this three-act play, Mercy continued to portray British rulers as villains and used code names for specific political figures. Mercy's mocking attacks on those in power made them seem less powerful and gave the revolutionaries hope that they might triumph in their cause.

The Group was published in 1775, the same year the American Revolution began. In *The Group,* Mercy continued the attack on Britain but added some new villains because Thomas Hutchinson had been recalled to Europe. She also boldly made the point that women should be legally freed from husbands who suffered no legal consequences under existing law for neglecting and abusing them. *The Group* was published in pamphlet form later that year in Boston, New York, and Philadelphia.

Mercy continued writing after the onset of the American Revolution. She branched into prose and added her first female characters in her new publications. General James Warren was away at war for long periods of time, and the two corresponded while Mercy remained home with their young family. Mercy and James had developed a close relationship with future president of the United States John Adams and his wife, **Abigail Adams** (1744–1818; see entry in volume 1) over the years. The two women drew support from one another during the war. They were both extremely intelligent people who had much in common, including their large families and political husbands. Mercy was sixteen years older than Abigail, but they were at ease in each other's company.

In May 1777, James Warren was appointed to the new Navy Board for the Eastern Department and was headquartered in Boston. He failed to win election to the Massachusetts House of Representatives in May 1778, and Mercy's writings began to move away from attacks on the British. Instead, her work expressed a growing disapproval of the new direction of American politics.

A new nation

As the draft of the constitution for the new country began to take shape, two distinct factions formed. The Federalists, under John Adams, supported the new constitution adopted at the Constitutional Convention in 1787. Those who criticized the proposed constitution and threatened to reject it were called Anti-Federalists. The Warrens were among the minority who opposed ratification of the Constitution in its final form. In 1779, James Warren declined selection as a possible member of the Continental Congress, in part because he was concerned about Mercy's health. She experienced severe headaches and was beginning to have problems reading and writing. The Warrens' fortunes continued to decline, and many of their powerful associates began to consider them politically suspect after Shays's Rebellion (see box). James Warren's political career revived in 1787 because his constituents appreciated his sympathy with the cause of the people during Shays's Rebellion. He was reelected to the Massachusetts House of Representatives and became Speaker of the House.

In 1788, Mercy wrote and published *Observations on the New Constitution,* which came out in both Boston and New York. The nineteen-page pamphlet criticized the U.S. Constitution because it originally lacked a bill of rights (a formal statement giving a group of people rights considered essential) and provided no term limits (restrictions on the length of time a person could hold public office) for elected officials or safeguards against a standing (professional) army. (The Bill of Rights was added to the Constitution and ratified on December 15, 1791.) Mercy continued to write and was finally able to publish a volume of poetry under her own name for the first time. Titled *Poems, Dramatic and Miscellaneous,* the book was issued in Boston in 1790. She dedicated this work to George Washington.

The year 1791 was a difficult one for Mercy. One of her sons, Winslow, was killed in action when the Native American forces of **Little Turtle** (c. 1752–1812; see entry in volume 2) defeated General Arthur St. Clair's army on November 4 in the Northwest Territory, west of the Appalachian Mountains. Although another son, Charles, had preceded him in death, Winslow was the son in whom Mercy had placed her hopes for the future of the Warrens.

Shays's Rebellion

In September 1786, a popular uprising called Shays's Rebellion broke out in Massachusetts; it was a protest against the financial policies of the new state government. Because of the war, Congress was nearly broke, commerce had suffered, and paper money was rare. This resulted in Revolution soldiers returning from the war to find that they had little money and could not afford to pay the high taxes demanded by the government. The government's response to the plight of these debt-ridden former soldiers was indifference in the courts. With the spirit of revolution still fresh in their minds, the people raised a ragged army to protest the court decisions and placed Daniel Shays (c. 1747–1825), a veteran of the Revolution, in command.

Participants in Shays's Rebellion demanded greater circulation of paper money, reduced taxes, and a break on their debts. The rebels' chief target was the courts, which were sending former soldiers to prison for debt. Their small army began to forcibly prevent courts in western Massachusetts counties from holding court sessions. Many of the upper social classes of Boston and eastern Massachusetts became alarmed, and the militia was ordered to put down the open revolt. But the state, like the rebel soldiers, had little cash. It had no way to pay the militia, and they refused to take to the field without guaranteed pay. Boston merchants took up a private collection to cover the expenses

Fighting erupts during Shays's Rebellion, a protest against the financial policies of the Massachusetts government. *(© Bettmann/Corbis.)*

of the military campaign, but this caused a negative public response because such an action clearly violated the U.S. Articles of Confederation, the nation's first constitution.

Shays's Rebellion was soon extinguished as the Massachusetts militia arrived at the U.S. arsenal in Springfield before the rebel force and successfully defended it from attack and capture. The rebels dispersed and were chased by the militia before being captured. However, Shays's Rebellion forced the country to go beyond the colonial thinking upon which the national government was built.

History of a revolution

For three decades, Mercy had been recording the events that took place around her as the young nation developed. She was impressed by the historic nature of the times she lived in and preserved her correspondence with the leading figures of the Revolution. She published the letters in 1805 under the title *History of the Rise, Progress, and Termination of the American Revolution*. The three-volume set provided an insider's view on the Revolution and the founding of the nation. It was offered for sale, an unusual occurrence for a work written by a woman, especially one of Mercy's social standing. Her daring set an important example for women authors who followed her.

History was received with critical acclaim by many, but it met with distinct disapproval from Mercy's longtime friend, John Adams. Mercy was sharply critical of Adams's character in her published letters. Vehemently disagreeing with his Federalist political position of favoring a strong central government, Mercy charged he was vain, corrupt, and undoing the gains made by the Revolution by leading the nation toward a monarchy. The two exchanged a series of heated letters beginning in the summer of 1807, and their friendship was severely tested until a mutual friend helped them reconcile in 1812. The ten letters from John Adams and six letters from Mercy were later published as *Correspondence Relating to Her History* in 1876. Although Adams did not care for Mercy's views, her letters to him did reveal a change in her former opinions. Mercy had come to appreciate the U.S. Constitution, which she had opposed in the 1780s. She wrote optimistically of American republicanism and its chances for survival.

By the early 1800s, Mercy's eyes gave her so much trouble that she gave up reading and writing on her own. Her eldest son, James Jr., assisted her in working with manuscripts and correspondence. During her final years, Mercy focused on the social issues of educational reform and equal rights for women. Except for her problems with eyesight, she remained in good health until the end of her life. Her beloved husband, James, died in 1808 after fifty-four years of marriage.

During her eighty-six years, Mercy had never traveled far beyond eastern Massachusetts. Except for a few years in Milton, Massachusetts, she had spent most of her life in historic Plymouth. She died at Winslow House on October 19, 1814, and was buried at Burial Hill in Plymouth. Notice of her death in Boston's newspapers competed with reports on the War of 1812 (1812–15), the latest conflict between America and Britain.

For More Information

Books

Anthony, Katharine. *First Lady of the Revolution: The Life of Mercy Otis Warren.* Garden City, NY: Doubleday, 1958. Reprint, Port Washington, NY: Kennikat Press.

Fritz, Jean. *Cast for a Revolution: Some American Friends and Enemies 1728–1814.* Boston: Houghton Mifflin, 1972.

James, Edward T., ed. *Notable American Women 1607–1950: A Biographical Dictionary.* Cambridge, MA: Belknap Press of Harvard University Press, 1971.

Richards, Jeffrey H. *Mercy Otis Warren.* New York: Twayne Publishers, 1995.

Web Sites

"Mercy Otis Warren." *The Massachusetts Historical Society.* http://www.masshist.org/bh/mercybio.html (accessed on August 22, 2005).

"Mercy Otis Warren (1728–1814)." *Sunshine for Women.* http://www.pinn.net/~sunshine/whm2002/warren.html (accessed on August 22, 2005).

George Washington

Born February 22, 1732 (Westmoreland County, Virginia)
Died December 14, 1799 (Mount Vernon, Virginia)

First U.S. president, military commander

Known as the Father of His Country, George Washington was commander of the Continental Army from 1775 through 1783, the entire period of the American Revolution. He then became the first president of the United States, serving from 1789 to 1797. The nation's capital and a state are named after him, as are numerous landmarks across the nation. As if in anticipation of his forthcoming historic role, Washington crafted a very formal, authoritative, and dignified persona for himself. In his military career, he defeated the British and won American independence, crushed the Native American resistance to U.S. settlement on the frontier, and decisively put down rebellions in the new republic. During his presidency, the new national government was formed, economic prosperity was established, and new treaties with Britain and Spain were signed. Perhaps one of his most crucial tasks was transferring the nation's overwhelming respect for him to the position of the president.

"It is our true policy to steer clear of permanent alliances with any portion of the foreign world; so far, I mean, as we are now at liberty to do it."

Family of wealth

George Washington was born in February 1732 in Westmoreland County of rural Virginia to Augustine Washington

479

George Washington. *(© Hulton Archive/Getty Images.)*

and Mary Ball. Augustine's first wife died, and he married Mary the year before George's birth. Augustine was schooled in England and kept busy managing his Virginia estates. George's ancestors received lands in England from King Henry VIII (1491–1547; reigned 1509–47), and they held various public offices there. However, political turmoil in England led Augustine's grandfather, John Washington (1631–1677), to immigrate to the Virginia colony in 1657. An ambitious man, John Washington acquired considerable land, built sawmills, and opened iron mines. John sent Augustine to England for his schooling. Augustine had four children with his first wife and six with Mary. He died in April 1743 when young George was just eleven. George's oldest half brother, Lawrence Washington, became his guardian. Being the eldest son, Lawrence inherited the well-developed estate of Little Hunting Creek from Augustine.

Lawrence raised George well. George spent his early years on a farm on the Rappahannock River near present-day Fredericksburg, Virginia. He learned much about the outdoors and farming, including tobacco growing and raising stock. He attended school locally off and on from seven to fifteen years of age. George was good at mathematics and learned surveying (examining and measuring land). The family grew larger when Lawrence married Anne Fairfax of the prestigious Lord Thomas Fairfax family. Lawrence built a house and named his 2,500-acre estate Mount Vernon. George grew up in the world of upper society, learning English manners and customs and gaining knowledge of the cultured world from Anne and Lawrence.

Land surveyor

Washington chose surveying as his profession. In 1748, Lord Fairfax (1692–1782), owner of 5 million acres in northern Virginia and the Shenandoah Valley, sent a party including sixteen-year-old Washington to survey some of his frontier holdings. It was one of Washington's first experiences living on the frontier for an extended period.

The following year, Lord Fairfax helped Washington obtain an appointment as a professional surveyor. For more than two years, Washington surveyed constantly throughout the northern Virginia region, often in wilderness settings that served to toughen him in body and mind. He also gained an interest in westward expansion and land speculation, making his first purchase—nearly 1,500 acres of western land—at age eighteen. Land speculation is the buying of cheap, undeveloped frontier land with the intent of reselling it to settlers at a higher price to make a profit. It was a common means of gaining wealth in early America.

Plantation owner

In 1751, Lawrence contracted tuberculosis. The Washington family, including George, went to Barbados in the West Indies in hopes that Lawrence would recover with the change in climate. There, George contracted smallpox, but he established a valuable immunity that would later protect him in his military life, when smallpox ravaged Continental Army troops. The family returned from Barbados the following year, but Lawrence soon died. At age twenty, George found himself the inheritor of Mount Vernon, one of Virginia's most prestigious estates.

For the next twenty years, Washington steadily increased the size of his estate to 8,000 acres and expanded the Mount Vernon house. He also experimented in the newest agricultural techniques. Though he owned forty-nine slaves by 1760, Washington disapproved of slavery. He refused to sell slaves, because he did not want to disrupt their families. As a result, he eventually owned three hundred slaves, more than he really needed.

Land speculation and tobacco farming through slave labor gained him solid acceptance among the Virginia upper class. Greatly concerned about public perceptions, Washington spent lavishly on clothes. He enjoyed theater, dancing, card games, fox hunting, billiards, horseracing, and duck hunting. At 6 feet 3 inches and 190 pounds, he was an excellent athlete. He had broad shoulders, heavy brows, a large straight nose, and piercing blue-gray eyes. He walked with a dignified air of invincibility. He excelled at firearms and horsemanship. During this period, he became very prominent in the community and was an active member of the Episcopal Church.

French and Indian War

George became active in military matters in the early 1750s. He was appointed an officer in the Virginia militia, the same position Lawrence had held. At this time the French were establishing fur-trading posts deeper into territory claimed by the British on the west side of the Appalachian Mountains. The French were also grooming friendly relations with Native Americans living in the area. In October 1753, Virginia's colonial governor, Robert Dinwiddie (1693–1770), sent Washington to warn the French in the Ohio River valley that they were trespassing on land claimed by Britain. Leading a small group of frontiersmen, Washington journeyed in winter conditions to a French outpost near Lake Erie. The French replied that they intended to settle the Ohio River area. After narrowly missing being shot in a skirmish with Native Americans and falling in a freezing stream, Washington brought the news back to Dinwiddie at Williamsburg in mid-January 1754.

Dinwiddie appointed Washington lieutenant colonel and gave him command of about 160 militiamen to take back to the Ohio River valley. Their assignment was to remove the French from the area. Washington and his troops left Alexandria, Virginia, in April 1754. The French by now had established a post at present-day Pittsburgh, Pennsylvania, which they named Fort Duquesne. Washington established a nearby position and on May 28, 1754, ambushed a small French detachment, killing its commander. These were the first shots of what would become the French and Indian War (1754–63), a struggle between the British and French over the control of lands in North America. The French soon counterattacked with a force of 1,200 soldiers and Native Americans, forcing Washington to surrender. Washington and his men were allowed to return to Virginia, unarmed, after promising not to build any more forts in Ohio for a year.

The British responded by sending regular army troops to Virginia in February 1755 under General Edward Braddock (1695–1755). Washington was appointed personal assistant to Braddock. Ignoring Washington's advice not to fight in an orderly, European fashion, Braddock's troops were ambushed by the French and Native Americans, suffering great losses, including Braddock himself. Washington led the survivors back to Virginia to safety.

Despite his defeats, Washington had showed coolness and great determination under fire. He rose to the position of commander of all Virginia colonial troops at twenty-three years of age. He also showed resolve by hanging deserters as an example to others. Washington was responsible for defending a 300-mile mountainous frontier with a force of only three hundred poorly paid, poorly fed, poorly clothed soldiers.

Finally, in November 1758, a combined force of British soldiers and Washington's colonial troops marched to Fort Duquesne to oust the French. However, the French burned and abandoned the post just before their arrival. The colonists renamed the location Fort Pitt (later known as Pittsburgh). Despite his victory, Washington was unhappy by the slowness of the war, the lack of support by Virginia leaders, and the failure of British commanders to give him a higher rank, which he felt he had been promised. As a result of the war, Washington had become a hero in America, but he had developed great hostility toward the British. Washington resigned with an honorary rank of brigadier general.

Return to civilian life

After resigning his military post, Washington got married. **Martha Washington** (1732–1802; see entry in volume 2) became the general's wife on January 6, 1759. Born Martha Dandridge, she was the widow of Daniel Parke Custis, with whom she had two children, John (nicknamed Jacky) and Martha (nicknamed Patsy). She was also one of the wealthier people in Virginia, owning some 15,000 acres and a large number of slaves. They proved an excellent match in temperament, and George showed great affection toward his two step-children. However, Jacky proved difficult and had a rebellious spirit. Patsy died in 1773, and her death proved a tragic loss for the family. Following Jacky's death in November 1781, George and Martha adopted two of his four children, Nelly and "Wash" Custis, and raised them at Mount Vernon as their own children.

As one of the wealthiest landowners in Virginia, Washington closely watched over the operation of his several wheat and tobacco farms during the following years. Washington had his own flour mill, blacksmith shop, brick kiln, carpenters, and stonemasons. He regularly ordered large amounts of supplies, including farm implements, from England. Mount Vernon was the location of many parties and much entertainment; its porch overlooked the Potomac River. Washington wore the finest clothes from London.

A political career

In addition to overseeing his landholdings, Washington began serving in the House of Burgesses (the local government) in 1759. From 1760 to 1774, he also served as justice of the peace for Fairfax County, with the court located in nearby Alexandria. As unrest grew in the colonies over British policies, Washington remained a loyal subject, even though he was irritated by the new rules, such as the restriction on expansion of colonial settlement beyond the Appalachians. This rule hindered his interest in land speculation. Through the 1760s, he steadily showed increasing signs of supporting those more radical opponents of new British taxes such as the Stamp Act of 1765.

As the spirit of rebellion grew, the royal governor of Virginia dissolved the House of Burgesses. Many of its members secretly gathered to continue conducting colonial business. Washington was one of those. However, he still favored using peaceful economic actions to protest British policies; he was not yet ready to take up arms. However, the Intolerable Acts, passed in 1774, imposed harsh measures on the colonies for their growing rebellious mood. The passage of this legislation firmly established Washington's opposition to the British monarchy.

Washington took part in the meeting of the colonial legislature on May 27, 1774, that called for formation of a Continental Congress later that year. He made a speech offering his military service against the British if needed. Washington was elected one of seven Virginia delegates to attend the first meeting of the Continental Congress in September 1774. He showed up at the meeting in Philadelphia in full military dress and provided advice on military matters to the Congress. The delegates chose a more peaceful course and sent a list of grievances to Britain. At this time, Washington continued shifting his viewpoint toward military action rather than sending petitions back to Britain. However, he still did not advocate complete independence for America.

Commander of the Continental Army

Washington assumed leadership of the Virginia militia in 1774 and was elected to the Second Continental Congress that met in Philadelphia in May 1775. By the time of the meeting, fighting had broken out between colonists and the British army near Boston on April 19, 1775. As the best-known military man in America, Washington was readily chosen as commander of the Continental Army in June. He refused to accept a salary but asked that his expenses be paid.

Washington took command of a loosely organized force of New England militia outside of Boston. For the next eight years, General Washington showed decisiveness in his actions as he strove to bring discipline to the inexperienced troops. Washington spent much of his energy mobilizing the states and Congress to contribute to the military mission.

On numerous occasions, the military campaign seemed on the brink of disaster, but Washington had adapted new military strategies of rapid movements that kept the army going. The new strategies avoided major confrontations with the larger British army that was better trained and equipped. Instead, the Continental Army focused on smaller skirmishes and quick retreats that kept the large British army on the move without major victories. Considering the ragged, underfed soldiers serving under him, this was a major accomplishment. Finally, in September 1781, Washington skillfully led the victory over a British force of seven thousand soldiers at Yorktown, Virginia. The events at Yorktown signaled that victory in the war was in reach, but the battles dragged on for two more years.

Morale among the troops remained low, and in May 1782 Washington angrily responded to a letter from troops suggesting he should be king and replace the ineffective Continental Congress. Washington believed that to establish a monarchy rather than a republic (a government run by officials elected by the public for the benefit of the public) would be contrary to everything for which they had sacrificed. Following the evacuation of British forces from New York in November 1783, Washington traveled to the Continental Congress meeting in Annapolis, Maryland, where he submitted his resignation on December 23. He also presented a detailed account of his expenses over the past eight years for repayment. He arrived home at Mount Vernon by Christmas Eve. At that time, the world was full of monarchs and military dictators, and Washington's voluntary resignation was unheard of. However, resigning brought Washington greater respect and admiration worldwide than his military exploits.

Back to Mount Vernon

Washington spent the next four years at Mount Vernon, making repairs from the years of general neglect. Having suffered great personal economic loss while away at war, he successfully began to make the plantation prosperous again. Also, being a leading figure of the new nation, he was obliged to regularly entertain foreign visitors, Native American delegations, and

George and Martha Washington with family and friends on the grounds of Mount Vernon. *(© Bettmann/Corbis.)*

visitors from other states. Rarely did the Washingtons have dinner alone.

Through the 1780s, Washington became dismayed with the functioning of the new nation under the Articles of Confederation, the nation's first constitution. He increasingly urged major governmental reforms including the need for taxing powers. However, Washington largely stayed away from politics and did not offer to help in forming a new government. Nonetheless, a meeting between representatives of Virginia and Maryland over navigation of the Potomac River was held at Mount Vernon in the spring of 1785. This meeting led to calls for a larger meeting to discuss a wider range of national issues. Washington encouraged such a meeting, and it took place in Annapolis, Maryland, in 1786, with delegates from five states attending. The Annapolis meeting called for yet another larger meeting in Philadelphia the following year to revise the Articles.

Reluctantly, Washington was selected as one of five delegates from Virginia to attend the meeting, later known as the Constitutional Convention. Washington arrived in Philadelphia in the summer of 1787, the day before the convention was scheduled to start, and was unanimously elected president of the convention on the first day. Serving as leader, he contributed very little to the debates, though he campaigned strongly for substantial changes. His commanding presence in the room, along with the presence of diplomat and scientist **Benjamin Franklin** (1706–1790; see entry in volume 1), helped bring the convention to a successful conclusion with an entirely new constitution. Washington's signature on the document likely secured its ultimate ratification by the states.

The first president

Following the Constitutional Convention, Washington hoped to return to Mount Vernon to run his plantation. However, he was the only person of prominence fully trusted by both those favoring and those opposing the new constitution. So upon adoption of the Constitution, Washington was unanimously elected the first president of the United States and **John Adams** (1735–1826; see entry in volume 1) of Massachusetts the first vice president. Many also believed Washington could give the most prestige to the new nation in dealing with foreign nations. Washington reluctantly accepted the post, not sure if he had the abilities to administer a government.

On April 16, 1789, Washington set out from Mount Vernon to New York, the temporary location of the new government. Along his journey were repeated celebrations as every town greeted him. Washington was the top symbol of the new nation. He was inaugurated on April 30 on the balcony of Federal Hall. Rather than the fine London clothing of his earlier years, he wore a brown suit made in America with white stockings and a sword. A month later, Martha traveled to New York to join George. She received a similar series of celebrations along the way.

Washington began the process of establishing how the president of the United States should behave. He paid a lot of attention to detail, trying to strike a balance between formal dignity and yet being accessible to the public as an elected official. He did not shake hands but rather bowed, wore a sword on his hip, and rode in a well outfitted four- or six-horse carriage. When he met guests, he stood on a raised platform, often wearing a black velvet suit and gold buckles, yellow gloves, cocked hat with ostrich plume, and powdered hair. His entertainment was private with good wines and good food. He decided to be addressed "Mr. President." He drew criticism from those opposed to a strong central government; they asserted that Washington was too formal and ceremonial, like a monarch. When the first Congress adjourned in September 1789, Washington began touring the nation to encourage unity, first to the Northeast and later to the South.

Building a government

When Washington first took office, there were no laws by Congress, no judiciary, and no executive departments. In 1789, the first Congress sent the Bill of Rights, the first ten amendments to the Constitution, to the states for ratification and established the judicial and executive departments. Washington had to fill some one thousand positions in the new government. He filled the key positions with people who spanned a range of political views. He believed this would help forge a common unity. He selected New York delegate **John Jay** (1745–1829; see entry in volume 1) as chief justice of the Supreme Court; Virginia politician **Thomas Jefferson** (1743–1826; see entry in volume 1) as secretary of state; New York politician **Alexander Hamilton** (1755–1804; see entry in volume 1) as secretary of the treasury; Virginia politician **Edmund Randolph** (1753–1813; see entry in volume 2) as the attorney general; former Continental Army general Henry Knox (1750–1806) as secretary of war; and Massachusetts politician Samuel Osgood (1747–1813) as postmaster general. The Constitution did not provide for a council of advisors for the president, but by late 1791 Washington began holding meetings among his department heads, referred to as his Cabinet. The purpose of the meetings was to have general discussion on governmental issues.

President George Washington with his Cabinet: (left to right) Henry Knox, Alexander Hamilton, Thomas Jefferson, and Edmund Randolph. *(© Bettmann/Corbis.)*

Through the next few years, Washington regretted the lack of unity within his Cabinet. He was distressed over growing political factions, which eventually led to political parties in the young nation. He consistently favored decisions and advice that came from Hamilton, who had served with him as a personal aide during the war. Hamilton put forward a bold plan of economic revival for the nation. The plan brought considerable criticism from those who feared a strong central government. Hamilton in particular clashed with Jefferson. Washington worked hard to keep them both in the administration.

A second term

The growing political divisiveness in the country led Washington to reluctantly make himself available for a second term in 1792. He was again unanimously elected with Adams remaining vice president. During his second term as president, Washington experienced considerable turmoil, both foreign and domestic. When France declared war on Britain in 1793, the division within his Cabinet grew too wide to resolve.

During the winter of 1793–94, Britain seized some six hundred American commercial ships. Hamilton favored keeping friendly relations with Britain. His economic plan depended heavily on taxes gained from imported British goods. On the other hand, Jefferson favored support of France, a nation that had assisted the United States during the Revolution and had signed an alliance treaty with the United States in 1778. Washington took a middle course, proclaiming neutrality (favoring no country) for the young nation. He knew the nation was totally unprepared for war and needed to maintain international trade relations to regain its economic footing. Washington then had the new French foreign minister, Edmond Charles Genet (1763–1834), removed from his post. Outside proper diplomatic channels, Genet was touring the nation raising support for France. Despite his removal, Genet had already influenced the creation of numerous Democratic-Republican societies around the nation, whose members actively opposed administration policies. Jefferson resigned in December 1793, unable to accept Hamilton's continued involvement in foreign affairs, which was Jefferson's area of responsibility as secretary of state.

To resolve the issue of ship seizures by the British, Washington sent Jay to negotiate a treaty. Though negotiating from a definite position of weakness—the United States had no real navy to threaten the British—Jay was able to obtain some trade concessions. Many in the United States, particularly among those favoring France, thought Jay had sold out to the British to protect Hamilton's economic programs. Despite much public uproar over the treaty, the U.S. Senate ratified it in August 1795. The Jay Treaty with Britain led to further political division in the nation. In March 1796, the U.S. House of Representatives requested presidential papers related to the treaty, and Washington refused to provide them, setting a precedent for maintaining a separation between the executive branch and the legislative branch; this is now known as executive privilege.

Following the Jay Treaty, President Washington sent diplomat Thomas Pinckney (1750–1828) to Madrid, Spain. His assignment was to negotiate a treaty giving Americans navigation rights to the Mississippi River and the port of New Orleans. Successfully achieved, the resulting Treaty of San Lorenzo proved highly popular among the public.

Other troubles were brewing within the United States. On the western frontier in the Northwest Territory, Native Americans had formed a strong alliance aided by British troops lingering in the area. The alliance sought to resist the spread of U.S. settlement into lands gained from Britain in the Treaty of Paris, the peace agreement that ended the American Revolution. The Native Americans dealt defeats to American forces sent to subdue the resistance in 1790 and 1791. The 1791 defeat included the loss of 690 soldiers under the command of General Arthur St. Clair (1736–1818), the heaviest loss in casualties to Native American forces in the history of the United States. Highly concerned about making the frontier safe for settlement, Washington ordered General **Anthony Wayne** (1745–1796; see entry in volume 2) to form a large military force, known as the Legion of the United States, and rigorously train them for two years. In the 1794 Battle of Fallen Timbers, Wayne's forces crushed the Native American alliance. The resulting 1795 Treaty of Greenville opened millions of acres of Native American lands to U.S. settlement.

During the same period that Washington was focused on taming the Northwest, farmers in western Pennsylvania revolted against the new taxes imposed by Hamilton's economic plan. The revolt is known as the Whiskey Rebellion (see box).

Farewell to public service

In 1796, Washington decided it was finally time for retirement; he did not want to pursue a third term. He waited until September to issue his Farewell Address. It was largely drafted by Hamilton and reviewed by others, but Washington put the final touches on it himself. The address warned against party

Whiskey Rebellion

The new national government established under the U.S. Constitution in 1789 had inherited a huge debt; the nation had borrowed large sums of money to wage the American Revolution. Secretary of the Treasury Alexander Hamilton was charged with developing a plan for putting the nation's finances on a firmer path. Among the number of proposals contained in Hamilton's plan was a tax on distilled liquor. Farmers in the western region of the United States grew corn. The only cost-efficient way of getting their crop to market was by distilling it into spirits, or whiskey. The whiskey was much easier to transport and brought a good price.

When the tax was adopted in 1791, frontier farmers from Georgia to Pennsylvania began protesting. They were short on cash to begin with and could not afford to pay more taxes. In addition, they felt that the federal government was not doing enough to protect them from Native American attacks. Their protests became increasingly violent, and they began harassing federal tax collectors. President George Washington saw this rebellion, known as the Whiskey Rebellion, as an opportunity to demonstrate the new powers of the national government. He selected western Pennsylvania as the location to exert new federal might. Washington personally led a force of almost thirteen thousand militiamen from four states to Pittsburgh, where some two thousand rebels

Pennsylvania protesters tar and feather a federal tax collector during the Whiskey Rebellion in 1794. (© Hulton Archive/Getty Images.)

had gathered. The large show of force by the government caused the rebels to scatter ahead of the army's arrival. Washington later granted a full pardon to two rebel leaders arrested and convicted of treason. He required them to take an oath of allegiance to the country. Congress repealed the whiskey tax in 1802.

The Whiskey Rebellion was the first occasion that the federal government exercised military authority over the nation's citizens and the only time in U.S. history that a sitting president commanded forces in the field.

politics and alliances with foreign nations. Washington had secured the West for settlement, brought economic prosperity through treaties with Britain and Spain, and most of all established an operating federal government.

In March 1797, with the inauguration of his vice president, John Adams, as the nation's second president, Washington returned to Mount Vernon. He gladly resumed his plantation operations and normal family life, though the household did continue receiving a steady stream of guests eager to visit with the former president.

The nation called for Washington's service again the following year in 1798 when war with France was looming. Adams requested that he serve as commander of a newly formed provisional army. Washington agreed but demanded that Hamilton be second in command and the more active in assembling a force. As it turned out, Adams was able to maintain peace with France through negotiations.

A tragic end

The end came suddenly to Washington's much heralded life. On December 12, 1799, Washington made his usual rounds inspecting his farm operations in cold and snowy conditions. He returned to Mount Vernon that evening tired and wet but refused to change clothes before entertaining at dinner. Late the following day, he came down with a throat infection and acute laryngitis. Personal doctors were summoned, but the treatment they performed seemed to weaken him further. With his strength steadily decreasing, Washington realized he was nearing death. He approached it with the same calmness he had shown in many crises during his life. He provided his personal secretary with instructions for his burial and died late the evening of December 14.

The entire country went into mourning. War hero Henry "Light-Horse Harry" Lee (1756–1818) wrote the famous words "first in war, first in peace, and first in the hearts of his countrymen," referring to Washington. Britain and Napoléon Bonaparte (1769–1821) of France paid tribute to Washington. Washington's will provided for freeing his slaves. He was the only Founding Father from Virginia to free his slaves and even provided pensions for the elderly and young.

The new nation's capital under construction was already named for Washington while he was still living. Later, a state was named after him, the only state named after an American individual. Counties in 32 states and 121 towns were named after him. A large prominent monument to Washington was dedicated in the nation's capital in 1885.

For More Information

Books

Brookhiser, Richard. *Founding Father: Rediscovering George Washington.* New York: Free Press, 1996.

Burns, James MacGregor, and Susan Dunn. *George Washington.* New York: Times Books, 2004.

Ellis, Joseph J. *His Excellency: George Washington.* New York: Knopf Publishing Group, 2004.

Ferling, John E. *The First of Men: A Life of George Washington.* Knoxville: University of Tennessee Press, 1988.

Schwartz, Barry. *George Washington: The Making of an American Symbol.* New York: Free Press, 1987.

Vidal, Gore. *Inventing a Nation: Washington, Adams, Jefferson.* New Haven, CT: Yale University Press, 2003.

Web Sites

Library of Congress. "Presidential Inaugurations: George Washington." *American Memory.* http://memory.loc.gov/ammem/pihtml/pi001.html (accessed on August 19, 2005).

Whiskey Rebellion—Whiskey Insurrection. http://www.whiskeyrebellion.org/ (accessed on August 19, 2005).

Martha Washington

Born June 2, 1732 (New Kent County, Virginia)
Died May 22, 1802 (Mount Vernon, Virginia)

First lady

"I am still determined to be cheerful and to be happy in whatever situation I may be, for I have also learnt from experience that the greater part of our happiness or misary [sic] depends upon our dispositions, and not our circumstances."

The lives of prominent eighteenth-century women were rarely recorded in any detail. Yet women played as vital a role as men in early America. Women managed the household duties, including food preparation and storage, sewing, giving birth to and caring for numerous children, and overseeing the health of the entire family. Martha Washington performed all these duties but on a grander scale than most women. She was a member of the wealthy planter class, which meant she had to oversee the household operations of large plantations. Her first husband, Daniel Parke Custis (1711–1757), was the richest man in Virginia. After his death, she remarried military hero and large landowner **George Washington** (1732–1799; see entry in volume 2). The wealth she brought to her second marriage ensured the success of Washington's plantation, Mount Vernon.

Washington became the first president of the United States and the most respected and honored American of the late eighteenth century. Few in the twenty-first century realize that at that time, Martha Washington was considered an American hero in her own right, cheered everywhere she

Martha Washington. *(© Bettmann/Corbis.)*

went. Her sense of duty to General Washington and his soldiers in the American Revolution (1775–83) became legendary. Further, Martha maintained an unfailing sense of duty to her family and to her role as wife of the first U.S. president, establishing rules of conduct that would guide future presidents' wives. Martha led the highest-profile life of any woman in the late eighteenth century. At the same time, her life, like the lives of almost all women of her generation, was ultimately defined by births and deaths of family members and by the religion that sustained her.

Childhood memories and learning skills

Martha Dandridge was born to John and Frances Dandridge in 1732 at Chestnut Grove, a 500-acre plantation on the Pamunkey River in New Kent County, Virginia. Chestnut Grove was 25 miles inland from Williamsburg, the only town of any size in colonial Virginia. In the 1700s, any farm with a house and at least a few hundred acres could be called a plantation. For comparison, the wealthiest Virginia resident, John Custis IV, owned more than 17,000 acres.

The Dandridge home was a new, comfortable, two-story structure reflecting a family rising in status within Virginian society. Martha's first childhood memories were probably the smells and sounds of rural Virginia—wood smoke, barnyard animals, food preparations, and sounds of activity in the slave quarters.

Like other eighteenth-century Virginia families, Martha's family lived in constant anticipation of visitors, who brought news and entertainment. Outside of Williamsburg, there were few inns for travelers. Even if they were complete strangers, travelers—including entire families and their slaves—were welcomed into rural Virginia homes with food and an overnight stay. Martha grew up in this welcoming atmosphere where at a moment's notice the women prepared large meals and saw to it that guests were comfortably housed. The welcoming skills Martha learned as a young girl would be used virtually every day of her adult life.

Martha was the eldest of eight children, and she developed her caregiving skills early as she helped watch over her siblings. She had three brothers and four sisters: John born in 1733, William in 1734, and Bartholomew in 1737, Anna Maria in 1739, Frances in 1744, Elizabeth in 1749, and Mary in 1756. By age fifteen, Martha had learned how to oversee a family's food preparation, clothing, health, and religious instruction.

"Debut" in Williamsburg

John and Frances Dandridge were not wealthy, but they were quite comfortable, secure enough to undertake the expense of taking their eldest daughter to Williamsburg to make her "debut." A debut in mid-eighteenth-century

The Veil of Secrecy

Martha Dandridge Custis Washington had a mulatto half sister, Ann, who grew up alongside Martha at the Chestnut Grove Plantation in Virginia. A mulatto is a person with white and black ancestry. In Ann's case, her father was Martha's father, John Dandridge, and her mother was the daughter of a Native American father and a black mother. It was very common in the 1700s and 1800s for mixed-race half brothers, half sisters, and cousins to grow up together on plantations. The mulatto children generally were born to plantation slave women who were made pregnant by white male residents—or sometimes the master—of the plantation or by white male visitors.

By the 1780s, there was a whole new generation of mixed-race children growing up at the Mount Vernon plantation, home to George and Martha Washington. For example, Betty, Martha's mulatto seamstress who had come to Mount Vernon as a small child, had given birth to two daughters fathered by a white Irish carpenter contracted to work at Mount Vernon for seven years. At the end of his seven years, he moved away but left his daughters behind. One of the girls, Oney, became Martha's personal maid.

There was always secrecy regarding the fathers of mulattoes. Fathering mulatto children was accepted as a routine part of plantation life. Mulattoes were favored as house slaves and often treated much better than field slaves. They had nice clothes to make a good appearance within the house; they also received better food and generally the lightest work assignments. From time to time, mulattoes were freed and even given parcels of land to live on and farm. This practice of favored treatment always raised questions about their parentage. However, birth records for mulattoes were never kept, and no one ever knew for certain who the fathers were.

Williamsburg meant attending a ball at the governor's palace, the grandest building in the colony, followed by more balls, concerts, dinners, and picnics. John and Frances probably ordered fine clothes from England for Martha and had her practice dance steps and her curtsy until both were perfect.

Martha, who had brown hair and hazel eyes, was extremely good-natured and made friends easily. At Williamsburg, Daniel Parke Custis was attracted to Martha. They began courting (dating) and fell in love. Twenty-one years older than Martha, Custis was the wealthiest bachelor in Virginia. Martha, on the other hand, stood to inherit no property. Daniel's father, John

A young Martha Washington. *(© Bettmann/Corbis.)*

Custis IV, did not approve of Martha as a wife for his son, but that was not surprising—he approved of no one.

Marriage to Daniel Parke Custis

Martha and Daniel married on May 15 in either 1749 or 1750; the precise year is uncertain in historical records. They lived at Daniel's home on the Pamunkey River. The home was known as the White House Plantation. Martha began her new life as a plantation mistress, drawing on the lessons she had learned from her mother. Martha's households would always be run exceedingly well.

Martha's first child, Daniel Parke Custis II, was born in November 1751 at White House Plantation. Her second was born in April 1753, a daughter named Frances Parke Custis. The third child, John Parke Custis, was born in 1754 and was always known as "Jacky." Daniel and Martha's fourth and last child was Martha Parke Custis, born in 1756. This daughter was called Patsy.

Family death

Deaths of family members in the eighteenth century were a common experience since people frequently died young from illnesses that are now treatable or curable. In 1754, Martha's life took a painful turn. Her firstborn son, Daniel, died in February 1754 at the age of two. Three years later, in April 1757, Martha lost her second child, Frances; then her husband died on July 8 at the age of forty-five. He had become ill on July 4, probably from a heart condition.

Only in her mid-twenties, Martha was now the wealthiest widow in all of Virginia. She would oversee the entire White House Plantation, which consisted of a large amount of cash and 17,779 acres spread over six counties and worked by 300 slaves. The pressure on Martha to administer her holdings was extreme. For help, Martha began considering remarriage.

Young Colonel Washington

In March 1758, Martha met the dashing young Colonel George Washington of the Virginia militia. Twenty-six years old, Washington stood more than 6 feet 3 inches tall with undeniable good looks that attracted women's attention. He had attained a hero's reputation during the French and Indian War (1754–63). Washington had schooled himself in the social manners of the day so as to present himself as a gentleman to Williamsburg society. He enjoyed theater and dancing and, like Martha, loved fine clothes.

Washington's financial condition was not unusual for a plantation owner: He had little cash but owned considerable property. Nevertheless, he had ordered farming equipment, furniture, and building supplies from England. These orders had thrown him into serious debt. Needing cash to sustain and further develop Mount Vernon, Washington hoped to marry a woman with money. Marrying to increase wealth was considered a wise practice in the 1700s. For Martha, marriage would allow her to share the management of the Custis fortune, and this would be a relief.

Washington inspired confidence and was known for his trustworthiness. Martha and George decided to marry after only three meetings and made their engagement official in June 1758. They chose January 6, 1759, as their wedding date. Although the marriage was a very practical choice for both of them, George and Martha clearly had a great affection for each other.

Mistress of Mount Vernon

In April 1759, Martha, five-year-old Jacky Custis, three-year-old Patsy Custis, and a large group of slaves traveled to George's Mount Vernon Plantation on the Potomac River. Mount Vernon would be Martha's home for the next forty years. George immediately began upgrading the Mount Vernon estate. With Martha's available cash, he was able to turn the land into a productive and profitable plantation.

Martha, now the mistress of Mount Vernon, oversaw the running of the main house and slave quarters while raising Jacky and Patsy. She seemed to relish her place in Virginia plantation life, overseeing domestic duties such as food preparation, entertaining a steady stream of visitors, and keeping family and slaves healthy. Martha always retired to her bedroom for an hour after breakfast to read the Bible and pray. Afterward, she checked the kitchen, the smokehouse, and the kitchen garden to be sure the slaves were properly carrying out their duties. Martha also spent much time administering medicine to those who were ailing.

A day rarely passed at Mount Vernon without visitors. Martha and George loved to entertain their steady stream of guests. The main meal was served at 3 PM. Martha spent the rest of her day visiting, gardening, or sewing.

Jacky and Patsy Custis

Martha also spent a great deal of time with her children. She taught Patsy the skills of managing a home. George hired tutors for Jacky, but Jacky proved to be an inattentive and lazy student. Martha tended to overprotect and spoil Jacky.

Martha and George's life at Mount Vernon was peaceful for the next thirteen years. Their worst problem concerned Patsy's health. Patsy had developed alarming "fits," which were diagnosed as epilepsy about 1769. Although many doctors were consulted, Patsy's epilepsy was never controlled. Meanwhile, Jacky had become a teenager and was very difficult to handle. He was sent to a school in Annapolis and in 1773 to King's College (later Columbia University) in New York, but he was never serious about his studies.

Tragedy struck the family on June 19, 1773. Patsy suddenly suffered a "fit" after Sunday dinner and died in only minutes. Martha and George were shocked and heartbroken. In October, eighteen-year-old Jacky returned from King's College to Mount Vernon to comfort his mother and stepfather. He announced he would not return to school but instead marry his sweetheart, Eleanor Calvert (1757–1811) of Maryland. Jacky and Eleanor were married at Mount Airy, Eleanor's home in Maryland, on February 3, 1774. Martha welcomed Eleanor as a daughter, and the two remained close for the rest of Martha's life.

Jacky and Eleanor split their time between Mount Airy and Mount Vernon. By the summer of 1774, Martha had begun to feel more cheerful, thanks to a steady stream of visitors, Eleanor's companionship, and Jacky's settling down. Martha resumed all her usual activities and her social life. However, her fifteen years with George at Mount Vernon were soon to end. The American Revolution (1775–83), the colonists' fight to gain independence from Britain, was about to commence. On June 18, 1775, George was named as commander of the new Continental Army. General Washington would not return to live at Mount Vernon for eight years.

American Revolution begins

While George was away, Martha was busy running the plantation, entertaining the usual stream of company, and caring for Eleanor, who was expecting her first child. Born in

September 1774, Eleanor's baby girl died at birth. At this same time, a disturbing newspaper article had accused Martha and her family of being Loyalists, supporters of the British and the king, and stated that Martha had separated from George. To prove such news wrong, Martha, Jacky, and Eleanor left Mount Vernon in November to join George in winter camp at Cambridge, Massachusetts. To show people that they supported the American cause, Martha dressed herself and Eleanor in homespun clothing, not the fine British clothing she had always worn at Mount Vernon.

Martha, Jacky, and Eleanor's trip to Cambridge convinced colonists that the Washingtons were united against Britain. This first trip to be near General Washington at winter camp began a series of yearly trips for Martha. Her arrival in camp each winter was much anticipated by the troops. She became as loved and honored as General Washington. All along her route, Patriots, those who supported American independence, greeted her and called her Lady Washington.

Winter camps

During the winter of 1776–77, Martha arrived at the Morristown, New Jersey, camp to join General Washington. She found the troops ragged, starving, and diseased. Churches in the town had become makeshift hospitals, and up to four soldiers were quartered in each home. The townspeople resented the heavy burden the men had placed on their community.

When Martha arrived, she immediately began sewing shirts and knitting stockings with woolen supplies she had brought from Mount Vernon. A number of Morristown's wealthier local women dressed up in their finery and paid a visit to Martha. They were surprised to find the wife of the great general plainly dressed and busily knitting. In her usual cheerful and positive manner, Martha discussed the need for women to help fill the needs of the soldiers by making and repairing clothes and other supplies. Martha managed to help win over the townspeople and in turn win their support for her husband and his troops. Martha was merely doing what she had learned to do in childhood, but on a larger scale: She was sewing, cooking, and providing health care for large numbers of people in a friendly and loving manner.

Martha's worst camp experience by far was at Valley Forge, Pennsylvania, located about 22 miles northwest of Philadelphia. She reached the camp in February 1778. Ten to eleven thousand men were in desperate condition, having camped there since a week before Christmas. Martha's arrival was like that of a relief agency; she brought various practical supplies, including wool, sewing materials, food, bandages, and medicine, without which the troops might not have survived. Martha continued to join George in winter camps throughout the war, her last camp being the winter of 1782.

Jacky and Eleanor Custis's children

Jacky and Eleanor's first surviving child, Elizabeth Parke Custis, had been born at Mount Airy on August 21, 1776. Since the birth, they preferred living at the roomy Mount Vernon and usually did not accompany Martha during her trips to the winter camps. A second daughter, Martha Parke Custis, was born on December 31, 1777, and Eleanor was pregnant again by fall of 1778.

Jacky purchased an estate, Abingdon, with a house and 900 acres, near Alexandria, up the Potomac River from Mount Vernon. He moved his family there before the birth of their third daughter, Eleanor Parke Custis—later known as **Nelly Custis Lewis** (1779–1852; see entry in volume 2)—on March 2, 1779. Baby Eleanor was soon nicknamed Nelly. Their fourth child, George Washington Parke Custis, known as Wash, was born in the spring of 1781.

Jacky Custis's death

In September 1781, General Washington made an unexpected stop at Mount Vernon. He was marching his soldiers south to Yorktown, Virginia, where French general Marquis de Lafayette (1757–1834) and his troops had the British army under General Charles Cornwallis (1738–1805) trapped. Jacky Custis, who had never shown the least interest in joining the army, was awed by the look of the men in uniform. Caught up in the exhilaration of the moment, Jacky decided he must accompany his stepfather to Yorktown. Washington's troops won the battle at Yorktown, and the British surrendered on October 17. However, the thrill of victory gave way to sorrow when Jacky, still at Yorktown, contracted camp fever and died on November 5, 1781. He was only twenty-seven years old and had been Martha's only living child.

Eleanor Custis was now a widow at twenty-four with four children under the age of five. Physically ill, Eleanor was in no condition to care for four small children, so George and Martha took the two youngest, Nelly and Wash Custis, to Mount Vernon. There was never a formal adoption, but George and Martha would raise them as their own.

A hero in her own right

Although George still had another year and a half to serve as commander of the Continental Army, Martha left her last winter camp, at Newburgh, New York, and returned to Mount Vernon in July 1782. Along the way, it became clear that Americans considered Martha an American hero in her own right. As she traveled through Philadelphia, citizens presented her with a carriage that had belonged to Pennsylvania's founder, William Penn (1644–1718). In Williamsburg she was honored with gold medals. With an American victory certain, George resigned his post on December 19, 1783, and arrived at Mount Vernon on December 24.

Five years at Mount Vernon

From December 24, 1783, until the spring of 1789, George and Martha lived at Mount Vernon. Their lifestyle was anything but calm and serene. When they returned to their plantation, its agricultural lands were in disarray. The plantation house was also suffering from years of neglect. The "general," as Martha now referred to George, spent long hours in his study catching up on the financial business of the plantation and planning new developments. Although all of Martha's Custis inheritance cash was long ago spent, the general embarked on an ambitious repair and building program. Two wings and a porch running the entire length of the house were added. The Washingtons also added a new kitchen, a washhouse, a dairy, a spinning house, a walled kitchen garden, an atrium for exotic plants, and an icehouse, the latest kitchen innovation of that time.

Many of the additions were sorely needed, because the Mount Vernon "family," George and Martha's relatives plus

General George and Martha Washington at home with their family.

(© Bettmann/Corbis.)

slaves, continued to increase rapidly in numbers. Also, a steady parade of guests arrived to visit and pay homage to the great general and his wife. Life at Mount Vernon was busy. By 1786, Martha was in charge of more than fifty slaves working in and immediately around the house—personal valets, butlers, waiters, cooks, coachmen, seamstresses, housemaids, washwomen, spinners, carpenters, general laborers, and gardeners.

Two family relatives were in residence at Mount Vernon: sixteen-year-old Fanny Bassett and George Augustine Washington. Fanny was Martha's niece, the daughter of Martha's sister Anna Maria, who had died in 1777. Fanny and Martha were like mother and daughter and became best friends. George Augustine was a nephew of the general. He had served in the war and was attempting to recover his health at Mount Vernon. Before long, Fanny and George Augustine fell in love; they married in the fall of 1785. By 1788, Fanny had a baby girl, Maria, and all lived at Mount Vernon. Although Martha apparently relished her life during the 1780s, she again would follow her husband, as duty to his country soon called.

Move to New York City

When the U.S. Constitution was ratified in 1788, the Electoral College unanimously elected Washington president of the new country. He was inaugurated on April 30, 1789, in New York City, the nation's temporary capital. Martha, Nelly, and Wash left for New York on May 16 after tearful goodbyes. Twenty-one-year-old Fanny was left in charge of Mount Vernon.

Crowds of people had cheered George all along his route to New York, and they did the same for Martha. In New York City, the presidential home was a three-story brick house at 10 Cherry Street (the structure no longer exists). The house was packed with people, including George, Martha, Nelly, Wash, and Tobias Lear (1762–1816), George's chief secretary who had come with them from Mount Vernon. Various other secretaries and aides also resided at the Cherry Street house, as did several house slaves, some of them from Mount Vernon.

No official etiquette (accepted conduct) yet existed for a president and his wife, so Martha had to develop her own rules for proper behavior. Martha faced decisions on this matter every hour and in the smallest detail. For example, she had to decide whether it would be more appropriate for her to greet someone by shaking hands, bowing, or curtsying.

Although Martha dressed simply, her clothes were made only of the finest silks and velvets. Her hair was groomed every day, but she then covered it in fine fashionable caps, high caps she hoped would make her look taller. Martha did not dress as elegantly as the women of high society, nor was she concerned about what the wealthiest of society thought of her. Some viewed the Washingtons as too plain, but others looked upon them as much too regal.

A gracious hostess

Part of Martha's job as the president's wife was to host social events at the presidential mansion. The first official entertaining she did was at a weekly event known as the Drawing Room. Held on Friday evenings, Drawing Rooms were a version of an open house or reception, open to women from prominent families. The president made an appearance, and refreshments were served. The first official state dinners welcoming diplomats were held on Thursday evenings. Martha always was present at the dinners, and she was sometimes the only woman at the table.

Even though Martha always appeared gracious, cheerful, and focused on doing her duty, privately she disliked that her every action was being judged; she, therefore, rarely left the presidential mansion. Martha felt that many of her duties as the president's wife were much less important compared to the responsibilities she was accustomed to assuming at Mount Vernon. However, her Drawing Rooms were packed every week. Martha loved being sociable and seemed to always put guests at ease. This was in contrast to George, whose ever-present concern for his presidential image made him seem very stiff. Martha and the children softened and enhanced George's public image by presenting him as a family man.

The U.S. Congress took a summer break beginning in late August 1790, and the Washingtons went home to Mount Vernon. Philadelphia was designated the new temporary capital for the national government, and on November 22 the Washingtons left Mount Vernon for their new home in the city that was considered at the time the center of American culture.

Move to Philadelphia

The Washingtons' new home was at 190 High Street (present-day 190 Market Street). George rented the home and had additions built for the family's large group of secretaries and slaves. Eleven-year-old Nelly was enrolled in school, but nine-year-old Wash was tutored at home.

The Thursday night official dinners and Friday evening Drawing Rooms continued in much the same manner as in New York but on a much grander scale in keeping with the social standards of Philadelphia. Appearance was everything in glittering, fashion-conscious Philadelphia, so Martha dressed in much more elegant gowns.

Polly Lear, Tobias Lear's wife, began to help Martha plan her social schedule. Polly took on the role that is now known as the social secretary for the First Lady. The words "First Lady" were not yet used; instead Martha was known simply as Mrs. Washington. With Polly's help scheduling social events, Martha soon enjoyed life in Philadelphia and made many friends. She no more felt a prisoner as she had in New York City.

Both Martha and George immensely enjoyed watching Nelly grow. At twelve, Nelly was a bright, cheerful, and highly energetic child. She loved school and took painting, music, and dancing classes. She was adored by Philadelphia society. Martha allowed Nelly to accompany her to teas, balls, and parties and let her help at receptions for diplomats. Wash, on the other hand, was an inattentive student, just as his father, Jacky Custis, had been. Martha made excuses for Wash and continued to spoil him terribly.

Second term

Martha assumed she, George, and the family would return to Mount Vernon at the end of George's first term in early 1793. Instead, pressure mounted for Washington to serve another four years as president. On March 4, 1793, Martha and her four grandchildren—Wash, Nelly, Elizabeth, and Martha Custis—all watched as George was sworn in for a second term.

In July, Polly Lear became ill during an outing with Martha and died eight days later. She apparently was one of the first victims of Philadelphia's 1793 yellow fever epidemic. The epidemic swept through the city in August, killing up to fifty people a day. In early September, Martha finally convinced George to leave the city for a few months until the epidemic came to an end. Martha, George, Nelly, and Wash left for Mount Vernon and returned to Philadelphia in the winter when it appeared safe.

In 1796, the Washingtons were able to spend the summer at Mount Vernon. George and Martha were both thrilled at the prospect of returning there permanently the next spring as private citizens. Upon her return to Mount Vernon, Martha was upset to learn that her personal maid, Oney, had run away just before the family had arrived back home. Oney was the daughter of Betty, the longtime seamstress at Mount Vernon. Oney escaped into a network of free blacks in Philadelphia.

George traveled back and forth to Philadelphia as government business demanded. He also worked on his farewell address, and it was published in the *American Daily Advertiser,* a Philadelphia newspaper, on September 19, 1796.

Between September 1796 and March 1797, the Washingtons attended many farewell dinners. At George's February 22 birthday ball, Martha dressed up in an extravagant orange and lemon gown and wore orange plumes in her hair; this uncharacteristically flamboyant outfit expressed how joyous Martha felt about leaving the scrutiny of public life and returning to her private life at Mount Vernon.

The new president, **John Adams** (1735–1826; served 1797–1801; see entry in volume 1), was sworn in on March 4, 1797. The entire Washington party left for Mount Vernon on March 9. They arrived in April, the most beautiful time of the year at Mount Vernon. They immediately set about making repairs, which were much needed after the family's eight-year absence. They resumed their routine of rising early. George split his time between correspondence and financial matters and riding over the property. Martha managed the house and many guests.

Martha had only two and a half years to spend with George at Mount Vernon. On December 12, 1799, on a cold snowy day, George rode on horseback as usual across the property. He later came to dinner but remained in his wet clothes and developed a sore throat by the next day. By the morning of December 14, he could hardly breathe, his throat almost swollen shut. Doctors were summoned, but George died that evening.

Martha never again lived in or even entered the large bedroom she and George had always shared. She took a small attic room a floor above, from which she could see the old family vault where George's body lay. Martha never fully recovered after the loss of her husband. At some point, she burned all correspondence between herself and George, presumably to keep the relationship private. Martha died the evening of

May 22, 1802. She was buried in a coffin beside George. Later, a new vault was built down the hill from the old vault, and the Washingtons' remains were moved there. The vault can still be viewed at Mount Vernon.

For More Information

Books

Brady, Patricia. *Martha Washington, An American Life.* New York: Viking, 2005.

Bryan, Helen. *Martha Washington: First Lady of Liberty.* New York: John Wiley and Sons, 2002.

Fields, Joseph E., ed. *Worthy Partner: The Papers of Martha Washington.* Westport, CT: Greenwood Press, 1994.

Norton, Mary Beth. *Liberty's Daughters: The Revolutionary Experience of American Women, 1750–1800.* Boston: Little Brown, 1980. Reprint, Ithaca, N.Y.: Cornell University Press, 1996.

Wilson, Dorothy Clarke. *Lady Washington.* Garden City, NY: Doubleday, 1984.

Web Sites

George Washington's Mt. Vernon Estates and Gardens. http://www.mountvernon.org/ (accessed on August 18, 2005).

National First Ladies Library. http://www.firstladies.org/Bibliography/MarthaWashington/FLMain.htm (accessed on August 18, 2005).

Anthony Wayne

Born January 1, 1745 (Waynesboro, Pennsylvania)
Died December 15, 1796 (Presque Isle, Pennsylvania)

General, politician

Gaining recognition as a general in the Continental Army during the American Revolution (1775–83), Anthony Wayne served in the first U.S. Congress before returning to a military role to defeat a strong Native American alliance. The alliance had formed west of the Appalachian Mountains in the Old Northwest to forcibly resist expansion of U.S. settlements into the region. Wayne demonstrated considerable courage and competence when the young nation needed leaders on the battlefield. He earned the nickname "Mad Anthony" for his fearless charges into enemy lines.

"Yet the resources of this country are great & if councils will call them forth we may produce a conviction to the world that we deserve to be free."

A surveyor

Anthony Wayne was born on New Year's Day in 1745 to Isaac Wayne and Elizabeth Iddings Wayne. He was their only child. His father and grandfather emigrated from Ireland and around 1724 settled on a 500-acre farm in Pennsylvania. The growing local community became known as Waynesboro. The Waynes also purchased a profitable tannery, where animal hides were processed for clothing and other uses.

Anthony Wayne. *(Library of Congress.)*

Young Anthony proved to be a very strong-willed youth and a challenge for the family; he often clashed with his father. He attended local schools until sixteen years of age. The family then sent Anthony to Philadelphia to attend a private academy operated by an uncle.

After two years of schooling at the Philadelphia academy, Wayne had acquired the skills of a surveyor. He found a job in 1765 with a Philadelphia land company and was sent to survey a large area of land in Nova Scotia, a province of Canada, in preparation for expanding settlement. After completing his job there, Wayne returned to Philadelphia and in March 1766 married Mary Penrose, daughter of a Philadelphia merchant. They had two children.

A Patriot for independence

After their marriage, Wayne and his bride moved back to the family property at Waynesboro. He took over operation of the tannery. Eight years later, in 1774, his father died, leaving Wayne the owner of substantial family property that provided a comfortable income.

As American colonists grew increasingly discontented with the policies of their British rulers in the early 1770s, Wayne became a leader of the Patriots (colonists favoring independence from Britain) in his region of Pennsylvania. In July 1774, he was selected as chairman of a county committee to draft a protest to the British government over the Coercive Acts, also known as the Intolerable Acts. This legislation was a series of four laws passed by British parliament in 1774 attempting to reestablish strict British control over the colonies. The following year, Wayne was appointed to represent the county at a provincial assembly to prepare for the American Revolution (1775–83), the colonists' fight for independence from Britain.

Military commander

Wayne's military role began on January 3, 1776, when the Continental Congress appointed him colonel of a Chester County regiment that he organized for the Continental Army. Wayne fought in key battles throughout the war. Late in the spring of 1776, he was sent to the Canadian front to reinforce U.S. troops struggling to capture Quebec. Despite Wayne's help, U.S. forces were unsuccessful, and Wayne was wounded in the retreat across the Canadian border. For that winter, Wayne was placed in command of two thousand troops under dismal conditions at Fort Ticonderoga.

By February 1777, Wayne rose to the rank of brigadier general, and in April he joined General **George Washington** (1732–1799; see entry in volume 2) and his troops in Morristown, New Jersey. Wayne showed skill and courage there and at the Battle of Brandywine in September 1777, where his forces suffered major losses while slowing the British advance on Philadelphia. He fought again in October at the Battle of Germantown, only to suffer another loss. In the winter of 1777–78, he wintered with General Washington at Valley Forge, Pennsylvania. In June 1778, Wayne led a valiant American charge in the indecisive Battle of Monmouth in New Jersey.

On July 16, 1779, in one of his greatest moments in the war, Wayne led a force of thirteen hundred men in a midnight attack against a British stronghold at Stony Point, New York, on the Hudson River. Seizing the fort, Wayne captured 575 British soldiers and fifteen cannons. The Continental Congress awarded Wayne a gold medal for the much-needed victory, which raised the hopes of the U.S. Army at a low point in the war.

Wayne followed Stony Point with victory at West Point, New York. He continued leading troops into combat further south under the command of Marquis de Lafayette (1757–1834) and won a victory in Green Spring, Virginia. He also directed troops under General Nathanael Greene (1742–1786) in battles in Georgia. He led Continental Army troops into Charleston upon withdrawal of the British army. In Georgia, Wayne's troops defeated Native American Cherokee and Creek forces allied with the British. Following the battlefield victories, Wayne negotiated treaties with the Creek and Cherokee in the winter of 1782–83. The state of Georgia rewarded Wayne for his war accomplishments with an 800-acre rice plantation.

Politics

By 1783, victory over Britain was secured. Wayne retired as a major general and returned home to Waynesboro a hero. Wayne began working on his Pennsylvania property again and getting involved in Pennsylvania politics. Wayne represented Chester County in the Pennsylvania General Assembly in 1784 and 1785. In 1788, he participated in the Pennsylvania constitutional ratification convention, where he favored creation of a stronger national government than that provided by the 1781 Articles of Confederation.

Wayne moved to Georgia following the Pennsylvania constitutional convention and settled on his rice plantation. In 1791, Wayne was elected to represent Georgia in the U.S. House of Representatives. He began serving in this position in

March 1791 but resigned the following March when his residency requirements for representing Georgia were questioned.

Opening the frontier

While Wayne was serving in the House, the U.S. Army met humiliating defeats in 1790 and again in 1791 at the hands of a strong Native American alliance in the Ohio River valley north of the Ohio River. Members of the Miami, Shawnee, Delaware, and Wyandot tribes were terrorizing settlers in the Northwest Territory. The alliance was led by **Little Turtle** (c. 1752–1812; see entry in volume 2) of the Miami and Blue Jacket (c.1745–c.1810) of the Shawnee. Created in 1787 by the Continental Congress, the Northwest Territory included the region north of the Ohio River to the Great Lakes and Canada, east to the Pennsylvania border and west to the Mississippi River. The present-day states of Ohio, Indiana, Illinois, Michigan, Wisconsin, and a portion of Minnesota were carved from the Northwest Territory. The 1791 defeat of General Arthur St. Clair (1736–1818) in Ohio was the worst defeat ever suffered by the United States in its battles with the Native Americans. Some 647 American troops were killed.

President Washington was anxious to establish control of the Northwest Territory and make it safe for American settlers. He appointed Wayne, who had just left his seat in the House, as major general in charge of a large new military force known as the Legion of the United States. During 1792 and 1793, Wayne trained this army at a newly established basic training facility in Legionville, Pennsylvania. Wayne's preparation of the troops set training standards for the army for many years. It was the first formalized basic training in the army.

In 1794, after negotiations with the Native American alliance failed, Wayne moved his force of one thousand men west to Fort Recovery in Ohio Country. They built forts as they proceeded. Then on August 20, Wayne's force engaged the alliance of two thousand warriors on the Maumee River just south of present-day Toledo, Ohio. It became known as the Battle of Fallen Timbers, named from the trees blown down by a recent major storm. Wayne was aided by the fact that the British had just signed the Jay Treaty with the United States. In the treaty, the British promised to stop providing support to Native Americans resisting western expansion of American

William Henry Harrison

A number of men who served under the command of General Anthony Wayne went on to gain fame of their own. One such person was William Henry Harrison (1773–1841). Harrison became a military hero and eventually the ninth president of the United States.

Harrison was born into a wealthy colonial family on a Virginia plantation. His father, Benjamin Harrison (c. 1726–1791), fully supported the fight for independence. He signed the Declaration of Independence in 1776, was a member of the Continental Congress from 1774 to 1777, and followed **Thomas Jefferson** (1743–1826; see entry in volume 1) as governor of Virginia from 1781 to 1784. Young William studied medicine in Philadelphia under the famous Dr. Benjamin Rush (1746–1813). However, he ran out of funds when his father died in 1791. So, having a real interest in military matters, Harrison enlisted as an army officer at age eighteen.

Harrison served as an aide to Wayne in the early 1790s, fighting the Native American alliance that was resisting American expansion on the frontier. He took part in the decisive Battle of Fallen Timbers in August 1794, which broke the Native American alliance in the Ohio Country. In 1798, President **John Adams** (1735–1826; served 1797–1801; see entry in volume 1) appointed Harrison secretary of the Northwest Territory and sent him to Congress as a territorial delegate the following year. In May 1800, Adams appointed Harrison governor of the newly established Indiana Territory.

Harrison negotiated a number of treaties with the Native Americans, opening up millions of acres to U.S. settlement in the future states of Indiana, Illinois, Wisconsin, and Missouri. However, in reaction to the treaties, a new alliance of tribes formed under the leadership of Shawnee leader **Tecumseh** (1768–1813; see entry in volume 2). Tecumseh's followers intended to stop further settlement in the region, but Harrison took command of a force of regular army and militia to combat the tribes. He delivered a major blow to the alliance in November 1811 at the Battle of Tippecanoe near present-day Lafayette, Indiana.

settlement. They also agreed to abandon their posts on American soil, which they had continued to occupy since the end of the American Revolution in 1783. Therefore, when the Native American warriors fell back from the battlefield at Fallen Timbers, they did not receive the backup they needed and expected from British troops at nearby Fort Miami. The Native American alliance was crushed.

Wayne followed the military victory with the Treaty of Greenville, signed on August 3, 1795. Wayne had convinced tribal leaders that continuing to defend the Northwest Territory was hopeless. As a result, the Native Americans ceded (gave up)

William Henry Harrison. (© *Bettmann/Corbis.*)

When the War of 1812 (1812–15) broke out, Harrison resigned as governor and was given the rank of major general to command all U.S. forces in the Northwest Territory. He was to combat British forces in the region and their Native American allies. On October 5, 1813, his troops delivered a major defeat to the British and Native Americans at the Battle of the Thames in Ontario, Canada. During the battle, Tecumseh was killed. The Native American resistance to American settlement was permanently stopped in the Northwest region. Harrison became a national hero and enjoyed the same popularity that Wayne had almost twenty years earlier.

After the war, Harrison had an illustrious political career, serving in the U.S. House of Representatives (1816–19), the Ohio Senate (1819–21), and the U.S. Senate (1825–28). After unsuccessfully running for president in 1836, he won in the next election in 1840. However, after giving a two-hour inauguration speech in freezing rain on March 4, 1841, in Washington, D.C., he died one month later of pneumonia. His grandson, Benjamin Harrison (1833–1901; served 1889–93), would become the twenty-third U.S. president in 1889.

most of Ohio and large parts of Indiana, Illinois, and Michigan. By destroying the confederation of tribes, Wayne opened large areas of the Northwest Territory for American settlement. Ohio became a new state less than a decade later, in 1803.

A sudden end

Following his success in Ohio Country, Wayne toured the newly abandoned British posts, setting up strongholds for U.S. control of the region. His national popularity was very high. He was even considered as a candidate for secretary of war when **Henry Knox** (1750–1806; see entry in volume 1) retired in December 1794. In late 1796, Wayne began his return home from the western frontier but died suddenly of complications from a case of gout (a disease affecting the joints and blood) at Presque Isle, now present-day Erie, Pennsylvania.

Many places and institutions in the former Northwest Territory are named after Wayne. These include the city of Fort Wayne, Indiana, the educational institution of Wayne State University in Detroit, and Wayne Counties in Ohio, Michigan, and Indiana.

For More Information

Books

Cleaves, Freeman. *Old Tippecanoe: William Henry Harrison and His Time.* New York: C. Scribner's Sons, 1939. Reprint, Newtown, CT: American Political Biography Press, 1990.

Nelson, Paul David. *Anthony Wayne: Soldier of the Early Republic.* Bloomington: Indiana University Press, 1985.

Preston, John Hyde. *A Gentleman Rebel: The Exploits of Anthony Wayne.* New York: Farrar & Rinehart, 1930.

Tucker, Glenn. *Mad Anthony Wayne and the New Nation: The Story of Washington's Front-Line General.* Harrisburg, PA: Stackpole Books, 1973.

Web Sites

"William Henry Harrison." *The White House.* http://www.whitehouse.gov/history/presidents/wh9.html (accessed on August 18, 2005).

William White

Born April 4, 1748 (Philadelphia, Pennsylvania)
Died July 17, 1836 (Philadelphia, Pennsylvania)

Episcopal church leader

William White has been called the chief architect of the Episcopal Church in America. His gifts as a theologian and an organizer, along with his family connections, made him an important leader during the development of the Church. He was largely responsible for creating the Constitution of the Protestant Episcopal Church in the United States. White helped organize the system of church government that remains the base of the modern Episcopal Church. As the rector (clergyman in charge of a parish) of a prominent Philadelphia, Pennsylvania, parish, White wrote extensively on the unity and future growth of Anglicanism, or the Episcopal Church, in the new nation. He was elected bishop of the diocese of Pennsylvania in 1786 and was presiding bishop of the Protestant Episcopal Church from 1795 until his death in 1836.

"Being invited to preach before a battalion, I declined and mentioned to the colonel ... my objections to the making of the ministry instrumental to the war."

Growing up

William White was born in 1748 to a wealthy Philadelphia family who had made their money in real estate. His father, Colonel Thomas White, was a lawyer and surveyor who held various public offices in both Pennsylvania and Maryland. His

William White. *(© Stapleton Collection/Corbis.)*

mother was Esther Hewlings. The White family was socially
connected with the affluent upper classes of Philadelphia, the
largest colonial city in America at the time. William graduated from the College of Philadelphia (later the University of
Pennsylvania) in 1765. Early in his education, he settled on a
ministerial vocation (career). In 1770, the twenty-two-year-
old White went to England for study and ordination (ceremony for giving ministerial authority) because there was no
Anglican bishop in the colonies. However, because he was
still quite young, his formal ordination did not occur until
April 25, 1772.

White returned to the United States as conflict between the colonists and British rulers was escalating. In 1772, he was elected assistant to the rector in his home church at Christ Church in Philadelphia. He was seen as a moderate revolutionary who made every effort to remain on good terms with the significant number of Loyalists (those who favored British rule) who were members of his parish. In 1773, William married Mary Harrison, the daughter of a former mayor of Philadelphia. William and Mary had eight children. William's sister, Mary White, married Robert Morris (1734–1806) in 1769 (see box). Morris was a successful businessman who became the chief financier of the Continental Army during the American Revolution (1775–83).

When the American Revolution officially began in 1775, White's rector, Jacob Duché (1737–1798), took sides with the Patriots (those favoring independence from British rule) and became chaplain to the Continental Congress. Duché reversed his allegiance when the British occupied Philadelphia in 1777. When Duché returned to England, White was then elected rector of the United Parish of Christ Church and St. Peter's. He remained in this position for the rest of his life.

White was also named chaplain to the Continental Congress in Duché's place. While serving the Congress, White became friends with several leading patriots, including **George Washington** (1732–1799; see entry in volume 2), who was an Episcopalian. White served as chaplain from 1777 to 1789.

The case of the Episcopal churches in America

White fully supported the cause of American independence but refused to use his pulpit to further the Patriots' cause. In the colonies, many prominent Loyalists were also Anglican clergymen with ties to the British civil authorities. This led people who considered themselves Patriots to characterize all Anglican clergymen as Loyalists, even though many of these clergy supported the Revolution. In the northern colonies, most Anglican ministers facing public hostility shut their churches. When the British withdrew from Boston in the spring of 1776, public religious services were no longer held. Anglican clergymen who remained in the United States could not conduct public worship. Instead, they went from house to house giving personal sermons to families. In the course of

Robert Morris

Robert Morris was known as the "financier of the American Revolution" because of his role in obtaining financial assistance for the colonies in their fight against the British. Morris was born in England in 1734 and moved to Maryland at the age of thirteen. His father died two years later. Morris apprenticed at the shipping and banking firm of the wealthy Philadelphia merchant Charles Willing (1710–1754). When Willing died, Morris joined his son to form Willing, Morris and Company, a firm that specialized in importation (bringing goods into the country), exportation (shipping goods out of the country), and general banking. This business made Morris one of the wealthiest and most influential citizens of Philadelphia. In 1769, Morris, a member of the Episcopal Church, married Mary White, the sister of future Episcopal bishop William White. Morris was elected to represent Pennsylvania in the Continental Congress from 1775 until 1778.

On August 2, 1776, Morris signed the Declaration of Independence. In March 1778, Morris also signed the Articles of Confederation as a representative of Pennsylvania. When Morris signed the newly created U.S. Constitution in 1787, he joined Roger Sherman (1721–1793) as one of only two people to have signed all three of the significant founding documents of the United States.

During the American Revolution, Morris remained in Philadelphia and gave critical financial support to the Continental government. Throughout the war, Morris's company imported arms and munitions and seized the cargo of British ships as they came into port. Morris obtained critically needed supplies for the army of General Nathanael Greene (1742–1786) in 1779, and in 1780 he raised more than a million dollars to contribute to George Washington's success in the Battle of Yorktown the following year. Morris served as superintendent of finance of the United States under the Articles of Confederation from 1781 until 1784. Along with **Alexander Hamilton** (1755–1804; see entry in volume 1) and **Albert Gallatin** (1761–1849; see entry in volume 1), Morris is considered one of the key founders of the American financial system.

On January 15, 1782, Morris went before the U.S. Congress to recommend the

their ministry, they performed marriages and baptisms, taught catechism (religious instruction), and attended to the needs of the sick and the dying.

Reflecting his allegiance to the new United States, on the Sunday before July 4, 1776, White stopped praying for the British king and altered other parts of his church services accordingly. By November, Pennsylvania was without Anglican church services everywhere except in Philadelphia. By the fall of 1778, thirty-year-old William White was the only Anglican

Robert Morris. *(Library of Congress.)*

establishment of a national mint (a place where money is produced) and a new coinage system, both later adopted. His portrait appeared on U.S. thousand-dollar notes from 1862 to 1863 and on ten-dollar silver certificates from 1878 until 1880. Morris, along with Oliver Pollock (c. 1737–1823), is

thought to also have played a role in the creation of the dollar sign.

In 1787, Morris was elected to the Constitutional Convention, where he nominated his friend George Washington as president of the convention. Washington appointed Morris as secretary of the Treasury in 1789 in the new U.S. government, but Morris declined the position. Morris served as a U.S. senator from 1789 until 1795.

In 1794, Morris began construction of a mansion in Philadelphia designed by the noted French architect **Pierre-Charles L'Enfant** (1754–1825; see entry in volume 2). During this time, Morris also became involved with some unsuccessful business deals. With Morris's debt mounting, the mansion remained unfinished and became known as "Morris's Folly." Morris was arrested and imprisoned for debt in Philadelphia's Prune Street prison from February 1798 until August 1801. His health suffered, and he spent the remainder of his life in retirement until his death on May 8, 1806. He was buried in the family vault of William White at Christ Church in Philadelphia.

clergyman left in Philadelphia. He was concerned about the unity and future growth of Anglicanism in the new nation. So in 1782, he wrote and published a pamphlet titled *The Case of the Episcopal Churches in the United States Considered*. In it, he recommended amendments to church structure that would conform with the new political values of the United States. He argued that, under the circumstances, the American church might proceed to ordain clergy without bishops in order to fill the desperate need. He also urged the use of the laity, or unordained church members, in carrying out church business. The High Church clergy (those who supported complete reliance on traditional church authority) in Connecticut and elsewhere posed strong resistance to White's proposal. They stressed the formal, liturgical character of Anglicanism that relied totally on formally established church authority and did not support American autonomy (right of self-government) in the Church that proposed giving laity greater powers.

The first efforts to reorganize the Anglican churches occurred in Maryland in November 1780. A convention was assembled composed of three clergymen and a number of laymen. They met to ask for public support for changes in the church during the troublesome times of the war. At the convention, organizers used the name "Protestant Episcopal Church" to replace their former designation as members of the Church of England, the official religion of England. They hoped that the name change would further distance their association with Britain. The name the Protestant Episcopal Church was eventually adopted by general agreement for the national church organization. The word Protestant was applied because it had come to describe any form of Western Christianity that owed no allegiance to the pope.

Taking care of business

The Anglican community faced more difficult decisions when the war ended with the signing of the 1783 Treaty of Paris. The establishment of an American branch of the Anglican Church holding the power to elect its own bishops became necessary. Ministers who remained in the United States had to decide whether they wanted to participate in the founding of a church that operated independently of the British king and the Church of England. The Revolution had left a general suspicion of Anglican disloyalty to American interests and raised some doubts about the Church's long-term survival in the United States. White and others envisioned an independent American church. They believed that once the church could be separated from all governmental ties it would be free to remodel itself.

After the Revolution, two different schemes emerged for structuring the American church. In 1783, the High Church clergy in Connecticut met to consider their situation. They decided the most pressing issue was the need for a bishop. The clergy elected Samuel Seabury (1729–1796) to fill the role, and he set sail for England, hoping to be consecrated (formally dedicated to religious service) by the bishops there. He did not receive consecration in England, so he journeyed to Scotland and was consecrated by the Scottish bishops on November 14, 1784. He then returned to Connecticut, where he organized his diocese on the English model. Meanwhile, in Pennsylvania and other states, the American church was organizing in the same way the nation was being organized, at the state and national levels as proposed by White.

White's pamphlet on church structure, along with his position as rector of the United Parish of Christ Church and St. Peter's, made him a prominent leader to whom both High Church clergy and those seeking reform in church authority (often referred to as Low Church) could turn for counsel. In 1784, the first meeting of clerical and lay delegates in New York City used White's suggestion for church structure. They agreed to continue using a modified English prayer book and recommended that each state should have a bishop. The delegates proposed that the national church should be governed by general conventions at which the bishops would meet with clergy and lay delegates.

The nature and authority of the Church

White helped write the *Constitution of the Protestant Episcopal Church in the United States of America.* It gave a republican form to the church's governing institutions by giving laypeople the power to participate in the election of church leaders. White also had an important role in writing the American revision of the English prayer book.

In 1785, White was elected president of the first meeting of the General Convention of the Protestant Episcopal Church, which met in Philadelphia. In the opening session, one of his first actions was to publicly recognize the consecration of Bishop Seabury. White fully supported Seabury in the hopes of promoting church unity in the United States. He worked in cooperation with Seabury to move the church's organizational efforts forward.

In 1786, the convention of the diocese of Pennsylvania elected White bishop. The Church of England and the British government were still wrestling with the problem of consecrating bishops who neither swore allegiance to the king nor obedience to the archbishop. They finally agreed to consecrate three such bishops in order to start the Episcopal Church in the United States. White was one of those bishops. He traveled to Lambeth Palace in England, and the archbishops of Canterbury and York consecrated him in February 1787.

The nature and authority of the Church

In 1789, Bishop White presided at the First General Convention of the Protestant Episcopal Church, where the constitution and prayer book were formally adopted. It was the same year that George Washington was inaugurated as the first president of the United States. By 1792, the Episcopal Church was finally established as an American denomination. It had a governing body, a national constitution, and the ability to consecrate new bishops. White was again called on to preside at the general convention in 1795. Because of White's long influential history with the Church, many bishops, priests, and laypersons looked to him as a father figure. They called on White to preside at every general convention until 1836.

Bishop White continued serving at his home parish in Philadelphia while attending to his national church duties. He was a trusted advisor to a new generation of leaders in the American Episcopal Church. White encouraged educational opportunities for women and helped found institutions for the deaf. White ordained **Absalom Jones** (1746–1818; see entry in volume 1), the first black American to be ordained by a major religious denomination.

As a public-spirited citizen and leader in Philadelphia, White was second only to diplomat and scientist **Benjamin Franklin** (1706–1790; see entry in volume 1) in popularity and respect. Toward the end of his life, White wrote *Memoirs of the Protestant Episcopal Church in the United States of America*. It is the only firsthand account of the events leading to the formation of the Episcopal Church. White's death in Philadelphia at the age of eighty-eight marked the end of an era for the Church.

For More Information

Books

Albright, Raymond W. *A History of the Protestant Episcopal Church.* New York: Macmillan, 1964.

Locke, David. *Episcopal Church (Great Religions of the World).* New York: Hippocrene Books, 1991.

Prichard, Robert W. *A History of the Episcopal Church.* Rev. ed. Harrisburg, PA: Morehouse Publishing, 1999.

Rhoden, Nancy L. *Revolutionary Anglicanism: The Colonial Church of England Clergy during the American Revolution.* New York: New York University Press, 1999.

White, William. *Memoirs of the Protestant Episcopal Church in the United States of America.* 3rd ed. Philadelphia: S. Potter & Co., 1880.

Web Sites

"William White, Bishop of Pennsylvania: 17 July 1836." *The Society of Archbishop Justus.* http://justus.anglican.org/resources/bio/202.html (accessed on August 18, 2005).

Eli Whitney

Born December 8, 1765 (Westborough, Massachusetts)
Died January 8, 1825 (New Haven, Connecticut)

Inventor, engineer, manufacturer

"One of my primary objects is to form the tools so the tools themselves shall fashion the work and give to every part its just proportion."

Eli Whitney is one of the most influential inventors in American history. Though most noted for inventing the cotton gin, he made his greatest contribution to industry by creating a manufacturing process for making muskets (firearms) with interchangeable parts. A part from one musket could fit any other musket he made. Whitney revolutionized industrial production by establishing the basis for the future assembly line and modern mass production. He was a pioneer in creating machine tools, which could make each part of a musket separately with consistent precision. With this new manufacturing process, unskilled workers could mass-produce items that were previously made very slowly by individual skilled craftsmen.

The cotton gin, on the other hand, was a mechanically simple device. Therefore, its importance was more in the social and economic realm. The cotton gin led to a booming Southern economy and greatly increased the use of slaves in the United States. Some eighty thousand slaves were brought into the United States between 1790 and 1808, the year that Congress finally banned the importation of slaves.

Eli Whitney. *(© Bettmann/Corbis.)*

Whitney's influence on agriculture in the South and manufacturing in the North was enormous. By 1815, Whitney's manufacturing system was widely known and used by other firearm makers; it was also used for making such diverse products as wooden clocks and sewing machines. By the mid-nineteenth century, the United States was supplying three-fourths of the world's cotton. Cotton made up some 60 percent of U.S. exports at that time.

A child with mechanical ability

Eli Whitney was born in December 1765 to Eli and Elizabeth Whitney in Westborough, Massachusetts, east of Worcester. They were a long-established family in the region. Ancestor John Whitney had emigrated from England to Watertown, Massachusetts, in 1635. The Whitneys were successful farmers in the Worcester area, and the older Eli also served as justice of the peace of Westborough. Young Eli grew up well cared for. His parents intended for him to go to college, but he was not interested in books. Farmwork did not appeal to him either. He had other interests, including working with his hands. Since early childhood, Eli had a great mechanical ability in working with tools found around the farm.

As he got older, Whitney made and repaired violins and at age fifteen began manufacturing nails. Nails were especially needed during the American Revolution (1775–83) to build various kinds of military buildings, bridges, forts, and defensive structures. Young Eli even hired a helper to meet orders for his nails. The demand for nails declined following the war, so Whitney turned to production of hatpins (pins used to secure women's hats on their heads) which sold well around the region.

Finally, at age at eighteen, Whitney decided that he would need a college degree to progress further. However, his parents were no longer financially able to pay for his college expenses. Therefore, Whitney began teaching at various schools to save money for college. He entered Leicester Academy in Leicester, Massachusetts, for final academic preparation before entering college. In May 1789, at twenty-three years of age, Whitney entered Yale College in New Haven, Connecticut. While pursuing his studies at Yale, he earned money repairing equipment at the college.

Off to the South

Whitney did well at Yale. Following graduation in the fall of 1792, he decided to pursue law studies. In order to earn money while studying law, he accepted a job as a tutor in Georgia. While aboard ship on his way from New England to Savannah, Georgia, he met **Catharine Littlefield Greene** (1755–1814; see entry in volume 1), widow of war hero General

Nathanael Greene (1742–1786). Realizing Whitney had no place to stay and little money, Greene invited him to stay at her plantation near Savannah, known as Mulberry Grove. There, he could make money by solving mechanical problems around the grounds.

While Whitney was staying at the plantation, many guests and neighbors dropped by for visits with Greene. Sitting in on the conversations, Whitney learned that the South's agricultural economy was struggling because the demand for tobacco was in decline. There was a high demand for cotton in Britain, but much of the land more than 50 miles from the coastline was not suitable for growing rice or black seed cotton with long fibers (called staples) that were common crops in the coastal area. However, a different variety of cotton, a short-staple cotton with sticky green seeds, could be readily grown on the plentiful higher, drier soils in the interior regions away from the coast. Separating the sticky seeds from the fluffy white cotton bolls was difficult. The green seed cotton could not be grown for profit since a single slave could separate only a pound of it each day using hand combs. Visitors to the plantation said a machine was needed to separate the seeds from the fibers. Greene suggested to Whitney that he could tackle the problem during his stay at the plantation. She would cover the costs of the development and provide a workshop.

The cotton gin

Taking the challenge, in ten days Whitney assembled a crude cotton gin ("gin" is short for engine) with which to experiment. By April 1793, he had a much improved though still simple model (see box). A slave could process 50 pounds of cotton a day with this device.

At the plantation, Whitney became friends with Phineas Miller, manager of the plantation. Miller was about the same age as Whitney and had graduated from Yale as well. The two decided to patent Whitney's new cotton gin and begin manufacturing the machine. They signed a partnership agreement in late May to manufacture machines and operate a cotton ginning business throughout the South. They dreamed of creating a monopoly and getting rich. (A monopoly is where a person or company has complete control over a product or a service.)

The Cotton Gin

Eli Whitney's invention to separate sticky seeds from short cotton fibers was very simple in design. It used a hand-cranked cylinder containing a series of teeth to separate the cotton from the seeds. This process was a mechanized version of the hand-combing method that slaves used to clean the cotton. Other gins had been in use at various times, so Whitney's creation was not altogether new. After Whitney's invention went public, many others built slight variations of the device.

Whitney's device included only a few basic parts: a hopper to feed the cotton into; a revolving cylinder with hundreds of short curved hooks placed in lines; and numerous wires spun through narrow grooves in a stationary piece. The seeds passed through the narrow grooves while the cotton fibers flowed through the revolving cylinder. Last in the process were bristles that combed the cleaned fibers from the wire hooks.

Shortly after Whitney's gins began operating, concerns arose that the cotton fibers were being unacceptably damaged. It took

The cotton gin, invented by Eli Whitney.
(© Underwood and Underwood/Corbis.)

over a year to determine that the machines did not unnecessarily harm the fibers. Larger versions of the cotton gin were soon developed besides those that were cranked by hand. The larger models could be driven by horses or water power.

Whitney returned to New Haven to begin producing the cotton gins to ship to Miller in Georgia. He received a patent on March 14, 1794. They suffered a setback in 1795 when Whitney's shop burned down. In addition, the cotton gin was such a simple device that others could easily reproduce it. Soon, many people were making and using cotton gins much like Whitney's. Whitney began a number of lawsuits to stop others from producing the cotton gins like his. However, the lawsuits proved unsuccessful and consumed a lot of time and money. By 1797, Whitney and Miller were out of business.

A personal economic bust

Though the cotton gin business did not bring its originators financial success, it did revive the Southern economy, which was now booming. The production of cotton doubled every decade following Whitney's invention. Before Whitney's cotton gin in 1792, the United States exported only 138,000 pounds of cotton. Just two years later, exports rose to 1.6 million pounds, and in 1795 cotton exports reached 6.3 million pounds. By 1800, the United States was producing 35 million pounds of cotton and exporting just over half of that. Although plantations expanded across the South and grew in size, the growth of cities and industry in the South was hindered by the emphasis on agriculture brought on by the cotton gin.

Perhaps feeling that Whitney and Miller deserved some reward for sparking the South's economic boom, the state of South Carolina gave them a payment of $50,000 in 1802. North Carolina, Tennessee, and Georgia also paid the partners for their effort. They received a total of $90,000. However, this still did not cover their expenses from the past ten years. Miller died in 1803 having lost money in the cotton gin venture. In 1812, Whitney's patent application needed to be renewed; however, Congress denied the renewal application.

Gun manufacturing

After seeing his cotton gin bring economic success to almost everyone but himself, Whitney tackled a different manufacturing project in 1797. The U.S. government was issuing contracts for the production of forty thousand military muskets. The prospects of war with France were growing, and the United States was readying its forces. Whitney submitted a proposal to build ten thousand muskets in just two years. This was a phenomenal rate of production for the late 1790s, especially for a person with no firearm-making experience and no factory, tools, or workers. The two existing U.S. armories had only produced one thousand muskets in the previous three years.

Whitney received a contract on January 14, 1798, for $134,000. Twenty-seven other gun manufacturers also

A busy Eli Whitney in his workshop. *(© Bettmann/Corbis.)*

received contracts. Whitney proposed to use a new method to produce firearms. He would create individual precision parts for the musket by machine, making each piece identical to others of its kind. This method allowed Whitney to use unskilled laborers rather than craftsmen, so he could make muskets much faster than other manufacturers and with less expense. Whitney became the first manufacturer in America to make a product with interchangeable parts. Until this time, muskets and other firearms were made one at a time by skilled craftsmen, with each part made specifically for that firearm. If a part broke, a new part would have to be made to fit that specific firearm.

Interchangeable parts

Whitney first found ten investors to provide money for his enterprise. He then purchased a 100-acre mill site with a 6-foot-high log dam on Mill River near New Haven. There, he built a factory and rebuilt the aging dam. The water spilling over the dam would provide the power to fuel his machines. He hired about fifty skilled workers to work on this initial phase of building the factory and the operating machines. Whitney also built a row of five stone houses for the married workmen and their families and a boardinghouse for single men. (This was the first time an American employer had provided residences for workers.) He also built a stone building for a store. The new community was named Whitneyville, the first manufacturing village in the nation. Whitney was unmarried and lived in a nearby farmhouse with three nephews and servants. He also brought in about a dozen mechanical apprentices at a time, and they stayed at the farmhouse, too.

Whitney then began designing and making the machines and tools he needed to make muskets. Expenses grew unexpectedly as the process unfolded, but he continued receiving financial support from investors. After overcoming numerous problems in designing his factory, which was the first of its kind, Whitney began producing muskets. However, he produced only five hundred the first year, rather than the four thousand called for in the government contract. Other problems arose, too, including a long severe winter that froze the flowing water that powered the machines. A yellow fever epidemic struck many of the workers, and Whitney had problems receiving supplies.

According to some accounts, when Whitney journeyed to Washington, D.C., in 1801 to request a time extension on his contract, he gave a memorable demonstration. Whitney set out a pile of parts, enough to make ten muskets, and challenged the government officials to assemble the muskets. They did it very successfully. The officials were greatly impressed with Whitney's ideas and gave him his extension.

A profitable business

Despite the continuous problems at the new factory, the government kept giving Whitney extensions to his contract as they remained greatly enthused by the process he was developing. Now unskilled laborers could produce a musket in simple steps; musket production was no longer a time-consuming, complex task that required a craftsman. The federal government adopted the manufacturing system in its two armories to produce firearms at a considerable savings. In the end, it would take eight years to produce a total of ten thousand.

At the beginning of the War of 1812 (1812–15), Whitney received another government contract; he was asked to manufacture fifteen thousand firearms. He also received a contract for another fifteen thousand firearms from the State of New York. Because of these government orders, Whitney's firearms business was much more profitable than his cotton gin enterprise.

The social life

Aside from the considerable time and energy that Whitney poured into his work, he also enjoyed refined life in society. He had a dignified manner and a pleasant personality; he also had strong opinions. Some claimed his greatest attribute was the perseverance he showed in developing his inventions.

On January 6, 1817, at fifty-one years of age, Whitney married Henrietta Frances Edwards, granddaughter of one of the great American religious figures in the eighteenth-century, Jonathan Edwards (1703–1758). They had four children, but one died young. Whitney died in New Haven in 1825. At first, two nephews took over operations and delivered another fifteen thousand muskets. His only son, Eli Whitney Jr., took over in 1842 and expanded the factory. In 1888, the Whitneyville factory was sold to Winchester Repeating Arms.

For More Information

Books

Gaines, Ann. *Eli Whitney*. Vero Beach, FL: Rourke Books, 2002.

Green, Constance M. *Eli Whitney and the Birth of American Technology*. Boston: Little, Brown, 1956.

Hall, M. C. *Eli Whitney*. Chicago: Heinemann Library, 2004.

Huff, Regan A. *Eli Whitney: The Cotton Gin and American Manufacturing*. New York: PowerPlus Books, 2004.

Patchett, Kaye. *Eli Whitney: Cotton Gin Genius*. San Diego, CA: Blackbirch Press, 2004.

Web Sites

Eli Whitney Museum. http://www.eliwhitney.org/cotton.htm (accessed on August 18, 2005).

John Witherspoon

Born February 5, 1723 (Gifford, Scotland)
Died November 15, 1794 (Princeton, New Jersey)

Protestant theologian, educator

"A good form of government may hold the rotten materials together for some time, but beyond a certain pitch, even the best constitution will be ineffectual, and slavery must ensue."

John Witherspoon was an American Founding Father, a noted clergyman, and an educator. He played an influential role in his home country of Scotland and in his adopted country, the United States. Witherspoon was the only clergyman to sign the Declaration of Independence. From 1776 until 1782, he served as a delegate to the Continental Congress, where he helped draft the Articles of Confederation, America's first constitution. After the American Revolution (1775–83), Witherspoon was twice elected to the New Jersey legislature.

Witherspoon served as president of College of New Jersey (now Princeton University) from 1768 until 1794. In his role as educator, he taught many students who became leaders in early American public life. His students included future U.S. senators, governors, U.S. Supreme Court justices, and the future author of the U.S. Constitution, **James Madison** (1751–1836; see entry in volume 2), who would one day become the fourth U.S. president. Witherspoon played an important role in the organization of a newly independent and national Presbyterian Church. In 1789, he opened its first general assembly with a sermon and presided until the election of the first moderator (assembly leader).

John Witherspoon. *(Library of Congress.)*

Twenty years in the Church of Scotland

John Witherspoon was born on February 5, 1723, the son of Anne, or Anna, Walker and James Witherspoon, a minister of the Church of Scotland. Witherspoon, one of six children in the family, was born in the village of Gifford in the parish of Yester, Scotland, 18 miles east of Edinburgh Castle. He received his early education at home before attending the preparatory school in Haddington, Scotland. At the age of thirteen, Witherspoon was considered advanced for his age and was admitted to the University of Edinburgh. He studied

Latin, Greek, logic, and philosophy. Witherspoon graduated in 1739, at the age of sixteen, with a master of arts degree.

Witherspoon went on to study theology (the research of religious truth and the nature of God) and gained a license to preach on September 6, 1743. He was called as minister of the Church of Scotland parish in Beith, Ayrshire, in 1745, where he was ordained, or formally became a minister. That same year, an invasion by Charles Edward Stuart (1720–1788), known as the Young Pretender, threw Scotland into turmoil. Stuart was trying to recapture the throne of England and Scotland for his family after his grandfather, King James II (1633–1701; reigned 1685–88), had been exiled to Italy for his Roman Catholic beliefs. Witherspoon joined other parish leaders in gathering troops to fight against the rebellion, but he was soon captured by Stuart's forces. He endured a brief but harsh imprisonment in Castle Doune near Stirling. In April 1746, Stuart's forces were defeated by the English army, ending the war. Stuart escaped to Europe where he remained for the rest of his life.

In reestablishing his life after the war, Witherspoon married Elizabeth Montgomery on September 2, 1748. The couple had ten children, five of whom died during childhood.

The Church of Scotland faced new challenges when Witherspoon was a young minister. Leaders in the Moderate, or liberal, Party of the church were challenging the Popular Party, which held a more traditional Christian faith. The Moderates were associated with closer ties to the government and selecting clergy by a central authority. The Popular Party favored continued independence of congregations and selecting their own ministers.

Witherspoon was an aggressive leader of the Popular Party, and in 1753 he published a witty satire (literary ridicule) about the Moderate Party called *Ecclesiastical Characteristics*. Published anonymously in Glasgow, Scotland, the pamphlet came out in multiple editions over the next few years from printers throughout Europe and North America. When his identity as the author became known, Witherspoon gained celebrity status. He continued his attacks on the Moderates' theology with additional publications. In June 1757, Witherspoon was asked to serve at the Laigh Kirk church in Paisley, near Glasgow. There, he continued his stand against the increasing liberalism (nontraditional views) of the Moderate

Party. In 1764, the University of St. Andrews awarded Witherspoon an honorary degree of doctor of divinity in recognition of his theological skills and leadership in the Popular Party.

Witherspoon moves to America

Witherspoon was gaining fame abroad and enjoying popularity at home as the lively theological debate went on in the Church of Scotland. American Presbyterians knew of Witherspoon through his writings, which established him as a man of orthodoxy (belief in long-standing church traditions and established doctrine) and a first-rate scholar. He also had a reputation for possessing a good sense of humor to accompany his commonsense philosophy. Witherspoon's name came up when the trustees of the College of New Jersey (see box) found themselves in need of a new president. In 1766, the New York and Philadelphia Presbyterians recruited Witherspoon to come to America to head the college and lead the Presbyterian Church. He was interested in the position, but his wife, Elizabeth, had no interest in leaving Scotland or her family and friends. She had a great fear of crossing the ocean to begin life in a new land, so Witherspoon regretfully declined the offer.

Though Witherspoon had already turned down the offer, negotiations were kept alive by the continued efforts of Benjamin Rush (1745–1813; see box), a young American and graduate of the College of New Jersey who was studying medicine in Edinburgh at the time. Rush spent several days with the Witherspoons, calming Elizabeth's fears and talking away her objections. He succeeded in persuading her to move to America, and final arrangements were made. Witherspoon packed up the family's belongings along with three hundred books to add to the college library. The Witherspoons and their five surviving children arrived in Princeton, New Jersey, on August 12, 1768. The students and faculty had arranged a warm reception to make the family feel welcome in their new country. The Witherspoons were greeted a mile out of town and escorted the rest of the way. When they got to the college, the family saw a candle illuminating each window of the institution in celebration of their arrival.

Witherspoon was forty-five years old when he became the sixth president of the College of New Jersey at Princeton.

Princeton University

Education in colonial America began with various religious denominations. They provided instructors and raised the funds to support schools and colleges, not only to ensure scholarly clergymen but also to develop enlightened citizens. The Congregationalists established Harvard and Yale, the Anglicans founded William and Mary, the Baptists established Brown, and the Presbyterians started Princeton.

A religious revival swept through the American colonies in the early eighteenth century. There was an urgent need for ministers to fill the vacancies in existing churches and in the new colonies. Because the Mid-Atlantic colonies showed the greatest need for higher education, several leaders of the Presbyterian Church met to plan the creation of a new institution in New Jersey. Of the original group who met, six were graduates of Yale and one was from Harvard. Their task was to create a new institution, erect buildings, secure financial support, and employ a competent faculty. The organizers solicited financial aid, and on October 22, 1746, New Jersey governor John Hamilton granted them a charter for their college. Trustees were chosen, and Jonathan Dickinson (1688–1747) was elected president of the new College of New Jersey. The college opened its doors in the spring of 1747 in Elizabeth, New Jersey.

When Dickinson died several months later, the infant college moved 6 miles down the road to Newark, where the new president, Aaron Burr Sr. (1715–1757), resided. Finances remained a concern during the early years of the school. In 1753, two delegates were sent to Britain and Ulster, Ireland, in hopes of securing funds for buildings and other financial need. They were successful in their mission, and plans went forward to build a new campus in the little village of Princeton. The quiet country town, once known as

He immediately went to work revising the college curriculum by adding the study of philosophy, history, and public speaking. Witherspoon insisted that his students master the English language so that they would be well equipped to take part in the political and social debates of the day. He introduced French as an elective for students who wanted to study a modern language, and he taught the classes himself. In addition to managing the college's affairs, Witherspoon taught a full load of courses and preached twice each Sunday.

The College of New Jersey had been founded for the express purpose of training young men in ministry to care for the

Nassau Hall, on the campus of Princeton University. *(© Roman Soumar/Corbis.)*

the village, the trustees built a massive stone building called Nassau Hall. Its name was given in memory of King William III (1650–1702; reigned 1689–1702), who was of the house of Nassau. The distinguished building itself was modeled carefully after King's College in Cambridge, England, but with less ornamentation.

Aaron Burr Sr. died in September 1757; three more school presidents died in office between then and the summer of 1766. At that time, the college sought out John Witherspoon from Scotland to serve as its sixth president. Witherspoon would serve from 1768 until his death in 1794.

The College of New Jersey officially became known as Princeton University in October 1896. Throughout its early history, Princeton carried out its purpose of training clergymen for the ministry and for public service. The institution played a major role in the creation and development of an independent America by training many notable graduates.

"Prince Town," was situated along the road halfway between Philadelphia, Pennsylvania, and New York City. Near the center of growing Presbyterian Church in America. A split in 1741 left the church divided into Old Side and New Light factions. The Old Side Presbyterians favored traditional means of worship at established churches with trained ministers. The New Light Presbyterians were influenced by the revival movement, which included ministers traveling across the country, often giving sermons in town markets or wherever crowds gathered. Witherspoon experienced great success in reuniting the quarreling sects. His moderate style and earnest desire to produce a well-educated clergy won him support from both sides.

Witherspoon became involved in trying to resolve some financial problems the college was having. He traveled extensively throughout the colonies, raising funds and recruiting

Dr. Benjamin Rush

The young nation was led by a number of bright professionals in the late eighteenth century. Dr. Benjamin Rush was the recognized leader in the medical field.

Rush was born in January 1746 near Philadelphia, Pennsylvania. His father, John Rush, was a farmer and gunsmith. After graduating from the College of New Jersey, later Princeton, in 1760, Rush served in a medical apprenticeship for six years before sailing to Scotland, where he received a medical degree from the University of Edinburgh. Rush returned to Philadelphia in 1769 and began his medical practice. He also taught medicine and chemistry at the College of Philadelphia, later the University of Pennsylvania Medical School. In 1770, Rush published the first American textbook on chemistry.

Rush also became a prominent Patriot during the American Revolution. He served in the Continental Congress in 1776, where he became one of the signers of the Declaration of Independence. He then served for a year as surgeon general for the Continental Army before resuming his practice and teaching. In 1787, Pennsylvania sent Rush as a delegate to the Constitutional Convention held in his hometown of Philadelphia. Rush supported the new constitution that was drafted at the convention and signed his approval alongside the names of the nation's Founding Fathers. In 1797, President John Adams appointed Rush treasurer

Benjamin Rush.

of the U.S. Mint in Philadelphia, a position he held for the rest of his life.

Rush was also a social activist supporting many causes, including education for women. He was also an outspoken critic of slavery and helped establish the abolitionist society (a group opposed to slavery) in Philadelphia. In his medical practice, Rush favored bloodletting, a controversial treatment that supposedly purged disease from a person's body by profuse bleeding. He conducted major bloodletting during the Philadelphia yellow fever epidemics of the 1790s, perhaps causing many deaths simply from the loss of blood. Rush also became a leading expert on mental health and authored the first American book on psychiatry in 1812.

students. He cultivated a great deal of goodwill even as he doubled the college's endowment (money donations) within the first year.

American Founding Father

By 1776, Princeton was attracting nearly as many students as highly popular Yale and enjoyed a record number of graduates. However, the American Revolution put Princeton in a difficult position: The town became a battleground, and at various times the main college building, Nassau Hall, was used as quarters by British and Continental Army troops. The military occupation destroyed much of the college campus and its most important piece of scientific equipment, the Rittenhouse Orrery. The orrery was an apparatus used to show the relative positions and motions of celestial bodies in the solar system. It was a prized possession. The library that Witherspoon had helped expand was also destroyed. Witherspoon worked hard at keeping college in session during the war years.

Witherspoon was a firm supporter of the American colonies in their war against Britain. On June 22, 1776, he was selected by New Jersey as a delegate to the Continental Congress in Philadelphia, Pennsylvania. Within days, Witherspoon voted for and affixed his signature to the Declaration of Independence. He was the only clergyman to do so. He served in the Continental Congress until November 1782 while he helped draft the Articles of Confederation. Witherspoon won the respect of his colleagues and was appointed to more than one hundred committees; many of the committees dealt with matters of considerable importance, such as negotiations with foreign powers. War also brought personal tragedy when Witherspoon's son James, a 1770 graduate of the College of New Jersey, was killed at the Battle of Germantown in Philadelphia in October 1777.

When American victory seemed certain and peace was at hand, Witherspoon resigned from Congress and returned to Princeton full-time in the fall of 1782. The campus buildings and the school's finances were in disarray. Student life in the early years of the republic was bleak because of the damaged facilities and the limited availability of food. Witherspoon set about rebuilding the college, a project to which he would devote the rest of his days. By July 1783, parts of Nassau Hall

A view of Nassau Hall (left) and the president's house, on the campus of Princeton University, 1764. *(© Corbis.)*

had been sufficiently repaired to serve a second purpose: For four months that year, the building housed the Continental Congress, bringing such statesmen as **George Washington** (1732–1799; see entry in volume 2), **John Adams** (1735–1826; see entry in volume 1), and **Thomas Jefferson** (1743–1826; see entry in volume 1) to Princeton.

Life after the Revolution

Witherspoon continued the work of restoration at Princeton even as he returned to public service in the New Jersey legislature in 1783. In 1787, Witherspoon was a member of the New Jersey convention that approved the U.S. Constitution. (New Jersey was the third state in the union to approve it.) Five members of the 1787 Constitutional Convention were former students of Witherspoon's. To Witherspoon, religion and politics were intertwined. Religious faith was essential to him if true liberty was to be achieved. Faith and liberty were so connected in his teaching that a generation of Americans was deeply affected. Witherspoon believed that a righteous people needed only limited governing; he therefore taught that a government's main purpose was simply to protect and defend its citizens.

Elizabeth Witherspoon, never fully content in her new country, died in 1789. Two years later, John Witherspoon married a twenty-four-year-old widow from York County, Pennsylvania, named Ann Dill. They had two daughters, but only one survived to adulthood. Health problems soon took their toll on Witherspoon. In 1784, he had had a shipboard accident that blinded him in one eye. A fall from his horse injured the other eye, causing it to steadily deteriorate. By 1792, Witherspoon was totally blind. When surgery failed to improve his situation, Witherspoon resigned himself to his fate and continued with his presidential duties with the help of an assistant. During Witherspoon's final years, his son-in-law, Samuel Stanhope Smith, increasingly carried more responsibility for college affairs and was himself elected president of the college in May 1795.

On November 15, 1794, the seventy-one-year-old Witherspoon died at home on his farm, known as "Tusculum," just outside of Princeton. On November 18, his body was brought to Nassau Hall, where it lay in state while grieving friends, colleagues, and students paid their last respects. Witherspoon was laid to rest in the president's lot at Princeton. He had dedicated his life to service, and he left both college and country in a better state than he had found them.

For More Information

Books

Brodsky, Alyn. *Benjamin Rush: Patriot and Physician*. New York: Truman Talley Books, 2004.

Collins, Varnum Lansing. *President Witherspoon*. Princeton, NJ: Princeton University Press, 1925. Reprint, New York: Arno Press, 1969.

Hawke, David Freeman. *Benjamin Rush: Revolutionary Gadfly*. Indianapolis, IN: Bobbs-Merrill, 1971.

Sloan, Douglas. *The Scottish Enlightenment and the American College Ideal*. New York: Columbia University Teachers College Press, 1971.

Wertenbaker, Thomas Jefferson. *Princeton 1746–1896*. Princeton, NJ: Princeton University Press, 1946. Reprint, 1996.

Web Sites

"John Witherspoon (1723–1794)." *Acton Institute for the Study of Religion and Liberty*. http://www.acton.org/publicat/randl/liberal.php?id=249 (accessed on August 17, 2005).

"John Witherspoon 1723–1794: Representing New Jersey at the Continental Congress." *Independence Hall Association*. http://www.ushistory.org/declaration/signers/witherspoon.htm (accessed on August 17, 2005).

Where to Learn More

The following list focuses on works written for readers of middle school or high school age. Books aimed at adult readers have been included when they are especially important in providing information or analysis that would otherwise be unavailable.

Books

Achenbach, Joel. *The Grand Idea: George Washington's Potomac and the Race to the West.* New York: Simon & Schuster, 2004.

Aikman, Lonnelle. *We, the People: The Story of the United States Capitol.* Washington, DC: U.S. Capitol Historical Society, 1991.

Ambrose, Stephen E. *Undaunted Courage: Meriwether Lewis, Thomas Jefferson, and the Opening of the American West.* New York: Simon & Schuster, 1996.

Ammon, Harry. *James Monroe: The Quest of National Identity.* New York: McGraw-Hill, 1971.

Anson, Bert. *The Miami Indians.* Norman: University of Oklahoma Press, 1970.

Appleby, Joyce O. *Inheriting the Revolution: The First Generation of Americans.* Cambridge, MA: Belknap Press, 2000.

Armento, Beverly J., Gary B. Nash, Christopher L. Salter, and Karen K. Wixson. *The American People: Creating a Nation and a Society*. New York: HarperCollins, 1994.

Berkin, Carol. *A Brilliant Solution: Inventing the American Constitution*. New York: Harcourt, 2002.

Bernstein, R. B. *The Constitution of the United States; with the Declaration of Independence and the Articles of Confederation*. New York: Barnes & Noble Books, 2002.

Billington, Ray Allen, and Martin Ridge. *Westward Expansion: A History of the American Frontier*. 5th ed. New York: Macmillan, 1982.

Borneman, Walter R. *1812: The War That Forged a Nation*. New York: HarperCollins, 2004.

Burns, James MacGregor, and Susan Dunn. *George Washington*. New York: Times Books, 2004.

Cerami, Charles A. *Jefferson's Great Gamble: The Remarkable Story of Jefferson, Napoleon, and the Men behind the Louisiana Purchase*. Naperville, IL: Sourcebooks, 2003.

Chernow, Ron. *Alexander Hamilton*. New York: Penguin Books, 2004.

Clark, Christopher, and Nancy A. Hewitt. *Who Built America? Working People and the Nation's Economy, Politics, Culture, and Society*. 2nd ed. New York: Worth Publishers, 2000.

Commager, Henry Steele. *The Great Constitution: A Book for Young Americans*. Indianapolis, IN: Bobbs-Merrill, 1961.

Danbom, David B. *Born in the Country: A History of Rural America*. Baltimore: Johns Hopkins University Press, 1995.

DeVoto, Bernard, ed. *The Journals of Lewis and Clark*. Boston: Houghton Mifflin Company, 1953. Reprint, 1997.

Dowd, Gregory Evans. *A Spirited Resistance: The North American Indian Struggle for Unity, 1745–1815*. Baltimore: Johns Hopkins Press, 1992.

Dreisbach, Daniel L., Mark D. Hall, and Jeffry H. Morrison, eds. *The Founders on God and Government*. Lanham, MD: Rowan & Littlefield, 2004.

Dunn, Susan. *Jefferson's Second Revolution: The Election Crisis of 1800 and the Triumph of Republicanism*. Boston: Houghton Mifflin, 2004.

Ehle, John. *Trail of Tears: The Rise and Fall of the Cherokee Nation*. New York: Doubleday, 1988.

Ellis, Joseph J. *His Excellency: George Washington*. New York: Knopf Publishing Group, 2004.

Farrand, Max, ed. *The Records of the Federal Convention of 1787*. Rev. ed. New Haven, CT: Yale University Press, 1966.

Feinberg, Barbara Silberdick. *Articles of Confederation: The First Constitution of the United States*. Brookfield, CT: Twenty-First Century Books, 2002.

Ferling, John E. *Adams vs. Jefferson: The Tumultuous Election of 1800*. New York: Oxford University Press, 2004.

Ferling, John E. *A Leap in the Dark: The Struggle to Create the American Republic*. New York: Oxford University Press, 2003.

Ferling, John E. *Setting the World Ablaze: Washington, Adams, Jefferson, and the American Revolution*. New York: Oxford University Press, 2000.

Ferris, Robert G., and James H. Charleton. *The Signers of the Constitution*. Flagstaff, AZ: Interpretive Publications, 1986. Reprint, 2001.

Franklin, John Hope, and Alfred A. Moss, Jr. *From Slavery to Freedom: A History of African Americans*. 8th ed. Boston: McGraw-Hill, 2000.

Freedman, Russell. *In Defense of Liberty: The Story of America's Bill of Rights*. New York: Holiday House, 2003.

Gilje, Paul A., ed. *Wages of Independence: Capitalism in the Early American Republic*. Madison, WI: Madison House, 1997.

Hawke, David F. *Everyday Life in Early America*. New York: Harper & Row, 1988.

Hays, Wilma P., and R. Vernon Hays. *Foods the Indians Gave Us*. New York: I. Washburn, 1973.

Hibbert, Christopher. *Redcoats and Rebels: The American Revolution through British Eyes*. New York: Norton, 1990.

Hoffman, Ronald, and Peter J. Albert, eds. *Religion in a Revolutionary Age*. Charlottesville, VA: United States Capitol Historical Society, 1994.

Horsman, Reginald. *The Frontier in the Formative Years, 1783–1815*. New York: Holt, Rinehart & Winston, 1970.

Horsman, Reginald. *The New Republic: The United States of America, 1789–1815*. New York: Longman, 2000.

Horton, James O., and Lois E. Horton, eds. *A History of the African American People: The History, Traditions, & Culture of African Americans*. Detroit: Wayne State University Press, 1997.

Huff, Regan A. *Eli Whitney: The Cotton Gin and American Manufacturing*. New York: PowerPlus Books, 2004.

Hurt, R. Douglas. *American Agriculture: A Brief History*. Ames: Iowa State University Press, 1994.

Irving, Washington. *Astoria, or, Anecdotes of an Enterprise beyond the Rocky Mountains*. Philadelphia: Carey, Lea, & Blanchard, 1836. Multiple reprints.

Isaacson, Walter. *Benjamin Franklin: An American Life*. New York: Simon & Schuster, 2003.

Jefferson, Thomas. *The Writings of Thomas Jefferson.* Edited by H. A. Washington. Washington, DC: Taylor & Maury, 1853–1854. Multiple reprints.

Kennedy, Robert G. *Mr. Jefferson's Lost Cause: Land, Farmers, Slavery, and the Louisiana Purchase.* New York: Oxford University Press, 2003.

Ketcham, Ralph L. *James Madison: A Biography.* New York: Macmillan, 1971.

Lambert, Frank. *The Founding Fathers and the Place of Religion in America.* Princeton, NJ: Princeton University Press, 2003.

Marini, Stephen A. *Radical Sects of Revolutionary New England.* Cambridge, MA: Harvard University Press, 1982.

Mattern, David B. *James Madison: Patriot, Politician, and President.* New York: PowerPlus Books, 2005.

Mattern, David B., and Holly C. Shulman, eds. *The Selected Letters of Dolley Payne Madison.* Charlottesville: University of Virginia Press, 2003.

McCullough, David G. *John Adams.* New York: Simon & Schuster, 2001.

McCullough, David G. *1776.* New York: Simon & Schuster, 2005.

McDougall, Walter A. *Freedom Just around the Corner: A New American History, 1585–1828.* New York: HarperCollins, 2004.

Middlekauff, Robert. *Glorious Cause: The American Revolution, 1763–1789.* New York: Oxford University Press, 1982.

Moore, Kay. *If You Lived at the Time of the American Revolution.* New York: Scholastic, 1997.

Morris, Richard B. *The Forging of the Union, 1781–1789.* New York: Harper & Row, 1987.

Morris, Richard B. *Witnesses at the Creation: Hamilton, Madison, Jay, and the Constitution.* New York: Holt, Rinehart, and Winston, 1985.

Murphy, Jim. *A Young Patriot: The American Revolution As Experienced by One Boy.* New York: Clarion Books, 1996.

Nash, Gary B., Julie R. Jeffrey, et al., eds. *The American People: Creating a Nation and a Society.* 4th ed. New York: Harper & Row, 1986.

Needleman, Jacob. *The American Soul: Rediscovering the Wisdom of the Founders.* New York: J. P. Tarcher/Putnam, 2002.

Norton, Mary Beth. *Liberty's Daughters: The Revolutionary Experience of American Women, 1750–1800.* Boston: Little, Brown, 1980. Reprint, Ithaca, NY: Cornell University Press, 1996.

O'Neill, Paul. *The Frontiersmen.* Alexandria, VA: Time-Life Books, 1977.

Padover, Saul K. *Jefferson.* New York: Mentor Books, 1970.

Patrick, John J. *The Young Oxford Companion to the Supreme Court of the United States.* New York: Oxford University Press, 1998.

Randall, Willard S. *Alexander Hamilton: A Life.* New York: HarperCollins, 2003.

Raphael, Ray. *People's History of the American Revolution: How Common People Shaped the Fight for Independence.* New York: New Press, 2001.

Remini, Robert V. *The Battle of New Orleans.* New York: Viking, 1999.

Richards, Leonard L. *Shays's Rebellion: The American Revolution's Final Battle.* Philadelphia: University of Pennsylvania Press, 2002.

Risjord, Norman K. *Jefferson's America, 1760–1815.* 2nd ed. Lanham, MD: Rowman & Littlefield Publishers, 2002.

Roberts, Cokie. *Founding Mothers: The Women Who Raised Our Nation.* New York: William Morrow, 2004.

Rutland, Robert A., ed. *James Madison and the American Nation, 1751–1836: An Encyclopedia.* New York: Simon & Schuster, 1994.

Simon, James F. *What Kind of Nation: Thomas Jefferson, John Marshall, and the Epic Struggle to Create a United States.* New York: Simon & Schuster, 2002.

Skeen, C. Edward. *1816: America Rising.* Lexington: University Press of Kentucky, 2003.

Smith, Jean Edward. *John Marshall: Definer of a Nation.* New York: Henry Holt & Co., 1996.

Stahr, Walter. *John Jay: Founding Father.* London: Hambledon and London, 2005.

Staib, Walter. *City Tavern Cookbook: 200 Years of Classic Recipes from America's First Gourmet Restaurant.* Philadelphia: Running Press, 1999.

Sugden, John. *Tecumseh: A Life.* New York: Henry Holt and Co., 1997.

Thompson, Charles L. *The Religious Foundations of America: A Study in National Origins.* New York: Fleming H. Revell Co., 1917.

Ulrich, Laurel Thatcher. *A Midwife's Tale: The Life of Martha Ballard, Based on Her Diary, 1785–1812.* New York: Knopf, 1990.

Vidal, Gore. *Inventing a Nation: Washington, Adams, Jefferson.* New Haven, CT: Yale University Press, 2003.

Wait, Eugene M. *America and the War of 1812.* Commack, NY: Kroshka Books, 1999.

Washburn, Wilcomb E., ed. *Handbook of North American Indians: History of Indian-White Relations.* Vol. 4. Washington, DC: Smithsonian Institution, 1988.

Weidner, Daniel W. *Creating the Constitution: The People and Events That Formed the Nation.* Berkeley Heights, NJ: Enslow, 2002.

Wilkinson, Charles F. *American Indians, Time, and the Law: Native Societies in a Modern Constitutional Democracy.* New Haven, CT: Yale University Press, 1987.

Wills, Garry. *Inventing America: Jefferson's Declaration of Independence.* Garden City, NY: Doubleday, 1978. Reprint, Boston: Houghton Mifflin, 2002.

Wood, Gordon S. *American Revolution: A History.* New York: Random House, 2003.

Wood, Gordon S. *The Creation of the American Republic, 1776–1787.* Chapel Hill: University of North Carolina Press, 1969. Reprint, 1998.

Zinn, Howard. *A People's History of the United States: 1492–Present.* Rev ed. New York: HarperCollins, 2003.

Web Sites

"African Slave Trade and Slave Life in the Americas." *University of Virginia.* http://hitchcock.itc.virginia.edu/Slavery/ (accessed on September 12, 2005).

"Alexander Hamilton: The Man Who Made Modern America." *The New York Historical Society.* http://www.alexanderhamiltonexhibition.org (accessed on July 29, 2005).

American Presidents. http://www.americanpresident.org/history/ (accessed on September 12, 2005).

"American Revolution." *The History Place.* http://www.historyplace.com/unitedstates/revolution (accessed on July 27, 2005).

"The American Revolution: Lighting Freedom's Flame." *National Park Service.* http://www.nps.gov/revwar (accessed on July 27, 2005).

"Articles of Confederation." *The Avalon Project at Yale Law School.* http://www.yale.edu/lawweb/avalon/artconf.htm (accessed on July 29, 2005).

Battle of Fallen Timbers. http://www.fallentimbersbattlefield.com (accessed on August 8, 2005).

"Ben's Guide to U.S. Government for Kids." *U.S. Government Printing Office.* http://bensguide.gpo.gov/9-12/documents/articles/ (accessed on July 29, 2005).

Carpenters' Hall. http://www.carpentershall.org (accessed on July 27, 2005).

"Comparing the Articles and the Constitution." *The U.S. Constitution Online.* http://www.usconstitution.net/constconart.html (accessed on July 29, 2005).

Eli Whitney Museum. http://www.eliwhitney.org/main.htm (accessed on September 12, 2005).

"Experience the Life: Religion." *Colonial Williamsburg.* http://www.history. org/Almanack/life/religion/religionhdr.cfm (accessed on August 9, 2005).

"Farming in the 13 American Colonies." *Social Studies for Kids.* http:// www.socialstudiesforkids.com/articles/ushistory/13coloniesfarm.htm (accessed on August 6, 2005).

The Federalist Papers. *University of Oklahoma Law School.* http://www.law. ou.edu/hist/federalist/ (accessed on September 12, 2005).

"The First American West: The Ohio River Valley, 1750–1820." *American Memory: Library of Congress.* http://memory.loc.gov/ammem/award99/ icuhtml/fawsp/fawsp.html (accessed on August 9, 2005).

"First Invasion: The War of 1812." *The History Channel.* http://www. historychannel.com/1812/ (accessed on August 2, 2005).

George Washington's Mt. Vernon Estates and Gardens. http://www. mountvernon.org/ (accessed on September 12, 2005).

The Historical Society of Pennsylvania. http://www.hsp.org (accessed on August 9, 2005).

"A History of American Agriculture." *Agriculture in the Classroom.* http:// www.agclassroom.org/teacher/history/ (accessed on August 6, 2005).

"History of the United States Mint." *U.S. Department of Treasury.* http:// usmint.gov/about_the_mint/mint_history/ (accessed on July 30, 2005).

Hurt, R. Douglas. "Agriculture." *Encyclopedia of North American Indians.* http://college.hmco.com/history/readerscomp/naind/html/ na_000500_agriculture.htm (accessed on August 6, 2005).

Independence Hall Association. *ushistory.org.* http://www.ushistory.org (accessed on July 29, 2005).

Independence Hall Association. "First Bank of the United States." *ushistory.org.* http://www.ushistory.org/tour/tour_1bank.htm (accessed on July 30, 2005).

"Independence National Historical Park." *U.S. National Park Service.* http:// www.nps.gov/inde/index.htm (accessed on July 29, 2005).

"Lewis and Clark National Historic Trail." *U.S. National Park Service.* http:// www.nps.gov/lecl/ (accessed on August 8, 2005).

Lewis and Clark Trail Heritage Foundation. http://www.lewisandclark.org (accessed on August 8, 2005).

"Liberty! The American Revolution." *Public Broadcasting Service.* http:// www.pbs.org/ktca/liberty/ (accessed on July 27, 2005).

Library of Congress. "The American Revolution and Its Era." *American Memory.* http://memory.loc.gov/ammem/gmdhtml/armhtml/armhome.html (accessed on September 12, 2005).

Library of Congress. "Fill Up the Canvas ... Rivers of Words: Exploring with Lewis and Clark." *American Memory.* http://memory.loc.gov/learn/ features/lewisandclark/ (accessed on September 12, 2005).

Library of Congress. "George Washington's First Inauguration." *"I Do Solemnly Swear": Presidential Inaugurations.* http://memory.loc.gov/ammem/pihtml/pi001.html (accessed on July 30, 2005).

Library of Congress. "Star-Spangled Banner." *American Memory.* http:// www.loc.gov/exhibits/treasures/trm065.html (accessed on August 2, 2005).

"Louisiana History." *Louisiana Department of Economic Development.* http:// www.crt.state.la.us/crt/profiles/history.htm (accessed on August 8, 2005).

Monticello, the Home of Thomas Jefferson. http://www.monticello.org/ (accessed on August 8, 2005).

Mount Vernon Ladies Association. *George Washington's Mount Vernon Estate & Gardens.* http://www.mountvernon.org (accessed on August 9, 2005).

National Constitution Center. http://www.constitutioncenter.org (accessed on July 29, 2005).

National First Ladies' Library. http://www.firstladies.org/Bibliography/index.htm (accessed on September 12, 2005).

New Advent: Catholic Encyclopedia. http://www.newadvent.org (accessed on August 9, 2005).

"New York State History." *The History Department at the University at Albany.* http://nystatehistory.org/ (accessed on August 8, 2005).

"Our Documents." *U.S. National Archives and Records Administration.* http:// www.ourdocuments.gov (accessed on July 29, 2005).

"Our Party: Our History." *The Democratic Party.* http://www.democrats.org/a/party/history.html (accessed on August 1, 2005).

"The Pioneers, Origin, and Organization of the AME Church." *The African Methodist Episcopal Church.* http://www.amecnet.org/history.htm (accessed on September 12, 2005).

"Postal History." *United States Postal Service.* http://www.usps.com/postalhistory/ (accessed on July 29, 2005).

"Presbyterian 101: Presbyterian Church History." *Presbyterian Church (USA).* http://www.pcusa.org/101/101-history.htm (accessed on August 9, 2005).

Public Broadcasting Service. "A Midwife's Tale." *American Experience.* http:// www.pbs.org/wgbh/amex/midwife/index/ (accessed on September 12, 2005).

"Religion and the Founding of the American Republic." *Library of Congress.* http://www.loc.gov/exhibits/religion/ (accessed on August 9, 2005).

"Shays' Rebellion." *Supreme Judicial Court Historical Society (Pennsylvania).* http://www.sjchs-history.org (accessed on July 29, 2005).

Supreme Court of the United States. http://www.supremecourtus.gov/ (accessed on September 12, 2005).

"Thomas Jefferson Digital Archive." *University of Virginia Library.* http:// etext.lib.virginia.edu/jefferson/ (accessed on August 2, 2005).

U.S. Courts. http://www.uscourts.gov (accessed on July 30, 2005).

U.S. Government Printing Office "The Constitution of the United States of America." *Ben's Guide to U.S. Government for Kids.* http://bensguide. gpo.gov/9-12/documents/constitution/index.html (accessed on July 29, 2005).

Whitten, Chris. *Founding Fathers Info.* http://www.foundingfathers.info (accessed on July 29, 2005).

Index

Italic type indicates volume
number;
Boldface indicates main
entries and their page
numbers;
(ill.) indicates photos and
illustrations.

"American System," of Henry Clay, *1:* 108–9

The American Village (Freneau), *1:* 152

Anglican Church, *2:* 425. *See also* Episcopal Church

during American Revolution, *2:* 523–26

structure of American Church, *2:* 526–27

Annapolis Conference, *1:* 189; *2:* 417–18, 486

Anthony, Susan B., *2:* 439

Anti-Catholicism, *1:* 95; *2:* 445

Anti-Federalists, *2:* 336. *See also* Democratic-Republican(s)

Gallatin, Albert, as, *1:* 161

Henry, Patrick, as, *1:* 104–5

and ratification of U.S. Constitution, *2:* 475

Warrens as, *2:* 475

Apekonit (William Wells), *2:* 312

Architect(s)

Latrobe, Benjamin Henry, *2:* 320–21

L'Enfant, Pierre-Charles, *2:* 271–78

Arlington House, *2:* 296

Armistead, George, *1:* 256

Armstrong, John, *2:* 388–89

Arnold, Benedict, *1:* 82

Articles of Confederation

foreign affairs under, *1:* 218

inadequate for governing, *1:* 188–89, 267; *2:* 333, 381, 417, 487

ratification of, *2:* 332

Asbury, Francis, *1:* **42–50**, 43 (ill.), 247–48

and AME Church, *1:* 38

becomes Methodist, *1:* 44–45

and Church of England, *1:* 44–45

and Hosier, "Black Harry," *1:* 39

as pioneer bishop, *1:* 48–49

volunteers as missionary to America, *1:* 45–48

Ash Lawn-Highland, *2:* 386

Ashburn, Joseph, *2:* 427

Ashley, John and Hannah, *1:* 141, 142 (ill.)

Assembly line, *2:* 530

Astronomy, *1:* 62, 66–67

Auteuil, *1:* 8–9, 26

B

Bache, Benjamin Franklin, *1:* 156

Ballard, Ephraim, *1:* 52

Ballard, Martha, *1:* **51–61**

begins diary, *1:* 54–56

interested in medicine, *1:* 54

as midwife and healer, *1:* 56–57, 59–60

as mother, *1:* 52

records economic contribution of women, *1:* 57–58

tells of social gatherings, *1:* 58–59

Baltimore

attack on (War of 1812), *1:* 254–56; *2:* 343, 426

as religious base, *1:* 48, 99–101; *2:* 445–46

Baltimore, Battle of, *1:* 256–57

Baltimore Cathedral (Basilica of the Assumption of the Blessed Virgin Mary), *2:* 321, 321 (ill.)

Bank(s)

Bank of Pennsylvania, *2:* 320

First Bank of the United States, *1:* 119, 192

national, *1:* 109, 240

Banneker, Benjamin, *1:* **62–70**, 63 (ill.)

as clock maker, *1:* 65

helps build new capital, *1:* 67–68

interested in astronomy, *1:* 66–67

works on almanacs, *1:* 67, 68–69

writes to Jefferson, Thomas, *1:* 62–63, 68

Barn raisings, *1:* 58

Barnstable, Massachusetts, *2:* 469

Barter economy, *1:* 57–58

Basilica of the Assumption of the Blessed Virgin Mary (Baltimore Cathedral), *2:* 321, 321 (ill.)

Bassett, Fanny, *2:* 507

Battle of Baltimore, *1:* 256–57

Battle of Bladensburg, *1:* 254–55

Battle of Brandywine, *2:* 515

Battle of Bunker (Breed's) Hill, *1:* 5–6

The Battle of Bunkers-Hill (Brackenridge), *1:* 74

Battle of Fallen Timbers, *1:* 88, 268; *2:* 309, 464, 492, 517, 518

and Britain, *2:* 387

Cabinet of, *1:* 238

and the courts, *1:* 239

death of, *1:* 244

and Declaration of
    Independence, *1:* 133, 229–30

dismantles Federalist policies,
    1: 239, 240; *2:* 340

election of 1796, *1:* 235–36;
    2: 338

election of 1800, *1:* 30, 84–85,
    119, 197, 236–38, 237 (ill.)

election of 1804, *1:* 119, 241–42

and Embargo Act, *2:* 341

entertains at President's House,
    1: 238–39

first years as president, *1:* 238–41

friendship with Madison and
    Monroe, *2:* 326, 331, 384

as governor of Virginia,
    1: 232–33

on Hamilton's economic plan,
    1: 234–35; *2:* 419–20

and Jay Treaty, *1:* 221

and Kentucky Resolution, *1:* 236;
    2: 339

and Lewis and Clark, *1:* 241;
    2: 282–83, 434–35, 436

and Louisiana Purchase,
    1: 240–41

and Madison, James, *2:* 318–19,
    326, 331–32, 335, 338,
    345, 384

and Marshall, John, *2:* 355

as minister to France, *1:* 233–34

Monticello, *1:* 228, 228 (ill.)

and *National Gazette,* *1:* 154–55,
    192

and public education, *1:* 231

and religious liberty, *1:* 231

as Republican, *1:* 192

second term as president,
    1: 241–42

as secretary of state, *1:* 192–93,
    234–35

as slaveowner, *1:* 231, 234

on slavery, *1:* 231, 233–34

as spokesman for common
    citizen, *1:* 224

and use of term "democracy,"
    1: 224

as vice president, *1:* 235–36

Jeffersonians, vs. Hamiltonians,
    1: 192–93

Jennison, Nathaniel, *1:* 139

Jennison v. Caldwell, *1:* 139

Jesuits (Society of Jesus), *1:* 95–96

Johnson, Richard Mentor, *2:* 467

"Join or die," *1:* 129

Jones, Absalom, *1:* 36, **245–51,**
    246 (ill.); *2:* 528

    leads Free African Society and
        African Church, *1:* 247–49

    purchases freedom, *1:* 246–47

    and St. Thomas African
        Episcopal Church, *1:* 249–50

Jones, John, *1:* 53

Judges, "midnight," *1:* 31, 239;
    2: 356

Judicial review, *2:* 355

Judiciary Act of 1789, *2:* 357

Judiciary Act of 1801, *2:* 352, 356

Junto, *1:* 125

K

Kennebec Proprietors, *1:* 53

Kentucky

    Clark, William in, *2:* 284

    and Clay, Henry, *1:* 105–6

    and Wilkinson, James, *1:* 88

Kentucky Resolution, *1:* 236; *2:* 339

Key, Francis Scott, *1:* **252–60,**
    253 (ill.); *2:* 426

    observes attack on Fort
        McHenry, *1:* 255–56

    serves in War of 1812, *1:* 254–55

    writes "Star-Spangled Banner,"
        1: 256–59

Key, Philip Barton, *1:* 254

A Key to Uncle Tom's Cabin (Stowe),
    2: 405

King, Rufus, *2:* 389

King's Mountain, Battle of, *2:* 453

Kispoko Town, *2:* 461–62

Knox County, Tennessee, *2:* 450, 456

Knox, Henry, *1:* **261–70,** 262 (ill.),
    264 (ill.); *2:* 490 (ill.)

    as Continental Army officer,
        1: 263–65

    and Native American
        negotiations, *1:* 268

    as secretary of war, *1:* 267–68

    and Washington, George, *1:* 263

Kortright (Monroe), Elizabeth,
    2: 382

Kosati, *2:* 361

Robards (Jackson), Rachel
    Donelson, *1:* 202, 209
Robertson, Donald, *2:* 329
"Rogues Harbour," *2:* 374
Roman Catholic Church
    Carroll, John, *1:* 93–101
    in Maryland, *1:* 95–101
    Seton, Elizabeth Ann, *2:* 441–49
Ross, Betsy, *2:* 423–30, 424 (ill.),
    429 (ill.)
    becomes a legend, *2:* 429–30
    as businesswoman, *2:* 427–28
    learns a trade, *2:* 424–25
    sews "Stars and Stripes,"
        2: 426–27
Ross, George, *2:* 425
Ross, John, *2:* 425
Royal Society of London, *1:* 127
Rush, Benjamin, *1:* 37; *2:* 518, 543,
    546, 546 (ill.)
Russell, Jonathan, *2:* 471

S

Sacagawea, *2:* 280 (ill.), **431–40,**
    432 (ill.), 435 (ill.)
    born to Snake people, *2:* 431–33
    joins Lewis and Clark
        expedition, *2:* 286, 433–36
    legend of, *2:* 439
    reunited with brother, *2:* 437
    sees the Pacific shore, *2:* 438
Sacramental meetings, *2:* 371
Saffron, *1:* 55
Sage, *1:* 55
Sailors, and almanacs, *1:* 69
St. Clair, Arthur, *1:* 268; *2:* 304, 307,
    308 (ill.), 492, 517
St. George's Methodist Church,
    1: 36
St. Joseph's Asylum, Philadelphia,
    2: 448
St. Louis, Missouri, *2:* 288, 435
St. Mary's Seminary, *1:* 99
St. Thomas African Episcopal
    Church, *1:* 245
San Ildefonso, Treaty of, *2:* 386
San Lorenzo, Treaty of (Pinckney
    Treaty), *2:* 421, 492
Saratoga (New York), Battle of,
    1: 115, 133
Sargent, Judith. *See* Murray, Judith
    Sargent

Sargent, Winthrop, Jr., *2:* 395, 397
Savannah, Battle of, *2:* 273
Savary de Valcoulon, Jean, *1:* 160
Scarlet fever (canker rash), *1:* 56
Schools, for free blacks, *1:* 182, 250
Schuyler, Elizabeth, *1:* 188
Schuyler, Philip, *1:* 83, 188
Scientists
    Banneker, Benjamin, *1:* 62–70
    Franklin, Benjamin, *1:* 127–28
Scotchtown Plantation, *2:* 316
Seabury, Samuel, *1:* 187; *2:* 527
Seaman (dog), *2:* 436
Second Bank of the United States,
    1: 211
Second Continental Congress. *See*
    Continental Congress, Second
Second Great Awakening, *2:* 369
Sedgwick, Catharine, *1:* 138, 140,
    143 (ill.)
Sedgwick, Charles, *1:* 146
Sedgwick, Susan, *1:* 146
Sedgwick, Theodore, *1:* 137,
    143–44
Sedition Act, *1:* 30, 156; *2:* 339
Seminole War of 1817–18, *2:* 389
Seminoles, *1:* 207; *2:* 362, 389
Separation of church and state,
    1: 225, 231
Seton, Elizabeth Ann, *1:* 99;
    2: **441–49,** 442 (ill.)
    converts to Catholicism,
        2: 443–44
    opens school in Maryland,
        2: 445–46
    organizes Sisters of Charity,
        1: 99; *2:* 446–48
Settlers, and Native American
    hostilities, *2:* 284, 307
Seven Buildings, Washington,
    D.C., *2:* 323
Seven Years' War. *See* French and
    Indian War
Sevier, John, *2:* **450–58,** 451 (ill.)
    as congressman, *2:* 456–57
    duels with Andrew Jackson,
        1: 204; *2:* 456
    as first governor of Tennessee,
        2: 455–56
    as governor of state of Franklin,
        2: 453
Sewall, Henry, *1:* 51
Shawnee, *2:* 306, 309, 459, 461,
    467, 517

W

Wabash River, *2:* 465

Walker, Quock, *1:* 138, 139

Wappoo Plantation, *2:* 409–10

War debt, American, *1:* 191

War hawks, *1:* 108; *2:* 342

War of 1812

    Battle of New Orleans, *1:* 205, 206

    Battle of the Thames, *2:* 467, 519

    British attack on Washington and Baltimore, *1:* 108, 254–56; *2:* 321–23, 426

    guns for, *2:* 538

    Harrison, William Henry, in, *2:* 519

    Madison, Dolley, and, *2:* 321–23, 343

    Madison, James, and, *2:* 342–44

    Monroe, James, and, *2:* 388–89

    and Native Americans, *2:* 311, 465–67

    "The Star-Spangled Banner," *1:* 256–59; *2:* 426

    Treaty of Ghent, *1:* 108

War of Jenkins' Ear, *2:* 409

Warren, James, *2:* 471, 474

Warren, James, Jr., *2:* 477

Warren, Mercy Otis, *2:* 469–78, 470 (ill.)

    and Adams, Abigail, *1:* 4

    comments on Constitution, *2:* 475

    publishes history of Revolution, *2:* 477

    writes to support Patriot cause, *2:* 472–74

Warren, Winslow, *2:* 475

Washington, Augustine, *2:* 479–81

Washington, D.C.

    attack on (War of 1812), *1:* 255; *2:* 343, 388–89

    building of, *1:* 67–68; *2:* 276

Washington, George, *1:* 116 (ill.); *2:* 298 (ill.), 429 (ill.), **479–95,** 480 (ill.), 487 (ill.), 490 (ill.), 496, 501–2, 506, 507 (ill.), 508–11

    and Adams, Abigail, *1:* 11

    becomes first president, *2:* 295–96, 488–89

    begins political career, *2:* 484–85

    Cabinet of, *1:* 234; *2:* 489–91, 490 (ill.)

    commands Continental Army, *2:* 485–86, 503

    at Constitutional Convention, *2:* 488

    and Custis, George Washington "Wash" Parke, *2:* 296–97

    death of, *1:* 100–101; *2:* 494, 511

    Farewell Address of, *1:* 195, 235; *2:* 337, 492–93

    on foreign affairs, *2:* 491–92

    as grandparent, *2:* 291–93, 294

    and Hamilton, Alexander, *1:* 187–88, 192; *2:* 337, 490–91

    inauguration of, *2:* 508

    and Knox, Henry, *1:* 264–65

    and Lewis, Nelly Custis, *2:* 291–303

    and Little Turtle, *2:* 310

    and Mount Vernon Conference, *2:* 487–88

    and neutrality, *1:* 222, 235; *2:* 491

    and new capital, *1:* 67

    and Northwest Territory, *2:* 308

    as officer in French and Indian War, *2:* 482–84

    and Pinckney, Eliza Lucas, *2:* 409, 414

    as plantation owner, *2:* 481–82

    on political parties, *2:* 490

    portraits of, *1:* 76–77

    as president, *2:* 489

    and Randolph, Edmund, *2:* 419

    reelected as president, *2:* 491–92

    as slaveowner, *2:* 482, 494, 507

    as surveyor, *2:* 481

    and Whiskey Rebellion, *1:* 28, 193; *2:* 493

Washington, George Augustine, *2:* 507–8

Washington, John, *2:* 480

Washington, Lawrence, *2:* 481

Washington, Martha, *2:* 298 (ill.), 484, 487 (ill.), **496–512,** 497 (ill.), 500 (ill.), 507 (ill.)

    and Adams, Abigail, *1:* 11

    during American Revolution, *2:* 504–6

    and Custis, George Washington "Wash" Parke, *2:* 296–97

    "debut" in Williamsburg, *2:* 498–500